# Hope and Uncertainty in Contemporary African Migration

This volume examines the relationship between hope, mobility, and immobility in African migration. Through case studies set within and beyond the continent, it demonstrates that hope offers a unique prism for analyzing the social imaginaries and aspirations which underpin migration in situations of uncertainty, deepening inequality, and delimited access to global circuits of legal mobility.

The volume takes departure in a mobility paradox that characterizes contemporary migration. Whereas people all over the world are exposed to widening sets of meaning of the good life elsewhere, an increasing number of people in the Global South have little or no access to authorized modes of international migration. This book examines how African migrants respond to this situation. Focusing on hope, it explores migrants' temporal and spatial horizons of expectation and possibility and how these horizons link to mobility practices. Such analysis is pertinent as precarious life conditions and increasingly restrictive regimes of mobility characterize the lives of many Africans, while migration continues to constitute important livelihood strategies and to be seen as pathways of improvement. Whereas involuntary immobility is one consequence, another is the emergence and consolidation of new destinations emerging in the Global South. The volume examines this development through empirically grounded and theoretically rich case studies in migrants' countries of origin, zones of transit, and in new and established destinations in Europe, North America, the Middle East, Latin America and China. It thereby offers an original perspective on linkages between migration, hope, and immobility, ranging from migration aspirations to return.

**Nauja Kleist** is a senior researcher at the Danish Institute for International Studies.

**Dorte Thorsen** is theme leader on gender and qualitative research in the Migrating Out of Poverty Research Programme Consortium, University of Sussex, UK and associate researcher at LPED, Aix Marseille Université–IRD, France.

# Routledge Studies in Anthropology

For a full list of titles in this series, please visit www.routledge.com

24 **Magical Consciousness**
An Anthropological and Neurobiological Approach
*Susan Greenwood and Erik D. Goodwyn*

25 **Diagnostic Controversy**
Cultural Perspectives on Competing Knowledge in Healthcare
*Edited by Carolyn Smith-Morris*

26 **Transpacific Americas**
Encounters and Engagements Between the Americas and the South Pacific
*Edited by Eveline Dürr and Philipp Schorch*

27 **The Anthropology of Postindustrialism**
Ethnographies of Disconnection
*Edited by Ismael Vaccaro, Krista Harper and Seth Murray*

28 **Islam, Standards, and Technoscience**
In Global Halal Zones
*Johan Fischer*

29 **After the Crisis**
Anthropological thought, neoliberalism and the aftermath
*James G. Carrier*

30 **Hope and Uncertainty in Contemporary African Migration**
*Edited by Nauja Kleist and Dorte Thorsen*

31 **Work and Livelihoods in Times of Crisis**
*Edited by Susana Narotzky and Victoria Goddard*

32 **Anthropology and Alterity**
*Edited by Bernhard Leistle*

33 **Mixed Race Identities in Australia, New Zealand and the Pacific Islands**
*Edited by Farida Fozdar and Kirsten McGavin*

# Hope and Uncertainty in Contemporary African Migration

Edited by Nauja Kleist and
Dorte Thorsen

NEW YORK AND LONDON

First published 2017 by Routledge

2 Park Square, Milton Park, Abingdon, Oxfordshire OX14 4RN
52 Vanderbilt Avenue, New York, NY 10017

*Routledge is an imprint of the Taylor & Francis Group, an informa business*

First issued in paperback 2019

© 2017 selection and editorial matter, Nauja Kleist and Dorte Thorsen; individual chapters, the contributors

The right of Nauja Kleist and Dorte Thorsen to be identified as the authors of the editorial material, and of the authors for their individual chapters, has been asserted in accordance with sections 77 and 78 of the Copyright, Designs and Patents Act 1988.

The Open Access version of this book, available at www.taylorfrancis.com, has been made available under a Creative Commons Attribution-Non Commercial-No Derivatives 4.0 license.

*Trademark notice*: Product or corporate names may be trademarks or registered trademarks, and are used only for identification and explanation without intent to infringe.

*British Library Cataloguing in Publication Data*
A catalogue record for this book is available from the British Library

*Library of Congress Cataloging in Publication Data*
Names: Kleist, Nauja, editor. | Thorsen, Dorte, editor.
Title: Hope and uncertainty in contemporary African migration / edited by Nauja Kleist and Dorte Thorsen.
Description: London ; New York : Routledge, [2017]
Identifiers: LCCN 2016017845 | ISBN 9781138961210 (hardback : alk. paper) | ISBN 9781315659916 (e-book)
Subjects: LCSH: Africa—Emigration and immigration—Case studies. | African diaspora—Case studies. | Hope—Case studies.
Classification: LCC JV8790 .H67 2017 | DDC 304.8096—dc23
LC record available at https://lccn.loc.gov/2016017845

ISBN: 978-1-138-96121-0 (hbk)
ISBN: 978-0-367-35898-3 (pbk)

DOI: 10.4324/9781315659916

Typeset in Sabon
by ApexCoVantage, LCC

# Contents

*Preface* vii
NAUJA KLEIST AND DORTE THORSEN

*List of Contributors* xi

1  Introduction: Studying Hope and Uncertainty in
   African Migration 1
   NAUJA KLEIST

2  How to Extract Hope from Papers? Classificatory
   Performances and Social Networking in Cape Verdean
   Visa Applications 21
   HEIKE DROTBOHM

3  Sticking to God: Brokers of Hope in Senegalese Migration
   to Argentina 40
   IDA MARIE VAMMEN

4  Zouglou Music and Youth in Urban Burkina Faso:
   Displacement and the Social Performance of Hope 58
   JESPER BJARNESEN

5  The Lack of Liberty Drove Us There: Spatialized Instantiations
   of Hope and Contested Diasporan Identity in the Liberian–
   American Transnational Field (1810–2010) 76
   STEPHEN C. LUBKEMANN

6  Prospective Moments, Eternal Salvation: The Production of
   Hope in Nigerian Pentecostal Churches in China 94
   HEIDI ØSTBØ HAUGEN

7 Hope and Uncertainty in Senegalese Migration to Spain: Taking Chances on Emigration but not Upon Return  113
MARÍA HERNÁNDEZ-CARRETERO

8 The Migratory Adventure as a Moral Experience  134
SYLVIE BREDELOUP

9 Death of a Gin Salesman: Hope and Despair among Ghanaian Migrants and Deportees Stranded in Niger  154
HANS LUCHT

10 Returning with Nothing but an Empty Bag: Topographies of Social Hope after Deportation to Ghana  173
NAUJA KLEIST

Index  193

# Preface

*Nauja Kleist and Dorte Thorsen*

This book started with a walk. On a warm afternoon in March 2008 Nauja, one of the co-editors of this volume, met Sam. She was heading across the campus of the University of Ghana, when a young man addressed her. 'Hi, are you from the States?' 'No, why?' Because, Sam explained in a broad American accent, he loved America but was deported a few years ago. What had started as a promising stay had gradually turned into an ill-fated adventure, mainly because he could not regularize his papers. Now Sam was studying business but badly wanted to return to the United States again, always on the alert for possible connections or opportunities to help him realize his dreams. Nauja studied Ghanaian migration policies at the time, but Sam's story added to her growing puzzlement about the gulf between policy-makers' ideas about well-managed migration and the sense among ordinary Ghanaians of feeling unable to realize their migratory aspirations. She was intrigued.

Meanwhile Dorte, the other co-editor, was doing research with adolescent boys from rural Burkina Faso who audaciously set off on migration to neighboring Côte d'Ivoire, sometimes without knowing where they would sleep on arrival and sometimes with insufficient money for the entire fare. They talked about being housed and fed temporarily by strangers and help extended by migrant relatives, but their accounts also dwelled on suffering. The boys were not pioneers but followed in the footsteps of older brothers, fathers, and grandfathers in trying to broaden their opportunities and move out of poverty. Dorte was astounded by her young interlocutors' disregard of barriers to their migration and how they had to negotiate border control, whether they had the right papers or not.

Gradually, our initial curiosity grew into a research program on new geographies of hope and despair in West African migration, developed and conducted with Ida Maria Vammen. We set out to explore the effects of restrictive mobility regimes for West African migration, taking our departure in a contemporary mobility paradox: that images and ideas of the good life, often taking place elsewhere, are circulated all over the globe, while access to legal international mobility circuits is a scarce resource for most people with non-Western citizenship. We then asked what this mobility paradox means for hope for West Africans migrants and their families, approaching hope as an analytical perspective that highlights anticipation and the simultaneous potentiality and uncertainty of the future.

Finalizing this book, the topic of hope, uncertainty, and migration seems more topical than ever. The emergence of the so-called refugee crisis, with one million people crossing the Mediterranean in 2015, has brought unprecedented public and political attention to migration. Poignant images have gone viral of the small body of Aylan Kurdi, washed ashore, and of the many men, women, and children on highways walking from the southern and eastern borders of the European Union. Meanwhile, most European states have implemented increasingly restrictive asylum and migration policies. In the process, the terms migrant and refugee have become conflated into one category, which is now widely connoted with persons whose mobility is considered illegal and purely motivated by economic motives. In this flawed logic, migrants are pulled by mirages of Europe, as soldiers of fortune, driven by ignorant hopes, while refugees' need for, and right to, protection has been downplayed unless they agree to remain in the so-called neighboring area.

This is a deeply problematic assumption which fails to take into account the multiplicity of political, sociocultural, and economic dimensions of mobility. It also ignores the ambivalence and precariousness of hope. Focusing on stereotypes, the webs of social relations, livelihood practices, collective social imaginaries, and aspirations remain hidden or are impugned. Likewise, the focus on boat migration easily overshadows the fact that most African migrants do not cross the Mediterranean in a rickety boat to Europe. Rather they tend to travel within their region or, increasingly, orient themselves towards destinations in the so-called Global South. A considerable number also find themselves stranded *en route*, emphasizing the importance of involuntary immobility and the many constraints that migrants face.

In this collection, we explore these other dimensions of African migration through nine case studies, ranging from countries of origin to destinations elsewhere in Africa, Europe, and further afield. The chapters analyze how migrants, their families, and local communities deal with the effects of restrictive mobility regimes and economic and political crisis, answering the following questions: What are the meanings and implications of hope in African migration? How is hope generated, distributed, brokered, or withheld in practices of mobility and situations of immobility—and how is it associated with different locations and futures? We thereby aim to put hope in context.

Finally, a note of thanks to all the people and institutions who have made this book possible. Research is a collective affair where we learn from other scholars and our interlocutors. It requires not only rigor but also openness to serendipity. An afternoon walk may be the first step in an unexpected direction. Whether those steps turn into something tangible—a research program or a book—depends on whether people want to talk and work with you. We have a lot to be grateful for. We thank the Danish Research

Council for Independent Research for generous funding. The chapters in this volume are partly based on papers from a panel at the 13th IUAES (International Union of Anthropological and Ethnological Sciences) congress in Manchester, 5–10 August 2013, and partly on new contributions. We are grateful to all participants in our panel, particularly to discussant Mattia Fumanti, University of St. Andrews. Likewise, we would like to thank all the contributors to this volume for their commitment; the two anonymous peer reviewers for their constructive and insightful comments on the entire manuscript; Jenny Money for her thorough language editing; great colleagues at the Danish Institute for International Studies (DIIS), especially Ida Maria Vammen, Ninna Nyberg Sørensen, Robin May Schott and Finn Stepputat, for commenting on and discussing different parts of the book; and finally the participants at the end-of-award conference 'Precarious Futures?', 16–19 September 2015, whose papers and discussions—although not meant for this book—helped to refine the final edition and argument.

We further thank the many interlocutors in Ghana, Burkina Faso, Côte d'Ivoire, Morocco, and elsewhere who have been so generous with their time, life stories, and ideas to help us understand some of the many aspects of migratory pathways. As her mother's four-year-long fight against cancer comes to an end, Dorte extends her thanks to the cancer treatment units, the palliative team, and her sister and father for doing much of the in-person care and to telecommunications for allowing care work at a distance. Nauja is grateful to her family, Sophia, Jonathan and Justin, for staying with her in Ghana during extended fieldwork trips and for their patience and love.

*Copenhagen and Brighton, December 2015*

# Contributors

**Jesper Bjarnesen** is a Senior Researcher at the Nordic Africa Institute in Uppsala, working on regional and war-related mobilities in West Africa, with a focus on inter-generational relations and urban youth culture in Burkina Faso and Côte d'Ivoire. He is also part of a research project on electoral violence and public protests in Burundi. He holds a PhD in cultural anthropology at the Department of Cultural Anthropology and Ethnology at Uppsala University and has published a dissertation on wartime mobilities in the context of the civil war in Côte d'Ivoire. He has previously done research on migrant aspirations and marginality in Senegal. He has published articles in *Migration Letters, Nordic Journal of African Studies*, and *Anthropology Southern Africa* and edited a theme section of *Conflict and Society*.

**Sylvie Bredeloup** is a Senior Researcher at the French Institute of Research for Development (IRD, LPED/Aix-Marseille University). Her research focuses on sub-Saharan African international migrations, including transit migration, programmed and precipitated return migration, and social and spatial changes in the cities in relation with mobility. Her publications include several books, the most recent being *Migrations d'aventures: Terrains africains* (Paris, CTHS, 2014), and over eighty articles in academic journals and books, such as the *Journal of African Cultural Studies, Urban Anthropology UAS*, and *Population, Space and Place*. Bredeloup is the coordinator of the regional research program 'Mobilities, Travels, Innovations and Dynamics in Mediterranean and sub-Saharan Africa' (MOVIDA), gathering together 55 African and European researchers.

**Heike Drotbohm** is Heisenberg Professor at the Department of Anthropology and African Studies at the University of Mainz in Germany. She conducted fieldwork in creole settings in Haiti, Cape Verde, Canada and the US, as well as Brazil. Her research focuses on transnational family arrangements, care in transnational social fields and return migration, and migrant deportation in particular. Drotbohm has published in the *Journal of Ethnic and Migration Studies, Citizenship Studies*, and *History of the Family* as well as in a number of books.

**Heidi Østbø Haugen** is a Postdoctoral Researcher in the Department of Sociology and Human Geography, University of Oslo; she has a PhD in Human Geography. Her research focuses on migration and trade between China and West Africa. Between 2009 and 2016, she carried out 16 months of ethnographic fieldwork among Africans in Guangzhou, South China. She has also travelled alongside some of her research participants to Nigeria, Ghana, Togo, and the Gambia. Her work on Sino-African migration is been published in, inter alia, *Ethnic and Racial Studies, International Migration* and *African Studies Review*. Prior to starting an academic career, she studied Chinese at Beijing Normal University and worked for the World Food Programme in Dakar. She is a steering-group member of the Chinese in Africa/Africans in China Research Network and has previously chaired the Nordic Association for China Studies.

**María Hernández-Carretero** is currently a Senior Researcher at the Norwegian Centre for Violence and Traumatic Stress Studies (NKVTS) in Oslo, Norway, where she does research on young refugees' experiences after resettlement in Norway. She was previously a doctoral researcher at the Peace Research Institute Oslo (PRIO) and has done research on migration imaginations and aspirations, the social dynamics of migration and migrant transnationalism, non-migrants' perspectives and experiences, and unauthorized migration by sea, including migrant views on risk and risk-taking and European migration control policies and practices. Her main empirical focus to date has been on Senegalese migration to Europe, particularly Spain. She has published in *Human Organization, the British Journal of Politics and International Relations* and *Journal of Ethnic and Migration Studies*.

**Nauja Kleist** is a Senior Researcher at the Danish Institute for International Studies, with a PhD in Sociology. Her research interests comprise transnational return migration and deportation, restrictive mobility regimes, remittances, diaspora mobilization, and states' migration–development policies. Another strand of research focuses on hope, reciprocity, belonging, recognition, and gender relations. She has, in particular, studied Ghanaian migration and Somali diaspora groups. Kleist has published in, for example, *African Affairs, Journal of Ethnic and Migration Studies, African Studies, African Diaspora* and in a number of books. She is the coordinator of the research program 'New Geographies of Hope and Despair', which examines the social effects of migration management for West African migrants.

**Stephen Lubkemann** is Associate Professor of Anthropology, International Affairs, and Africana Studies at The George Washington University, and is the Co-Director of the GWU Diaspora Research Program. Lubkemann's research investigates social, political, and economic transformation in war-torn societies, and diasporas and their relationship to political and economic development. He currently coordinates a major international project on diaspora impacts in post-conflict societies as well as the African Slave Wrecks Project. His publications have appeared in numerous journals and include the award-finalist book *Culture in chaos: An anthropology of the social condition in war* (Chicago 2008).

**Hans Lucht** is a Senior Researcher and anthropologist at the Danish Institute for International Studies (DIIS) in Copenhagen. He holds a PhD in Anthropology from the Department of Anthropology, University of Copenhagen. Lucht's research focuses on undocumented migration from West Africa to Europe and his book *Darkness before daybreak—African migrants living on the margins in Southern Italy today* (University of California Press) won the 2012 Elliott P. Skinner Book Award from the Association for Africanist Anthropology.

**Dorte Thorsen** is Theme Leader on Gender and Qualitative Research in the Migrating Out of Poverty Research Programme Consortium, University of Sussex, UK and Associate Researcher at LPED, Aix Marseille Université–IRD, France. Her research focuses on African migrations; one strain explores the experience of migrants from sub-Saharan Africa living in urban Morocco, another children's and youth's migration from rural Burkina Faso to urban areas in Burkina Faso and Côte d'Ivoire. She is involved in research on intra-household dynamics, migration, and youth aspirations in Bangladesh, Ghana, Indonesia, Rwanda and Vietnam. She has published widely on the issue of adolescents' migration, e.g., the monograph *Child migration in Africa* (Zed Books, with I. Hashim), book chapters and journal articles in *Canadian Journal of Africa Studies*, *International Development Planning Review*, and *Hommes et migration*.

**Ida Marie Vammen** is a PhD Fellow in the Department of Anthropology, University of Copenhagen. She is part of the research program 'New Geographies of Hope and Despair', anchored at the Danish Institute for International Studies. Her current work revolves around the recent transatlantic migration flow from West African to South America, exploring how different social and legal possibility structures and constraints influence the migrants' livelihood strategies and notions of hope, risk, and failure, as well as their transnational family relations.

# 1 Introduction

## Studying Hope and Uncertainty in African Migration

*Nauja Kleist*

Contemporary migration is characterized by a mobility paradox: the increased reach and accessibility of communication, media and transport technologies mean that people in many parts of the world are exposed to visions of the good life elsewhere. At the same time, because of growing inequality, paired with restrictive mobility regimes, the vast majority of people in the Global South are excluded from the circuits of legal mobility, not least on the African continent.

This volume uses hope as an analytical prism through which to examine the mobility paradox in African migration. For millions of Africans, migration constitutes one of the ways in which to cope with uncertainty and difficult life situations. The volume analyzes migrants' temporal and spatial horizons of expectation and possibility and how these horizons link to mobility practices in contexts of uncertainty and precariousness. Such analysis is pertinent, we argue, because deepening marginalization and increasingly restrictive regimes of mobility define the lives of many Africans, while migration continues to offer important livelihood strategies. The consequences are the intensification of high-risk migration, such as the crossings over the Sahara Desert and the Mediterranean Sea, involuntary immobility when (aspiring) migrants cannot leave their countries of origin or are stranded in transit zones surrounding the desired destinations (cf. Carling 2002; Lubkemann 2008), and, finally, the emergence and consolidation of new destinations in the Global South and BRIC countries, like China, Brazil, and Argentina.

We argue that hope constitutes a fruitful analytical framework in which to link questions of political economy and mobility regimes with analyses of the collective social imaginaries and aspirations which imbue migration projects—to examine the social effects of the mobility paradox, in other words. We approach hope in a broad sense as an anticipation of the 'not-yet' (Bloch 1986), characterized by simultaneous potentiality—faith or confidence in the future—and uncertainty. As Lubkemann suggests in this volume, hope can be perceived as the 'sustenance of the possibility of a (desired) alternative to a (currently lived) reality'. Hope is neither a description of the present nor pure fantasy. It is linked to social imaginaries understood as 'what enables,

DOI: 10.4324/9781315659916-1

through making sense of, the practices of a society' (Taylor 2004, 2). Hope is grounded within the realm of the thinkable or imaginable and hence has a strong collective and normative dimension. It may inspire action (Cole and Durham 2008; Sarro 2015), make people cope with suffering and difficult life situations (Zigon 2009), or lead to resignation and passivity (Crapanzano 2003). Being embedded in uncertainty, hoping is different from knowing or from having absolute faith. Hope can be disappointed and may remain a distant horizon. Yet uncertainty may also invoke hope in that the future remains unpredictable (Cooper and Pratten 2015a; Johnson-Hanks 2005). In that sense, hope offers a particular take on uncertainty, one which emphasizes potentiality and anticipation rather than fear and doubt.

Approaching hope as an analytical framework thus implies examining both potentiality and uncertainty. The focus on potentiality means analyzing social imaginaries of the good life or 'sparks' of faith or confidence, however frail; uncertainty implies examining precarious or unpredictable life conditions and how the hoping subject deals with them. A hope perspective enables us to analyze how visions of the good life or future are generated and distributed, and how horizons of possibility and expectations are linked to different places and temporalities. It thus illuminates meaning-making practices and the potentiality of life, to explore how and whether migrants maintain or create a sense of anticipation or faith in the future in uncertain and precarious situations.

There has been a revival of interest in hope and the future in anthropology and social philosophy since the turn of the millennium (e.g., Crapanzano 2003; Miyazaki 2004; Rorty 1999; Thompson and Zizek 2013; Webb 2007). Key themes include temporality (Appadurai 2013; Cole and Durham 2008; Dalsgård *et al.* 2014; Miyazaki 2004; 2006; Piot 2010), social change (Castells 2012; Hage 2003; Zournazi 2002), and uncertainty (Cooper and Pratten 2015b; Horst and Grabska 2015; Johnson-Hanks 2005). Despite the centrality of mobility and migration in contemporary life, studies of mobility and immobility constitute a surprisingly small strand of the anthropological literature on hope (for exceptions, see Cole 2014; Hage and Papadopoulos 2004; Kleist and Jansen 2016; Lucht 2011; Mar 2005; Narotzky and Besnier 2014; Pine 2014; Vigh 2009). Our volume contributes to this literature in three ways—first, by suggesting an analytical framework for studying hope in relation to migration and (im)mobility, second, by situating African migration in the mobility paradox, and, third, by exploring hope in a range of ethnographically grounded and theoretically informed case studies on the continent and beyond.

The chapters focus primarily on West African migration. As a region, West Africa has been shaped by mobility for centuries. From the transatlantic slave trade, forced labor migration, and seasonal mobile livelihoods to inter-continental migration to Europe, North America, and emerging destinations in Latin America and Asia, West Africa is characterized by long-established mobility practices (e.g., Akyeampong 2000). Reflecting this nature, the volume is global in geographical scope, with case studies set in neighboring countries in West Africa, zones of transit on the continent, and new and established destinations further afield to migrants' countries of origin in the case of aspiring migrants or returnees. The chapters analyze how African migrants contend with and circumvent impediments to their mobility: how they struggle with perilous situations, generate strategies to accumulate material and symbolic wealth and grasp new opportunities, and their imaginative work in insisting on the possibility of devising a meaningful life, but also elaborate on extended periods of waiting, and of suffering, shame, and social death when migration projects fail and hope is postponed or lost.

To avoid misunderstandings, let me also emphasize what we do *not* do in this volume. We do not claim that migration is determined by migrants' individual hopes alone, as a kind of reversed rational-choice approach where 'information' has been replaced by hopes or dreams. Such an approach would ignore not only situations of conflict and violence but also the structural opportunities and constraints, including the sometimes restraining sets of social and economic obligations and expectations in which much migration is embedded. It also lends itself to the perception shared by many policymakers that migrants are uninformed and unrealistic soldiers of fortune whose mobility can be prevented through information campaigns about the hardships of life in Europe or other destinations. Not only is this a misguided perception, but it also reflects a theoretically flawed conceptualization of hope as naïve optimism and individual desires. Rather, the volume as a whole emphasizes the pertinence of social and collective hope as well as anxiety, frustration, periods of waiting, shame, and failure, as much as achievement and notions of meaningful futures. A focus on hope thus offers a fundamentally ambivalent perspective.

The remainder of the introduction is structured in the following way. First, I elaborate on the mobility paradox; second, I present an analytical framework for studying the relationship between hope, mobility, and immobility; and third, I situate the chapters in relation to three overall themes: repositories of hope, temporality, and existential (im)mobility.

## The Mobility Paradox: Stratified Globalization and Restrictive Mobility Regimes

Two sets of conditions make the analysis of migration, mobility, and immobility in relation to hope particularly relevant today: widespread crisis and rising inequality, and the consolidation and expansion of restrictive mobility regimes.

Crisis and precarity constitute permanent conditions of life for many people today (Cooper and Pratten 2015b; Hage 2003; 2009; Horst and Grabska 2015; Standing 2014). Stratified processes of globalization marked by privatization, the expansion of markets, and deregulation have deteriorated the living conditions of millions of people (Sassen 2014). Likewise conflict, political instability, everyday violence, and the effects of securitization create or deepen precarity. Such processes can be observed all over the world—including Africa, with its history of IMF-induced structural adjustment programs since the 1980s and, in many countries, the continuous deregularization of the economy and cut-back of state services (Ferguson 2006; Harrison 2005). Hence, whereas the global financial crisis unleashed in 2008 exacerbated conditions of precarity, it did not create them alone (cf. Makhulu et al. 2010). Indeed, in many African countries and elsewhere in the world, a sense of enduring crisis or marginalization is experienced as a permanent life condition, which has led to a diminished belief in the state's capacity to secure a good life (Johnson-Hanks 2005; Narotzky and Besnier 2014). Crisis may indeed be the context, rather than the exception, as Vigh (2008) has suggested.

One of the implications of this observation is the pertinence of uncertainty (Cooper and Pratten 2015a; Horst and Grabska 2015). Two sources of uncertainty can be distinguished: imperfect knowledge and the unpredictability of the future (Williams and Baláz 2012, 168). As Horst and Grabska (2015) point out, both sources are relevant in relation to conflict and displacement—and indeed to a range of other situations. Johnson-Hanks has described how life in Cameroun is characterized by such extreme unpredictability that 'plans are always tenuous, partial, more hope than conviction' (2005, 369). This, however, does not mean that uncertainty is implicating passivity or resignation. Rather, uncertainty can be productive, constituting 'a social resource [which] can be used to negotiate insecurity, conduct and create relationships and act as a source for imagining the future with the hopes and fears this entails' (Cooper and Pratten 2015a, 2; cf. di Nunzio 2015). Uncertainty implies an at least preliminary lack of closure and hence a space for hope.

Rising inequality constitutes another relevant dimension for examining the mobility paradox. Inequality in an African context is not novel, of course, given the history of the extraction of human and natural resources over several centuries, from the slave trade to colonization and postcolonial predatory regimes in some parts of the continent. Inequality today, however, is also linked to the contemporary processes of stratified globalization, as indicated above. Some African economies are booming. Seven out of ten of the fastest-growing economies in the world between 2011 and 2015 were African, yet income inequality increased in the same period (Chotikapanich et al. 2014, 3). One dimension of the African 'lion economies' and high growth rates is precisely increasing inequality, where some get rich and richer—quickly and visibly—while the number of poor people is rising (Chotikapanich et al. 2014; Mubila et al. 2012). Another dimension is that the spectacles of modernity and conspicuous consumption of global and national elites—such as corporate buildings made of steel and glass, luxury cars, and expensive consumer brands—are plainly visible in African capitals and major cities. To be seen but not to be touched or lived in. Likewise, there are construction booms of comfortable private residences in many places, often owned by international migrants (Graw and Schielke 2012; Makhulu *et al.* 2010; Smith and Mazzucato 2009).

Inequality may inspire migration, especially in those parts of Africa with a well-developed culture of migration (Graw and Schielke 2012), where migration is often seen as one of the few possible ways to change one's situation for the better. As is well documented in the literature on West African migration, internal, regional, and intercontinental migration constitutes established livelihood strategies, modes of fulfilling social obligations, sending remittances, pursuing further education, or establishing access to opportunities for oneself or one's family (Akyeampong 2000; Awedoba and Hahn 2014; Cligget 2003; Cole 2014; Graw and Schielke 2012; Horst 2004; Kabki *et al.* 2004; Nieswand 2013; Riccio 2008). Whereas most West African migration takes place within the region (Ratha *et al.* 2011), there is significant migration not only on and outside the continent, including Europe and North America, as well as to emerging destinations in Asia and Latin America.

However, the consolidation of contemporary regimes of mobility (Glick Schiller and Salazar 2013) has made access to legal migration an increasingly unequally distributed privilege. This is the second aspect of the mobility paradox. Restrictive immigration policies in Europe—and indeed most places in the world—filter and divide migrants into desired and undesired categories, according to qualifications, labor shortage, and assessment of migrants' perceived intentions or likelihood to overstay their visas or engage in other kinds of unauthorized activity (Gammeltoft-Hansen 2011). Migrants are thus subjected to risk assessment in terms of (what may develop into) irregular entry to or stays in Europe or other (perceived) destinations, even when their mobility may be perfectly legal at the outset. The result is that the majority of Africans are *de facto* excluded from legal migration to Europe and other parts of Africa outside their home region. The maritime border zones of the Mediterranean Sea and the Atlantic Ocean, which simultaneously link and separate North and West Africa from Europe, are heavily patrolled through the use of increasingly sophisticated surveillance technology. Furthermore, European border control is increasingly externalized and carried out in collaboration with local authorities and private companies in transit and departure areas in African countries, including territorial waters and coastal and inland areas (Andersson 2014; Carling and Hernández-Carretero 2011; Gammeltoft-Hansen 2011; 2013; Lemberg-Pedersen 2013; Streiff-Fénart and Segatti 2014).

This development has made unauthorized migration more difficult, dangerous, and expensive. This is a global tendency. African migration, however, is the most affected in the world when counting fatalities within the continent and especially towards Europe (Brian and Laczko 2014). Between January and September 2014 were registered the deaths of 3,072 people crossing the Mediterranean on the way to Europe, of whom 30 per cent were of sub-Saharan (mainly West and Central African) origin (2014, 25). In 2015, the registered number of dead or missing persons between January and the middle of December was 3,605[1] and this number continues to increase. Zooming further out, there were an estimated 22,294 fatalities between 2000 and 2014, making the Mediterranean by far the deadliest border region in the world (Brian and Laczko 2014). Crossing the Sahara to reach Libya or other North African countries for the purpose of work or onward migration is another deadly migration route, with 1,790 reported fatalities between 1996 and 2013 (2014, 24), although these figures are most certainly under-reported.

The high number of fatalities is testimony to the fact that restrictive mobility regimes do not put an end to high-risk and unauthorized migration. What is more, the waning of legal migration possibilities does not only concern intercontinental migration to established destinations; the EU's global approach to migration management has repercussions for intra-African migration in terms of more restrictive border control within the continent. Migrants experience prolonged blockages in so-called transit zones, partly or wholly funded and implemented by the EU. The borderlands in Niger and Libya (Brachet 2010; Bredeloup and Pliez 2011) and Senegal, Mauretania and Morocco (Andersson 2014; Streiff-Fénart and Segatti 2014) provide well-known examples. Likewise, the EU has funded and supported migration management programs in a range of sending countries, focusing on the prevention of (what is expected to become) irregular migration into Europe, for instance through the introduction of biometric identification, intensified and technologized document control and sensitization campaigns (Andersson 2014; Kleist 2015). Such blockages and impediments may terminate, deter, or defer migration through detention or deportation (Andersson 2014; Andrijasevic 2010). Likewise, they may cause prolonged periods of immobility while waiting for mobility 'openings' (Poutignat 2012) or connections (Alpes 2011), or while accumulating funds (Lucht 2011). They constitute thresholds, as Jocelyne Streiff-Fénart and Aurelia Segatti (2014) argue.

The growth and consolidation of global and local inequalities, in combination with restrictive mobility regimes, exacerbate conditions of uncertainty in relation to migrants' livelihoods and possible futures, as described above. However they also generate new geographies of hope. Whereas Western countries have been affected by the economic crisis unleashed in 2008, rising economies in the South are reshaping the distribution of possibilities globally, following their emerging markets and high growth rates. One of the consequences is the emergence of new migration destinations, due to the combination of restrictive mobility regimes in established destinations and economic growth in the BRIC countries (Brazil, Russia, India and China) and a range of other states.

The authors in this volume explore these transformations, examining how precarious living conditions, restrictive mobility regimes, and new opportunities frame contemporary African migration and the hopes underpinning it.

## Situating Hope: Potentiality, Uncertainty and Social Imaginaries

Hope is a tricky concept to pin down, with its simultaneous vernacular and theoretical usages, ranging from everyday aspirations to eschatology and existentialism. The contributors to this volume do not necessarily employ the same hope theories but do share an overall approach to hope as 'a socially mediated human capacity' (Webb 2007, 68). This implies attention to the situatedness of hope, i.e., the social imaginaries and realities that hope is embedded in or inspired by. Furthermore, as indicated above, hope as an analytical perspective implies attention to simultaneous potentiality and uncertainty of future. Below I elaborate on these two interrelated dimensions in more detail.

According to Ernst Bloch, perhaps the most well-known of the hope theorists, hope is 'the most human of all mental feelings' (1986, 75), constituting the antithesis to despair, fear, and anxiety. In Bloch's opus magnum *The Principle of Hope* (1986), he calls for a temporal reorientation of philosophy from retrospection to the future (cf. Miyazaki 2004), approaching hope as an anticipatory consciousness towards the 'not-yet-become' (Bloch 1986, 11) and as embedded in the conditions of the present. This has become an influential position in hope theories. As Craig Browne notes:

> From Ernst Bloch through to Richard Rorty, discussions of hope in philosophy and social theory have highlighted the significance of anticipation and the practical consequences of projections that simultaneously emerge in the present but point beyond it.
>
> (2005, 68)

The focus on anticipation is central for our understanding of hope. The emphasis on potentiality implies confidence in the future but also entails the possibility of failure and slippage (Whyte 2002; Zigon 2009). The hoping subject does not know if or when uncertainty turns into certainty and the potentiality of hope evaporates or materializes. Hope is not static but may change, be transformed, weakened, or strengthened. Such a perspective thus emphasizes the temporality and elasticity of hope—how it is related to processes of becoming and horizons of expectation and possibility (Graw and Schielke 2012; Narotzky and Besnier 2014). However, the modes and content of hope are situated in overall socio-economic and socio-cultural setups, in specific times and places (cf. Cole and Durham 2008).

The situated nature of hope thus accentuates attention to its collective and social dimensions and how they are related to social imaginaries and collective visions of the good and meaningful life and future within particular societies and groups. This is what Ghassan Hage (2003) calls *social hope*.[2] Migration and mobility are important elements of social hope in some societies, connoting potentiality and hope at the symbolical and material levels despite the uncertainty and risk that migration may imply. Hage emphasizes the role of the nation-state as the most important actor in generating and distributing social hope to the population—so-called *societal hope*. Societal hope consists of visions of the good life and achievement within society. Such visions may be related to upward social mobility, security, and/or social recognition or symbolic capital in a Bourdieusian sense (Bourdieu and Wacquant 1992). The power of societal hope is 'the ability to maintain an *experience* of the *possibility* of upward social mobility' (Hage 2003, 13, emphasis in original)—in spite of existing structural constraints and inequalities. Inspired by Bloch, we may say that societal hope is an example of how the state puts the potentiality of the 'not-yet' to work.

Hage's concept of societal hope calls for attention to the political visions of a good life and to the question of who are included in or excluded from these visions. They direct attention to the link between individual hopes and the socio-cultural and politico-economic circumstances in which social hope is generated, distributed, and mapped (cf. Narotzky and Besnier 2014). However, in large parts of Africa, and indeed elsewhere in the world, societal hope for (aspiring) migrants and their families is challenged on at least two fronts. First, by protracted crisis in many countries and precarious life conditions, as described above. Second, by the 'disjunctive sets of "flows" of people, goods, images and ideas' in the present moment of globalization (Cole and Durham 2008, 14; cf. Appadurai 1996; 2013). Such flows may widen and increase social hope through providing alternative visions of the good life and sources of knowledge about how to realize these visions, and where they are supposed to take place. This indicates that the role of the state in generating societal hope is ambivalent to say the least. Indeed, the chapters in this volume amply show that societal hope is not necessarily the most important mode of social hope for migrants and their families. Rather, it is a key concern to distinguish between the different kinds of social hope and their spatial location.

In what follows, the chapters are situated in relation to three dimensions: first, repositories of hope; second, spatial and temporal dimensions of hope; and third, connections between existential and physical (im)mobility in relation to postponed or lost hope.

## Repositories of Hope: Locating Social Hope and Its Pathways

Migration is linked to ideas of different places and the opportunities or constraints they are perceived to offer in a stratified and unequal global world (Mar 2005; Vigh 2009). Such perceptions may be grounded in images circulated in the media and public culture and through social networks. As the chapters in this volume show, much migration is inspired by the success of peers or previous generations of migrants, pointing to the role of social imaginaries and of the past in shaping visions of the future (cf. Sarro 2015). This calls for simultaneous attention to be paid to the content of hope—for instance, to the visions of the good life and how they are associated with certain places—and to the underpinning notions of how to realize or cultivate such hope. In other words, to different sources of knowledge, institutions, and forces that are perceived as brokering or facilitating social hope, however ambivalent or uncertain they may seem to be.

The contributions to this volume examine how notions of opportunities and meaningful lives and futures are located in different places, sources of knowledge and spheres of life. Four such repositories of hope are identified: papers and bureaucracies (Drotbohm and Vammen), spiritual and religious institutions (Haugen, Vammen, Bredeloup, and Lucht), public culture (Bjarnesen), and social networks (especially Drotbohm, Bredeloup, Hernández-Carretero, Lucht, and Kleist).

**Heike Drotbohm** shows how social hope is generated in the interaction with administrative and classificatory regulations of migration regimes in Cape Verde. Analyzing how aspiring migrants understand the relationship between bureaucratic classification and their gendered life and family positions, she shows that the process of visa application at the American Embassy is experienced as a social performance, based on (perceived) knowledge of the logics of the American mobility regime. Whereas the would-be migrants say that they must convince the consular officer of their eligibility through having something or somebody left behind to ensure their return to Cape Verde—for instance, small children—consular officers disregard such ideas as ill-informed rumors. However, Drotbohm points out that the bureaucratic procedures and outcomes of visa applications are so uncertain and incoherent that visa applicants may maintain an, albeit delimited, hope for a future in the United States.

The relationship between legal papers and hope is also central in **Ida Maria Vammen**'s chapter on a regularization program for undocumented Senegalese in Buenos Aires, Argentina. The implications are quite different, however. The amnesty was a result of a lobbying campaign by a Senegalese diaspora association in collaboration with Argentinian human-rights lawyers and NGOs. Vammen examines the conflictual understandings of the program from the point of view of the association on the one hand, and undocumented Senegalese street-hawkers on the other, analyzing how the different actors are seen as 'brokering hope', as she coins it. Whereas the association perceived the amnesty as an expression of brokering societal hope in Argentina through obtaining political rights, the street-hawkers were convinced that it was the work of God. This view was endorsed by a visiting *marabout* and interpreted as religious confirmation of their moral virtue as a group. In their view, social hope was embedded in moral and religious being, rather than in state logics. Religious practice and guidance thus constitute a source of knowledge and a repository of hope for these migrants, rather than the relatively delimited societal hope distributed by the Argentinian state.

**Jesper Bjarnesen** demonstrates how hope can be located in public culture. Focusing on young migrants of Burkinabé heritage who fled from

Côte d'Ivoire to Burkina Faso with their families following the conflict in 2000–05, Bjarnesen shows how this group of young people finds hope in the Ivorian music style of Zouglou and its urban and cosmopolitan mode of life and personal comportment. Having been born and raised in Côte d'Ivoire, these young migrants face challenges of integration in Burkina Faso and of establishing livelihoods in a context characterized by prejudice and competition for scarce resources. Bjarnesen shows how the consumption of Zouglou music and the performance of a confident Zouglouman style serve as a repository of knowledge for a hoped-for future—for instance, through lyrics offering advice on how African migrants should behave in a European metropolis. The social performance of Zouglou thus entails hopefulness, exemplifying how social hope may also be generated in the collective consumption of public cultural flows.

Finally, the chapters emphasize the importance of social networks. The role of family members, friends, experienced migrants, and connection men in supporting, advising, informing, or dreaming about migration runs through almost all the chapters in this volume. Social networks are pertinent in the much-practiced 'migration talk', as Drotbohm terms it, when (aspiring) migrants seek and exchange knowledge about the challenges of visa application, living in a new environment, or handling the hazards of journeys (see also Bredeloup and Hernández-Carretero). Connection men, return migrants, or religious authorities may serve as particularly important sources of knowledge on migration (Vammen, Haugen, Lucht, and Kleist), but social hope may also be generated in the visible or imagined achievement of successful migrants, when they visit, or through the material outcomes of their migration, such as houses, remittances, or prestigious consumer goods (cf. Makhulu et al. 2010). Indeed, much migration is fed on 'inherited hope', as Bjarnesen puts it: following in the footsteps of earlier generations of migrants and repeating their success, as also shown by Bredeloup, Hernández-Carretero, and Kleist.

Social hope is thus exchanged and mediated in and through different repositories and sources of knowledge, including but certainly not delimited to formal channels of information. Rumors, lyrics, sermons, and the ubiquitous migrant houses generate alternative understandings of how migration may be a pathway to a meaningful future and how to realize it. This points to the question of temporality—to when the visions of the good life are supposed to take place—to which I now turn.

## The Time of Hope: Near and Distant Futures

The second overarching theme in the book is the relationship between hope and temporality in migration. A key feature of hope is its futurity; or more precisely, hope may be a key aspect of the future. Following Cole and Durham (2008), the future can be conceptualized as having three dimensions: imaginations of the future through 'specific representations of temporality'; the ways in which individuals orient themselves to the future, for instance, through hope; and, finally, how individuals create the future through 'designing and normalizing new kinds of practices', which may also generate hope in the process (2008, 10).

However, to state that hope is related to the future does not indicate when this 'not-yet' is (imagined to be) taking place. Jane Guyer's (2007) analysis of temporal reorientation in the post-cold war period is useful to consider here. Guyer claims that there has been 'a strange evacuation of the temporal frame of the "near future"' (2007, 409) which has become increasingly 'punctuated', being scheduled by dates, terms, and events that structure everyday life and postpone the meaningful future—the 'not-yet' in Bloch's terms—to an abstract long-term perspective. Guyer shows this through the examples of evangelic and macro-economic thinking. In the first case, meaningful existence is located in prophetic time or 'end time' (cf. Piot 2010) marked by the Second Coming of Christ; in the second case it is postponed to the long run of macro-economic development, where the payoff of economic interventions (or their absence) is supposed to take place. In both cases the result is an extreme long-sightedness and a 'gap between an instantaneous present and an altogether different distant future' (Guyer 2007, 417). Reframing Guyer's thoughts in a hope perspective, we can say that a central question is when and where the potentiality of hope—where 'the good' may happen—is perceived to be taking place.

In this volume, we identify three distinct answers to this question: spatial transposition of hope in the context of the moral breakdown of the present (Lubkemann), temporal reorientation from the future to the present (Haugen), and the postponement of hope to the distant future (Hernández-Carretero, Lucht, and Drotbohm).

**Steven Lubkemann** examines discourses and practices of diasporicity in relation to historical and contemporary considerations of 'return' to Liberia among the descendants of the transatlantic slave-trade in the middle of the nineteenth century and refugees from the civil war in the 1980s and 1990s, respectively. He argues that diasporicity as a social practice is characterized by the sense of attachment *elsewhere* but that this sense is determined by histories and present conditions of structural violence—in this case in relation to slavery and racism in the United States—rather than by originating elsewhere. Thus, in situations of a morally broken down present, hope may be located in a (potential) parallel existence within this *elsewhere*. Diasporicity, then, constitutes a spatialized instantiation of hope, rather than a temporal one. Diasporicity, Lubkemann suggests, may be 'usefully conceived as a particular instantiation of hope which is constructed through processes of social imagination that rely upon spatialization'. Hope is not located in the future, in other words; it can only be imagined in another place.

Such a spatial transposition of hope stands in contrast to temporal reorientations of hope from the future to the present (Miyazaki 2004; Pedersen 2012). Inspired by Ernst Bloch, Hirokazu Miyazaki (2004; 2006) has called for a temporal reorientation of the retrospective nature of philosophy from the past to the future. Miyazaki approaches hope as a method, focusing on the 'prospective momentum entailed in anticipation of what has not-yet-become' (2004, 14)—on sparks of hope in the present. However, Miyazaki also examines how certain concepts and ideas serve as sources of hope taken up by individuals or groups to reorient their knowledge and engagement with the world through changing their modes of life and hence transforming their presence in the process. In such cases, temporal reorientation concerns how the presence is reimagined 'from the perspective of the end' (2006, 157) through the pursuit of particular actions and modes of life. Just as the future cannot be reduced to hope, this approach shows that hope cannot be reduced to a phenomenon exclusively of the future.

Temporal reorientation is central in **Heidi Østbø Haugen**'s chapter on a Pentecostal Nigerian migrant church in Guangzhou, China. The church is mainly patronized by Nigerian traders who often find themselves in difficult and uncertain situations in relation to their businesses and legal situation. Haugen demonstrates how a Nigerian pastor and congregants make sense of and cope with these challenges through religious messages and practices that not only praise achievement, success, and prosperity, and hence generate hope for the future, but also articulate and perform the (hoped-for) achievement as facts of the present, regardless of the challenges they face. The seemingly fantastic promises of wealth constitute a reality still in the making—in the state of the 'not-yet' to use Bloch's term—which can be appreciated, as Haugen argues, for the social momentum they produce, rather than their accuracy. The Pentecostal prosperity gospel thus constitutes a method for practicing hope in the present as well as in the distant future of prophetic time.

In many migration projects, however, the aim is to establish a better life and future 'back home' through saving money, sending remittances, and gaining experience. In these cases the temporary horizon of hope is located in the future. This is indeed the case in **María Hernández-Carretero**'s chapter on the striking difference between decisions to migrate from Senegal to Spain and decisions to return. Hernández-Carretero shows how migrants have been willing to confront considerable uncertainty when migrating to Spain but insist on being well-prepared and hence to minimize uncertainty when returning to Senegal. She argues that this is grounded in pressures and expectations from their family and peers as well as the migrants' perceptions of the capacity of the Spanish and Senegalese states, respectively, to deal with crisis. Whereas they regard the economic crisis in Spain as temporary, Senegal is perceived to be in a state of permanent crisis without much societal hope. In line with Guyer's reflections on temporal reorientation and her distinction between the near and the distant future, Hernández-Carretero shows that the realization of the hoped-for life may be postponed to the distant future while the present and the immediate future is put on hold in the context of crisis, conflict, unemployment, or simply the absence of hoped-for opportunities. Whereas long-term hope may be preserved, the present and immediate future is evacuated.

These perspectives demonstrate the volatility of the temporal horizons of hope. Practicing hope through temporal reorientation locates hope in the present and spatial transposition locates it in an *elsewhere*, whereas many migration projects locate hope in—what is hoped to be—the near future. However, in some cases, hope is postponed or suspended to a more distant future, pointing to the possible failure of migration projects.

## Existential (im)Mobility: The Perseverance and Failure of Hope

The third theme in this volume focuses on the role of hope in delayed or failed migration projects. This concerns the social and existential repercussions when migrants get stranded *en route* and end up in protracted periods of involuntary immobility (Carling 2002; Lubkemann 2008), when they cannot meet the expectations of family members or themselves to send money, let alone return in glorious or just remotely respectable ways or, worst of all, when they come back empty-handed. These are not trivial concerns in the context of economic crisis, political conflict, and restrictive regimes of mobility that characterizes much African migration today. By implication, large numbers of people are excluded from legal or safe migration, their journeys and the outcomes of migration projects are highly uncertain, and the risk of failure is high.

However, as already stated, this has not brought migration to a halt. In spite of uncertainty and possible dangers, migration keeps on connoting potentiality and hope at the symbolical and material levels for many (aspiring) migrants in situations characterized by precarious or stagnating living conditions. Indeed, one of the tensions inherent in the mobility paradox, described in this introduction, is the 'schism between the culturally expected and the possible' (Vigh 2009, 95; cf. Graw and Schielke 2012). Migration is one way of endeavoring to resolve this schism. This may be through sending remittances and/or maintaining or fulfilling other social obligations. However, migration may also be the expression of a related desire to move on in life which, in many cases of African migration, is closely related to fulfilling social and economic expectations and hence become a proper adult man or woman (Cole 2014; Vigh 2006).

The sense of being socially on the move or going somewhere in life has been conceptualized as existential mobility[3] by Ghassan Hage (2009; Hage and Papadopoulos 2004). Hage distinguishes between physical and existential mobility and describes the latter as 'an intrinsic feature of how we experience our humanity' (Hage and Papadopoulos 2004, 112). According to Hage, one of the drivers of migration is a sense of existential stuckedness or of moving too slowly. Migration is 'a powerful trope for imagining oneself as being socially on the move [. . .] and a way of imagining a possible escape from a frozen future', as Gaibazzi has noted in relation to young Soninke men in the Gambia (2014, 173). In other words, the urge to go somewhere in life (existential mobility) may be dealt with through physical mobility. Conversely, existential immobility or 'stuckedness' refers to the feeling of not going anywhere in life, of being stuck.

The connection between existential and physical (im)mobility and how migrants cope with hardship and suffering is explored throughout the chapters. Migration may constitute a moral experience or adventure (Bredeloup and Vammen) where migrants maintain a sense of moving forward in life in spite of challenges. However, for many migrants, involuntary immobility corresponds to a sense of existential immobility, of 'not moving well enough' (cf. Jansen 2014) or even moving backwards, hence a sense of abjection in Ferguson's terms (2006; 2008). As the chapters show, migrants may experience immobility during migration when they are stuck *en route* (Lucht) or in the country of destination (Hernández-Carretero). Other authors show how aspiring migrants and deportees may find themselves in situations of involuntary physical and existential immobility before migration (Drotbohm) or after deportation (Kleist).

Exploring the moral and existential dimensions of hope in the context of uncertainty, involuntary immobility, or delayed or failed migration projects, the chapters point not only to the perseverance of hope but also to its limitations. Taking departure in the notion of migration as *adventure* in Francophone West and Central Africa, **Sylvie Bredeloup** argues that migration constitutes a moral experience for young migrants in their search for moral independence as well as their desire to live a different life, finding fulfillment and returning in a successful way. The social hope invested in migration thus relates to both the process of migration itself and to its outcome. *Adventure* is seen as a stage in life, that of youth, which is to be followed by settling down in socially respectable ways; it may thus be characterized as a hopeful practice. However, in the case of failure—when migrants fail to meet the expectations of their families, their peers, and themselves—*adventure* and other kinds of migration project are embedded in shame and social death.

Failed migration projects may cause migrants to postpone their return. Yet many migrants show a remarkable perseverance in maintaining a sense of hope, in spite of structural constraints and seemingly hopeless situations, whether caused by economic crisis, conflict, or unlucky personal circumstances. Such perseverance is a remarkable feature of **Hans Lucht**'s chapter on Ghanaian migrants in Niamey, Niger, a hub for sub-Saharan migrants waiting or preparing to cross the Sahara to reach Libya. Whereas most migrants spend some time in Niamey waiting for good travel connections or accumulating resources, others end up being stranded, neither being able to move forward nor wanting to return empty-handed. Taking departure in the funeral of a Ghanaian man, Lucht unpacks the migration circumstances and the lost or suspended hopes of a group of stranded Ghanaian migrants.

Living from hand to mouth and in spite of extreme challenges, this group still maintains the hope that their lives will change for the better and that they may once again go back to Ghana in a successful way. Lucht proposes that such perseverance of hope can be understood as a sense of 'existential continuity between one's efforts and the responses they generate'. Not giving up hope indicates a continuing faith that one's efforts will pay off, if not in this lifetime, then in the afterlife.

Whereas the stranded Ghanaians in Niamey refuse to return empty-handed, such refusal is not possible for deportees and other kinds of forced returnee. As shown in several chapters in this book, this mode of return is perceived as the worst possible way of returning, as an unthinkable move, and a catastrophe for both the migrant and his or her family—to be avoided at all costs. In the final chapter of the book, **Nauja Kleist** examines life after deportation in the context of high-risk overland migration from Ghana to Libya and onwards to Europe. Whereas deportees may be seen as successful if they return with money and resources, returning in an untimely way and empty-handed is embedded in feelings of shame and a sense of individual failure, despite widespread knowledge of the dangers and uncertainty related to high-risk migration. Kleist argues that this social conundrum can be understood as an expression of the local persistence of social hope in the lack of convincing and desirable alternatives. Whereas the Ghanaian state distributes societal hope that emphasizes a prosperous future in Ghana through education and hard work, dismissing high-risk and irregular migration, large parts of the population feel excluded from realizing these visions and continue to place social hope in migration as a pathway to a better future. Individualizing failure thus enables the continued collective and social hope for a better life through migration.

These and other chapters in the volume thus demonstrate that the analysis of hope is not equivalent to examining success, achievement, or optimism. Rather, they highlight how much African migration is characterized by challenges and potential failure, although that individual and especially social hope may be maintained, even in the face of seemingly invincible constraints and difficulties.

## In Conclusion: The Ambivalence and Precariousness of Hope

In this introduction, I have argued that hope constitutes a fruitful analytical framework in which to examine the social imaginaries underpinning African migration in the contemporary moment, characterized by inequality, protracted crisis, and restrictive mobility regimes. Whereas the paradoxes of mobility in the late twentieth and early twenty-first centuries have been elaborated on in other anthropological and sociological literature, the contribution of this volume is to link and employ theories of hope with studies of migration and (im)mobility. This provides us with new and insightful ways of examining why and how migration continues to play such a pertinent role in the practices and perceptions of a good and meaningful life, in spite of sometimes formidable challenges.

The framework of hope analysis that I have proposed is based on an understanding of hope as a social and collective phenomenon that encapsulates the simultaneous potentiality and uncertainty of the future. With inspiration from, in particular, Ernst Bloch and Ghassan Hage, I have outlined four dimensions of this framework which are also reflected in the chapters. First, a *distinction between societal hope and other modes of social hope*. This implies examination of the institutions and actors who generate, distribute, and broker collective visions of the good and meaningful life. Second and relatedly, different *repositories of hope*, i.e., the sources of knowledge and spheres of life which provide or inspire social hope in relation to migration. The most central repositories of hope examined in the chapters are social networks, religion, legal papers, and public culture. Third, analysis of the *temporal and spatial horizons of different modes of hope*, where we have identified three models: the spatial transposition of hope in a broken-down present, the temporal reorientation to the present, and the postponement of hope. Fourth, the *relationship between existential and physical im(mobility)*. This calls for attention to be paid to the ways in which migration projects may be disrupted, delayed, or fail, to how hope may be suspended or lost, and to the glimpses of anticipation that tomorrow—or next year—might be different to today and yesteryear, even in seemingly hopeless situations.

Theoretically, this volume thus demonstrates the value of including a hope perspective in migration studies and the pertinence of adding a spatial and mobility dimension to the expanding hope literature. Empirically, it emphasizes the ambivalence and precariousness of social hope in migration in the context of the contemporary mobility paradox. In the face of crisis, conflict, or stasis, many migrants (and other sectors of the population) find visions of a meaningful future and how to realize it in spheres of life other than those distributed by the state they live in or originate from. This reflects dwindling faith in the (nation-)state's ability to secure a meaningful future and provide societal hope for its citizens which, again, adds to the explanation of the importance of migration as a pathway of hope today.

Finally, we make it abundantly clear that an analytical focus on hope should not necessarily be perceived as a hopeful exercise (cf. Crapanzano 2003; Sarro 2015). Migration projects do not always succeed and many migrants find themselves being exploited or 'stuck', without opportunities for sending remittances, moving on to new locations, or returning in socially acceptable ways. Some migrants die or disappear, whereas others are deported empty-handed, facing shame and social death. Hence, the link between mobility and hope is not only embedded in uncertainty but is also precarious. The contributions to this volume do not constitute a celebration of hope in migration but, taken together, they draw attention to how the ambivalent and precarious nature of social hope is exacerbated and amplified by the mobility paradox.

## Acknowledgement

I am grateful for insightful comments and suggestions on earlier versions of this chapter from the two anonymous reviewers, and from Dorte Thorsen, Ninna Nyberg Sørensen, Ida Vammen, Sine Plambech, and Adam Moe Fejerskov.

## Notes

1. Data.unhcr.org/mediterranean/regional.php, accessed 14 December 2015. No information on the nationality of dead or missing persons in 2015 could be found.
2. Rorty coined the notion of social hope, referring to the stories which members of a society 'need to be able to tell themselves [. . .] about how things might get better' (quoted in Schneiderhan 2013, 429).
3. Hage also uses the term 'upward symbolic mobility' rather than 'existential mobility' in his conversation with Papadopoulos (2004).

## References

Akyeampong, E. 2000. Africans in the diaspora: The diaspora and Africa. *African Affairs* 99 (395): 183–215.
Alpes, M. J. 2011. *Bushfalling: How young Cameroonians dare to migrate*. PhD thesis, University of Amsterdam, Institute for Social Science Research.
Andersson, R. 2014. *Illegality, Inc.* Oakland: University of California Press.
Andrijasevic, R. 2010. From exception to excess: Detentions and deportations across the Mediterranean space. In *The deportation regime: Sovereignty, space and the freedom of movement*, eds. N. De Genova and N. Peutz, 147–165. Durham and London: Duke University Press.
Appadurai, A. 1996. *Modernity at large: Cultural dimensions of globalization*. Minneapolis and London: University of Minnesota Press.
Appadurai, A. 2013. *The future as cultural fact: Essays on the global condition*. London and New York: Verso.
Awedoba, A. K., and H. P. Hahn. 2014. Wealth, consumption and migration in a West African society: New lifestyles and new social obligations among the Kasena, Northern Ghana. *Anthropos* 109 (1): 45–55.
Bloch, E. 1986. *The principle of hope*. Cambridge: MIT Press.
Bourdieu, P., and L. Wacquant. 1992. *An invitation to reflexive sociology*. Cambridge: Polity Press.
Brachet, J. 2010. *Blinded by security: Reflections on the hardening of migratory policies in central Sahara*. Oxford: University of Oxford, International Migration Institute Working Paper No. 26.
Bredeloup, S., and O. Pliez. 2011. *The Libyan migration corridor*. Fiesole: Robert Schuman Centre for Advanced Studies, European University Institute, Research Report.
Brian, T., and F. Laczko. 2014. *Fatal journeys: Tracking lives lost during migration*. Geneva: International Organization for Migration.
Browne, C. 2005. Hope, critique, and utopia. *Critical Horizons* 5 (1): 64–86.
Carling, J. 2002. Migration in the age of involuntary immobility: Theoretical reflections and Cape Verdean experiences. *Journal of Ethnic and Migration Studies* 28 (1): 5–42.

Carling, J., and M. Hernández-Carretero. 2011. Protecting Europe and protecting migrants? Strategies for managing unauthorised migration from Africa. *British Journal of Politics and International Relations* 13 (1): 42–58.

Castells, M. 2012. *Networks of outrage and hope: Social movements in the Internet age*. Cambridge and Malden: Polity.

Chotikapanich, D., G. Hajargasht, W. E. Griffiths and C. Xia. 2014. *Inequality and poverty in Africa: Regional updates and estimation of a panel of income distributions*. Rotterdam: Paper prepared for the IARIW 33rd General Conference, 24–30 August.

Cligget, L. 2003. Gift remitting and alliance building in Zambian modernity: Old answers to modern problems. *American Anthropologist* 105 (3): 543–552.

Cole, J. 2014. Producing value among Malagasy marriage migrants in France: Managing horizons of expectation. *Current Anthropology* 55 (S9): S85–S94.

Cole, J., and D. Durham, eds. 2008. *Figuring the future: Globalization and the temporalities of children and youth*. Santa Fe: School of Advanced Research Press.

Cooper, E., and D. Pratten, eds. 2015a. Ethnographies of uncertainty in Africa: An introduction. In *Ethnographies of uncertainty in Africa*, eds. E. Cooper and D. Pratten, 1–16. Basingstoke and New York: Palgrave Macmillan.

Cooper, E., and D. Pratten, eds. 2015b. *Ethnographies of uncertainty in Africa*. Basingstoke and New York: Palgrave Macmillan.

Crapanzano, V. 2003. Reflections on hope as a category of social and psychological analysis. *Cultural Anthropology* 18 (1): 3–32.

Dalsgård, A. L., M. D. Frederiksen, S. Højlund and L. Meinert, eds. 2014. *Ethnographies of youth and temporality: Time objectified*. Philadelphia: Temple University Press.

di Nunzio, M. 2015. Embracing uncertainty: Young people on the move in Addis Ababa's inner city. In *Ethnographies of uncertainty in Africa*, eds. E. Cooper and D. Pratten, 149–172. Basingstoke and New York: Palgrave Macmillan.

Ferguson, J. 2006. *Global shadows: Africa in the neoliberal world order*. Durham: Duke University Press.

Ferguson, J. 2008. Global disconnect: Abjection and the aftermath of modernism. In *Readings in modernity in Africa*, eds. P. Geschiere, B. Meyer and P. Pels, 3–17. London: International Africa Institute.

Gaibazzi, P. 2014. Home as transit: Would-be migrants and immobility in Gambia. In *The challenge of the threshold: Border closures and migration movements in Africa*, eds. J. Streiff-Fénart and A. Segatti, 163–176. Lanham: Lexington Books.

Gammeltoft-Hansen, T. 2011. *Access to asylum: International refugee law and the globalization of migration control*. Cambridge: Cambridge University Press.

Gammeltoft-Hansen, T. 2013. The rise of the private border guard: Accountability and responsibility in the migration control industry. In *The migration industry and the commercialization of international migration*, eds. T. Gammeltoft-Hansen and N. Nyberg Sørensen, 128–151. London and New York: Routledge.

Glick Schiller, N., and N. B. Salazar. 2013. Regimes of mobility across the globe. *Journal of Ethnic and Migration Studies* 39 (2): 183–200.

Graw, K., and S. Schielke. 2012. Introduction: Reflections on migratory expectations in Africa and beyond. In *The global horizon: Expectations of migration in Africa and the Middle East*, eds. K. Graw and S. Schielke, 7–22. Leuven: Leuven University Press.

Guyer, J. I. 2007. Prophecy and the near future: Thoughts on macroeconomic, evangelic, and punctuated time. *American Anthropologist* 34 (3): 409–421.

Hage, G. 2003. *Against paranoid nationalism: Searching for hope in a shrinking society*. Annandale, NSW and London: Pluto Press and Merlin.
Hage, G. 2009. Waiting out the crisis: On stuckedness and governmentality. In *Waiting*, ed. G. Hage, 97–106. Melbourne: Melbourne University Press.
Hage, G., and D. Papadopoulos. 2004. Ghassan Hage in conversation with Dimitris Papadopoulos: Migration, hope and the making of subjectivity in transnational capitalism. *International Journal for Critical Psychology* 12: 95–117.
Harrison, G. 2005. Economic faith, social project and a misreading of African society: The travails of neoliberalism in Africa. *Third World Quarterly* 26 (8): 1303–1320.
Horst, C. 2004. Money and mobility: Transnational livelihood strategies of the Somali diaspora. *Global Migration Perspectives* 9: 1–19.
Horst, C., and K. Grabska. 2015. Introduction. Flight and exile: Uncertainty in the context of conflict-induced displacement. *Social Analysis* 59 (1): 1–18.
Jansen, S. 2014. On not moving well enough: Temporal reasoning in Sarajevo yearnings for 'normal lives'. *Current Anthropology* 55 (S9): S74–S84.
Johnson-Hanks, J. 2005. When the future decides: Uncertainty and intentional action in contemporary Cameroon. *Current Anthropology* 46 (3): 363–385.
Kabki, M., V. Mazzucato and E. Appiah. 2004. 'Wo benanE a EyE bebree': The economic impact of remittances of Netherlands-based Ghanaian migrants on rural Ashanti. *Population, Space and Place* 10 (2): 85–97.
Kleist, N. 2015. Policy spectacles: Promoting migration–development scenarios in Ghana. In *Mobility makes states: Migration and power in Africa*, eds. J. Quirk and D. Vigneswaran, 125–146. Pennsylvania: University of Pennsylvania Press.
Kleist, N. and S. Jansen. 2016. Introduction. Hope over Time-Crisis, Immobility and Future-Making. *History and Anthropology* 27 (4): 373–392.
Lemberg-Pedersen, M. 2013. Private security companies and the European borderscapes. In *The migration industry and the commercialization of international migration*, eds. T. Gammeltoft-Hansen and N. Nyberg Sørensen, 152–172. London and New York: Routledge.
Lubkemann, S. C. 2008. Involuntary immobility: On a theoretical invisibility in forced migration studies. *Journal of Refugee Studies* 21 (4): 454–475.
Lucht, H. 2011. *Darkness before daybreak: African migrants living on the margins in Southern Italy today*. Berkeley, Los Angeles and London: University of California Press.
Makhulu, A.-M., B. A. Buggenhagen and S. Jackson. 2010. Introduction. In *Hard work, hard times: Global volatility and African subjectivities*, eds. A.-M. Makhulu, B. A. Buggenhagen and S. Jackson, 1–27. Berkeley, Los Angeles and London: University of California Press.
Mar, P. 2005. Unsettling potentialities: Topographies of hope in transnational migration. *Journal of Intercultural Studies* 26 (4): 361–378.
Miyazaki, H. 2004. *The method of hope: Anthropology, philosophy, and Fijian knowledge*. Palo Alto, CA: Stanford University Press.
Miyazaki, H. 2006. Economy of dreams: Hope in global capitalism and its critiques. *Cultural Anthropology* 21 (2): 147–172.
Mubila, M., L. Lannes and M. S. Ben Aissa. 2012. Income inequality in Africa. In *Briefing Notes for AfDB's Long-Term Strategy*, 1–6. Tunis: African Development Bank.
Narotzky, S., and N. Besnier. 2014. Crisis, value, and hope. Rethinking the economy: An introduction to Supplement 9. *Current Anthropology* 55 (S9): S4–S16.
Nieswand, B. 2013. The burger's paradox: Migration and the transnationalization of social inequality in southern Ghana. *Ethnography* 15 (4): 403–425.

Pedersen, M. A. 2012. A day in the Cadillac: The work of hope in urban Mongolia. *Social Analysis* 56 (2): 136–151.
Pine, F. 2014. Migration as hope: Space, time and imagining the future. *Current Anthropology* 55 (S9): S95–S104.
Piot, C. 2010. *Nostalgia for the future: West Africa after the Cold War*. Chicago and London: University of Chicago Press.
Poutignat, P. 2012. Migration at the level of individuals: Life trajectories in Mauretania and Spain. In *The challenge of the threshold: Border closures and migration movements in Africa*, eds. J. Streiff-Fénart and A. Segatti, 177–196. Lanham: Lexington Books.
Ratha, D., S. Mohapatra, C. Özden, C. Plaza, W. Shaw and A. Shimeles. 2011. *Leveraging migration for Africa: Remittances, skills, and investments*. Washington, DC: The World Bank.
Riccio, B. 2008. West African transnationalisms compared: Ghanaians and Senegalese in Italy. *Journal of Ethnic and Migration Studies* 34 (2): 217–234.
Rorty, R. 1999. *Philosophy and social hope*. London: Penguin.
Sarro, R. 2015. Hope, margin, example: The Kimbanguist diaspora in Lisbon. In *Religion in diaspora: Cultures of citizenship*, eds. J. Garnett and S. Hausner, 226–242. London: Palgrave Macmillan.
Sassen, S. 2014. *Expulsions: Brutality and complexity in the global economy*. Cambridge, MA and London: The Belknap Press of Harvard University Press.
Schneiderhan, E. 2013. Rorty, Addams, and social hope. *Humanities* 2: 421–438.
Smith, L., and V. Mazzucato. 2009. Constructing homes, building relationships: Migrant investments in houses. *Tijdschrift voor Economische en Sociale Geografie* 100 (5): 662–673.
Standing, G. 2014. *The precariat: The new dangerous class*. London and New York: Bloomsbury Academic.
Streiff-Fénart, J., and A. Segatti. 2014. Threshold policies: Discourses and practices of control and closure. In *The challenge of the threshold: Border closures and migration movements in Africa*, eds. J. Streiff-Fénart and A. Segatti, ix–xviii. Lanham: Lexington Books.
Taylor, C. 2004. *Modern social imaginaries*. Durham and London: Duke University Press.
Thompson, P., and S. Zizek, eds. 2013. *The privatization of hope: Ernst Bloch and the future of utopia*. Durham and London: Duke University Press.
Vigh, H. 2006. Social death and violent life chances. In *Navigating youth, generating adulthood: Social becoming in an African context*, eds. C. Christiansen, M. Utas and H. E. Vigh, 31–60. Uppsala: Nordic Africa Institute.
Vigh, H. 2008. Crisis and chronicity: Anthropological perspectives on continuous conflict and decline. *Ethnos* 73 (1): 5–24.
Vigh, H. 2009. Wayward migration: On the imagined futures and technological voids. *Ethnos* 74 (1): 91–109.
Webb, D. 2007. Modes of hoping. *History of the Human Sciences* 20 (3): 65–85.
Whyte, S. R. 2002. Subjectivity and subjunctivity: Hoping for health in Eastern Uganda. In *Postcolonial subjectivities in Africa*, ed. R. Werbner, 171–190. London and New York: Zed Books.
Williams, A. M., and V. Baláz. 2012. Migration, risk and uncertainty: Theoretical perspectives. *Population, Space and Place* 18 (2): 167–180.
Zigon, J. 2009. Hope dies last: Two aspects of hope in contemporary Moscow. *Anthropological Theory* 9 (3): 253–271.
Zournazi, M. 2002. *Hope: New philosophies for change*. Annandale: Pluto Press.

# 2 How to Extract Hope from Papers?
## Classificatory Performances and Social Networking in Cape Verdean Visa Applications

*Heike Drotbohm*

### Introduction

Emilia,[1] a young woman living in my neighborhood on the Cape Verdean island of Fogo, had been waiting for weeks for Laura, a good friend, who was living in the United States at that time. The day Laura came for a visit, she, Emilia and another friend, Mauricio, sat in front of Emilia's house. When I passed by, they asked me to join them and Emilia told me that they were school friends who had all finished the *liceu*—the local secondary school—in the same year. Then she instantly changed the topic and said, 'You know, Heike, I am carrying hope, twice'. She giggled and I hesitated, not sure what to say because I was aware that Emilia was pregnant and that, for several weeks already, her swelling belly had been watched by the entire neighborhood. I thought that her allusion to 'hope' was related to this intimate condition and that she might want to tell me something about her longed-for baby. Sitting down I said, 'Sure. Lucky you! But twice?' To my surprise she did not talk about her pregnancy but, instead, explained that she had just received an invitation to an 'interview' at the American Consulate in Praia, the capital of Cape Verde. Then she continued: 'Having a very young baby will make it much easier to travel. The baby is my *"linki"*.[2] Laura knows a lot about this. She will help me (*'dar apoio'*) and, with the baby, all this [the visa application] won't be a problem. All is in order now, and we're finally going to make it'.[3] In this dialogue, Emilia—whose particular perspective will follow at a later stage of this chapter—connected her positive attitude towards the visa application to two complementary features: firstly, she assumed that her pregnancy and, hence, the presumed changing bureaucratic category, might improve her chances in the administrative process. Secondly, she counted on the support which her friend Laura, who had successfully migrated before, had promised to provide.

In this text I will explore how young Cape Verdeans manage to progress their emigration plans despite the unpromising circumstances. Just like her friends, Emilia had grown up in an African context in which any attempt to access the international circuits of work, business, or leisure travel is somewhat unrealistic. However, despite the negative experiences of others who were in the same situation, but who failed at some point in the course

DOI: 10.4324/9781315659916-2

of this long and often delayed process, Emilia was able to maintain an optimistic attitude. In what follows I argue that the ability to continue on the bumpy, contingent, and often frustrating path of visa application depends on the dynamics between the bureaucracies of border-crossing, the support provided by social networks, and legal classifications which change over a person's life course.

Evidently, contemporary forms of mobility are hard to imagine without understanding the social meaning of migration rights. As several authors argue, the present era of migration control has become the final stronghold of state sovereignty. While nation-states, on the one hand, are losing control over many realms of social life, they implement a wide variety of measures for regulating border-crossing and entry and migrant's rights—such as their access to residency, employment, social services, and citizenship (Bauböck 1991; Bosniak 1991; Dauvergne 2004; Morris 2002; Sassen 2006). Today, migration scholars examine law not as a containment of regulation, but rather as a social field in the Foucauldian sense, wherein technologies of control, supervision, and discipline are created, stretching from consulates, border-control agents, the military and the police, to prisons, factories, schools, and health and social services (Donnan and Wilson 2010; Fassin and D'Halluin 2005; Feldman 2012; Heyman 2009; Hyndman 2000; Salter 2006).

The procedures of the modern administrative state constitute a highly selective and porous process, differentiating between and allowing entry only to a certain category of eligible non-citizen populations. Whereas the documentary requirements for border-crossing are demanding and costly, the rules and regulations are usually not only unequal and selective but also arbitrary and incoherent. Most of all, the bureaucracies of international travel are discretionary and imply an assessment of 'moral worth' or 'deservedness' of the applicant, judging his or her financial, social, and moral capacities and determining the likelihood that she or he will create security problems in the receiving country. Those intending to migrate have to explore their individual mode of potential transit; they have to understand not only the formalities and requirements, but also the scope for interpretation and the loopholes through which they might be able to pass. In this process, entry visas, as a supplement to a country's citizens passport—which are issued by the consulates of the countries of destination prior to the envisaged journey—can turn into fetishized objects of desire (Heyman 2001; 2009; Hoag 2010; Jansen 2009; Salter 2006).

In many parts of contemporary Africa, obtaining access to international travel constitutes the most vital and promising social sphere, in which a better, more prosperous and more secure life can be imagined. In his 2010 book, *Nostalgia for the future*, Charles Piot examines the desire and the attempt to obtain a visa for going abroad as being part of a particular historical post-Cold War crisis, in which local connections to the global diaspora generate new fantasies about exile and global membership. In a comparable vein, Phillip Mar (2005) discusses doubt about a positive political future as a key element of the local *'zeitgeist'*, in which hope emerges as an 'intellectual emotion' motivating migration processes, which are assumed to provide access to better living conditions. In his article on migration from Hong Kong to Australia, he describes 'social hope' as 'a particularly open-ended and speculative practice, that encompasses long spans of time, steep curves of cultural learning and social attunement, risks and investments that occur across generations' (Mar 2005, 365). Drawing on Hirokazu Miyazaki's (2003) elaboration on hope as a way to study critiques and utopian alternatives to capitalism, Mar (2005) suggests approaching hope in order to examine how processes of knowledge formation are produced in the context of transnational migration. This approach can be complemented by Simon Turner's (2015) work on Burundian refugees in Nairobi, who live in conditions of extreme uncertainty. Turner confirms this understanding of hope as a collective, utopian perspective and argues that, for many of these refugees, an 'open-ended' form of hoping is the only possible way, as it helps to imagine a life beyond the current state of suffering. In contrast to this, he observes 'goal-directed' modes of hoping in institutionalized contexts, such as refugee camps, churches, or international NGOs, where the promise to improve contemporary living conditions can be understood as a key commodity. He further argues that 'hope may be seen as a mode of governing, shaping the desires and aspirations of subjects through hope' (Turner 2015, 177). This connects to 'societal hope', as described by Kleist in the introduction to this volume.

In this chapter I base my argument on these theoretical assumptions of the collective and institutionalized aspects of hope and examine the striking paradox between the pessimism of a life trajectory across national borders, which turns out to be barred for the majority of young Africans on the one hand, and their continuing perseverance on the other. More precisely, I will study how those who intend to migrate manage to persist despite the obstacles of visa bureaucracy, how they organize their knowledge, and nurture their optimism in the course of a bumpy and often barrier-strewn route. After this introduction, I first outline the particularities of the Cape Verdean transnational field and focus on the impact of migration on local forms of social stratification. Next, I return to the three individuals introduced at the beginning of this chapter and reflect on their specific conditions for and experiences of travel. The crucial impact of support networks as well as the duty to submit to expectations and claims articulated therein, will then be addressed. Finally, I turn to hope fostered in the institutional sphere through bureaucratic classifications and the discretionary power of migration officers, whose attitude and room for maneuver need to be interpreted by those islanders who wish to go abroad.

To support my argument I rely on ethnographic fieldwork carried out between 2006 and 2008 on Fogo and Brava, two small islands lying to the south-west of the Cape Verdean Archipelago. I integrated my own family life into São Filipe, Fogo's main town, and traveled occasionally to the island's interior as well as to the neighboring island of Brava. During these twelve months of fieldwork, I combined participant observation with semi-structured or narrative interviews as well as ego-centered network techniques. Subsequently, I also visited family members living in Lisbon and in Boston. Whereas this research was actually concentrated on the dynamics between mobility and immobility within cross-border family networks, the desire, intention, or plan to travel appeared constantly as a side strand of information among the islanders, especially of those belonging to the younger generation.

## Rights of Passage as a *rite de passage* in Cape Verde

The small West African country of Cape Verde offers itself particularly well for the study of the meaning of hope in the context of migration regimes, because the imagination and the speculation about possible avenues to migration have long shaped everyday life in the archipelago. Since the mid-fifteenth century, Portuguese traders used these ten islands, located approximately 550 miles west of the coast of Senegal, as trading posts for trafficking in slaves, sugar, and cotton. Being a constituting element in the context of African Atlantic economies (Guyer 2004), the Cape Verdean population gained an international reputation and accumulated wealth by means of creating bonds with other Atlantic trading populations—be they in Portugal, along the Upper Guinea Coast or in Brazil (Batalha 2004). The decline of slavery, which began in the middle of the nineteenth century, signaled drastic economic changes; hence the search for new economic foundations began. Cape Verde is a desert country and its local agriculture provides only few crops. There is hardly any national industry, to the extent that 90 per cent of all food and consumer goods need to be imported. Due to demographic growth, the country faced severe famine during years of drought and frequent food crises marked life on the islands until the 1960s (Bigman 1993). Because of these conditions, spatial mobility and global networking turned from being a privilege into being an essential means of survival.

Already during these hard times, the emigration of individual family members, their strongly felt absence on the islands, and the collective waiting for their material support or greetings sent from abroad all constituted essential elements of everyday social life on the islands. Those traveling were accompanied by the hopes of their loved-ones, who integrated the vision about the dangers of the Atlantic crossings as well as the burden of living and toiling abroad into their daily talks, imaginations, songs, and prayers (Halter 1993). Over the course of history, migration destinations changed. Whereas, at the beginning of the nineteenth century, Cape Verdeans regularly crossed the Atlantic to make new lives in North America (particularly in Massachusetts), once their country became politically independent from Portugal in 1975 there emerged strong flows of labor migration to Portugal, the Netherlands, Luxembourg, France and, more recently, Italy. A considerable number of Cape Verdeans can also be found in the other ex-Portuguese

African colonies such as Guinea Bissau, São Tomé and Principe, Angola and Mozambique (Batalha 2004; Carling and Batalha 2008; Drotbohm 2009; Halter 1993).

After centuries of Cape Verdean migration, the diaspora population now outnumbers the 550,000 inhabitants of the ten islands. Today, Cape Verde can be understood as a 'migration culture'—i.e., that social practice and the perception of self and society cannot be understood without taking into consideration the dynamics between physical and spatial mobility and social stratification (Carling and Åkesson 2009). Lisa Åkesson (2004) describes migration as 'making a life', which captures the local population's perception of migration as only according social recognition by means of cross-border migration. Certainly, not everybody in Cape Verde is able to travel and leave the country and some never even leave the island on which they were born. However, during my fieldwork I rarely came across someone who did not have one or more family members living outside Cape Verde. Comparable to van Gennep's (1909) interpretation of a *rite de passage*, which accompanies a person's maturation and status shifts in the moment of biographical transition, a Cape Verdean who manages to organize and realize cross-border migration gains recognition and respect in his or her community of origin (see also Chavez 1992; Monsutti 2007). The access to 'rights'—be it to visas, to territorial entry, or to other types of immigrants' rights eventually obtained after reaching the country of destination—is considered a crucial and longed-for element in defining the position, the capacity, and the ability of the individual aspirant or migrant. Hence, 'rights' are part and parcel of the 'rite' of passage, during which the successful migrant transforms his or her spatial as well as social position, especially towards those remaining in the country of origin. Under ideal circumstances, she or he is expected to establish a stable life abroad, acquire economic capital, and support family and friends back in the country of origin (Drotbohm 2016). Support, here, infers not only the sending of remittances and other kinds of material support, but also, particularly, the responsibility to help others to migrate (Carling 2008; Gaibazzi 2014; Khoo 2004; Menjívar 2006). Hence, successful cross-border migration in Cape Verde today can be understood as a quasi-ritualistic process, which is initiated and observed on a communal level and contributes to social stratification by dividing people into 'achievers' compared to 'aspirants' or 'failed' individuals. A successful migration transforms a person's social position and generates social expectations and hopes for a better future—not only for her or himself, but also within her or his social networks extending across national borders.

## Uneven Biographical Conditions of Travel

Whereas many Cape Verdeans travel regularly between the islands and some eventually also travel to other African countries,[4] the term *migrason* refers to those types of international mobility which will bring *uma vida midjo*, a better life, and generally indicates places in North America or in European countries. The peripheral position of the Cape Verdean Archipelago implies that a clandestine crossing of these borders is quite unlikely. Most islanders aspiring to gain entry into Europe or North America plan for a 'documented' border-crossing and concentrate on the process of visa application, with its regulations, requirements, classifications, and measures. '*Arrangar a lei*'—literally 'to arrange the law'—is a common expression in Cape Verde, describing the contingent and unpredictable social process of visa application. Those intending to migrate are aware of the fact that criteria of capacity and eligibility are not fixed and permanent but change over the course of a person's lifetime.

The three school friends—Laura, Emilia, and Mauricio—presented in the introductory vignette had shared similar conditions at a particular moment in time. They spent their childhoods on the same minor Cape Verdean island and in the same town, had succeeded in continuing their education after primary school, and had witnessed the changing conditions for international travel and visa application within their social networks. Contrary to their mothers and fathers, some of whom had been traveling on a Portuguese passport, Cape Verde's political independence in 1975 complicated entry into the most popular destination countries.[5] In recent decades, Portugal's signing of the Schengen Agreement in 1995 in particular, and the events around 9/11, which were followed by a fusion of migration control and security measures on both sides of the Atlantic, contributed to barring visa applications from poor countries, especially Africa.

Despite these deterrents, the three friends imagined themselves going abroad one day in the future. They were also aware that they each faced highly distinct starting conditions, which might oblige them to 'travel on different tickets' in order to realize their plans. Laura, who had been introduced as 'the visitor' in the initial vignette, had always been convinced that she would one day be able to leave the country. During one of our talks, she told me that her father had been a successful lawyer, living in the country's capital city, Praia, and that he often traveled and worked in Boston, Massachusetts. Although he had not married Laura's mother but lived with his wife and children on the neighboring island, he had always affirmed his fatherhood and supported Laura socially and financially. Laura, who had been a diligent and talented student, dreamt of following in her father's footsteps and entering his profession after finishing college. In order to support this aim, her father had arranged for her to undertake an internship at a friend's law firm in Boston. By the time we met, Laura was still working there. The continuity of her stay in Boston, however, had remained undecided. Laura had entered the United States on a tourist visa and had received a temporary residence permit through her labor contract at the law firm. Simultaneously, she persistently tried to win a scholarship to a public university. When we met, the challenge of establishing a long-term legalized stay in the United States was still unresolved, and she even feared that she might not be able to re-enter the United States after her short visit to the islands.

Unlike for Laura, nurturing such precise migration plans would have been a mere illusion for the two other friends. Mauricio had grown up in the same neighborhood, together with his parents and an older sister. Some years ago his mother had been granted a special visa which enabled her to travel to Portugal and receive proper medical treatment for a severe renal disease. Although her husband and her two children had expected to follow her within a short time, '*arrangar a lei*' proved to be difficult for Mauricio's mother, who commuted between clinics and several social-service offices and tried to get all the documents prepared. During the first two years of her absence, she called nearly every Sunday and promised her children that, sooner or later, everything would be fine. Some months ago, only Mauricio's sister received her papers and succeeded in obtaining a visa for Portugal. Mauricio, however, was expected to continue working in his father's grocery shop and in the family's gardens; he would eventually be able to follow them abroad at a later point in time—depending on his mother's health and her ability to stabilize her economic foundation in Portugal. He was still at this uncertain waiting stage when we met.

Of the three of them, Emilia was the only one who never had any kind of precise migration plans. In her own words, she had always been a lazy student and knew that she would never receive a student scholarship of any sort to enable her to go abroad. Her personal linkage transcending national borders was 'some kind of uncle' in Canada, but definitely not someone who would want her to join him. Emilia had never considered migration to be a realistic future project. Rather, as she told me, she felt able to adapt to constantly changing circumstances and to make the best of it. When, recently, she fell in love with a young man living on a neighboring island, and fell pregnant, she knew that he would probably not be reliable enough to support her adequately. At the same time, however, her pregnancy made her reconsider her ability to care properly for her as-yet-unborn child, and she began to assess her options for going abroad. Whereas some friends had suggested that she participate in the 'visa lottery' of the U.S. Embassy, others underlined the particularly opportunistic issue of her pregnancy, which will be explained in more detail below.

Despite their different biographical situations, all three had shared a positive, even utopian, attitude towards their personal futures. They had dreamed of opportunities away from their country of origin, even while having to cope with the unexpected temporalities of migration, the prevailing uncertainties, the experience of delay, or in Mauricio's case, the frustration of an eventual failure. The perseverance of hope, I argue in the following section, is nurtured not only by a person's individual capacity to continue this uneven trajectory. Essential elements are, first, the bureaucratic procedures of migration regimes, which are imprecise and incoherent enough to allow the individual to believe in the eventuality of him or her overcoming this obstacle, and, second, a social environment which not only encourages an optimistic attitude but also provides support in various ways. In this process, as the next section will show, would-be migrants' attitudes move from a collective and rather vague imaginary of a life abroad, to a more individualized mode of hoping, which supports them in organizing the required social backing and particular kind of knowledge.

## From Aspiration to the Organization of Support and Knowledge

In contemporary Africa, those who make up the poor, uneducated, and young social strata are highly aware of the uneven distribution of migration potential. In everyday life, the general ways and opportunities to migrate, and the individual attempts and failures, as well as changes in the legal conditions for international travel, are constantly discussed in the public realm as some kind of daily 'migration speak'. As Jørgen Carling (2001) made clear in his work on Cape Verdean migration, we need to differentiate between people's aspirations to migrate and their ability to do so in order to understand why some individuals manage to migrate whereas others do not. In his aspiration/ability model, he analyzes both characteristics on two analytical levels. First, analysis on the macro level, which he understands as a particular social, economic, and political environment of emigration which may hinder or facilitate attempts to migrate. Second, he refers to certain characteristics, such as age, gender, and the social status of the person aspiring to migrate. As he points out several times in his article (Carling 2002), interpersonal relations, social networks, and households complicate a clear distinction between aspiration and ability, as these features also considerably affect the outcome of migration plans.

My own empirical observations in Cape Verde confirm this crucial meaning of the meso level, where plans and strategies for migration are drawn up and fostered. The shift from a vague wish to a precise action is generated within a social environment which provides not only moral backing, but also the necessary organizational information as well as practical and financial support. In other words, emigration can never occur on an individual level. To facilitate a person's journey, economic resources need to be calculated and social relations need to be activated within families and households. In most migratory contexts, migration is encouraged, generated, and facilitated by 'sponsors', who see the financial and organizational support they provide as a kind of investment, which might eventually generate a positive outcome for themselves (Lindquist 2012). Even if a migrant fails and is unable to pay back his or her debts, the sponsoring person's reputation will be strengthened in the respective social environment. At the same time, migration sponsors are usually aware of the fact that not everybody will be able to sustain the burdensome and often prolonged process of visa application, and, hence, some focus their backing on certain chosen individuals.

In his article on visa application procedures in the Gambia, Paolo Gaibazzi convincingly elaborates on the kinship networks necessary for obtaining a visa there. He argues that young Gambian men intending to travel first have to prove that they are 'fit for migration' within their personal networks in order to receive the appropriate and requisite type of support. In this West African case, the backing essential for migration tends to engender kinship reciprocities as well as intergenerational dependencies. Young Gambians are forced to remain obedient and submissive *vis-à-vis* senior kin; hence, it is not only state actors, such as consular officials, but also older family members who turn into an additional regulatory authority for migration. According to Gaibazzi, 'The visa regime actually pushes young Soninke men into the system of support, thereby sustaining the norms and uncertainty of social certification' (Gaibazzi 2014, 51). Complementarily, Obadare and Adebanwi (2010) reflect on the role of religious or spiritual authorities in Nigeria, who might also approve of the individual travel plan, depending on their reading of the obstacles the would-be migrant might face.

In addition to a docile attitude *vis-à-vis* the authorities, other individual characteristics such as age or gender may impact on the decision as to who might qualify for support. The individual positions of the three friends differed considerably in this respect. Whereas Laura felt embedded and supported in multiple ways by her wealthy father, Mauricio experienced quite the opposite: his older sister was felt to be more 'valuable' in Lisbon, where their mother was suffering from ill health. In addition to this gendered preference, age might be a second criterion: often, amongst siblings, those born earlier are expected to travel before the others, since being officially a minor is often a prerequisite for travel on the basis of family reunification—a criterion which might disappear in the course of time. Hence, a relative's decision to postpone or reject a claim for support eventually boils down to quite rational decisions based on the calculation of a family's resources, capacities, and needs. From the perspective of the would-be-migrants, however, delays allow room for interpretation and usually throw up serious doubts about the trustworthiness of their social environment. In Mauricio's case, his mother's repeated promises to take him to Lisbon fed his continuing expectations, but his sister's migration reinforced a sense of gendered inequality and rivalry within his family. In the end, Mauricio struggled with a growing fear that he was being misinformed or cheated on and, hence, eventually not 'deserving' to migrate.

In general, visa application procedures are a particularly blurred field of social practice which requires the help of others. Just filtering the correct information from a consulate's website, leaflets, brochures, or other types of informational material requires the ability to master a foreign and bureaucratic language to an advanced level, which usually discourages many potential travelers. Additionally, several forms need to be downloaded from the Internet, filled out electronically and uploaded again, a technique requiring assistance in many cases. In Cape Verdean towns and villages, teachers or other individuals with higher education often serve as trusted translators and help to interpret broadly held formulations, to make sense of incomprehensible rules, and comply with technical necessities. In some cases, these are migrant returnees who are well informed about the most recent changes in migration law as well as the tips, tricks, and traps to watch out for.

Getting access to the right type of knowledge is considered crucial for being a successful applicant. Laura, who was able to rely on a very supportive network, but whose father did not live permanently in the United States, profited not only from his contacts but also from her ability to differentiate between the different types of application procedure. Through her personal networks she had learned that neither the work permit she had been promised nor her official application to a U.S. university while still being in Cape Verde would have constituted good grounds for a visa application. In order to distinguish herself from the many others who intended to study abroad, she concentrated her application process on a tourist visa, which can be obtained much more easily providing that the applicant possesses a sponsoring letter from an American citizen who can prove his or her independent political and financial status. Additionally, her father helped her to fill out the forms, paid her travel to the country's capital and the requisite visa-processing fees. Laura's trajectory recalls Mar's (2005) understanding of hope as being part of a long process of cultural and social learning that needs to be transmitted across generations.

Finally, I want to return to the collective dimension of hope. Islanders, like Laura, who were able to improve their individual opportunities and conditions and successfully obtain a visa, are usually immediately contacted by friends and relatives who wish to acquire additional, non-official, information through her experiences. Within her friendship networks, Laura instantly had to serve as a resource person, supposedly assisting those who lacked sufficient understanding of the formal requirements. Many migrants told me about the 'turning point', when their successful application transformed them into a positive role-model. Zé, a man in his thirties who had presented himself at the American Consulate in Praia some weeks before our encounter, told me about his best friend, who had not only photocopied his filled-out application forms, but also asked him about the entire procedure of self-presentation, the queuing in front of the consulate, the type of person receiving him, the size and the aesthetics of the office, and the kinds of questions asked by the consulate official. Finally, his friend took note of all these details and discussed each of Zé's answers again and again. By means of accessing this type of knowledge, those aspiring to migrate expect to find out about the 'hidden secrets' of visa application and try to transform the inconsistent initial information into a more precise and reliable level of understanding.

## Hope and Empathy in 'Classificatory Performances'

The social support and knowledge thus acquired need to be understood as necessary prerequisites for confronting arbitrary and incoherent state bureaucracies, which enact governmental policies of migration on a discretionary basis.

Obadare and Adebanwi (2010), referring to the Nigerian context, describe the visa application process as a 'space of abjection and humiliation'. What was once the 'open-endedness' of hope has to turn into a 'goal-directed' attitude (Turner 2015), as the individual is supposed to focus on the very precise and individual bureaucratic steps to be taken in order to be successful. As already mentioned, traveling requires a wide range of fees to be paid and documents to be obtained which are all considered crucial criteria for eligibility. These documents—processing fees, return tickets, proof of professional qualifications and of possession of adequate finances to live abroad independently, health certificates, and a clear criminal record—will be pre-screened by immigration officers working at the consulate. 'The mobile subject is configured by the receiving state in terms of health, wealth, labor/leisure, and risk' writes Mark Salter (2006, 176) in his reflection on the intersection between border regimes and the individual in the moment of visa application. He underlines the crucial meaning of confession, i.e., the applicant's ability to narratively fit into the conceptual schema of migration managers who pre-screen the individual's body and characteristics before giving (or rejecting) admission.

Would-be-migrants are fully aware of the fact that their papers need to be perfectly complete, but that even this still does not guarantee actual access to a visa. A person who has managed to assemble and fill out the appropriate forms and hand them in at the consulate has to wait for the case to be processed and to receive an invitation to a personal interview. In Cape Verde, this period until '*a chamada*' ('the call') can last several months or even longer, during which time the visa applicant has to cope with feelings of uncertainty and fears of failure. It was during this phase of her own visa application that Emilia informed me about her 'double hope'. After the short encounter together with her friends, I contacted her again, curious about her particular story and her most recent efforts to migrate. Once more she began the conversation by stating how optimistic she was that this time she would be granted a "non-immigrant visitor's visa" to the United States. Then she talked about the different types of visa and the sorts of people who, according to her, are usually granted them:

> It's not easy to go abroad if you don't have much to offer. To provide you with a visa, they want you to have 'strong ties', you need to be well connected to your home country. They want to be sure that you won't stay over there and they want to see this on paper. They want a good work contract, or a full bank account, material things, a house—everything which can prove that you will certainly return. This kind of proof is difficult for young people, who do not have much to offer, you can imagine. I don't have a house or a big car. But I have my baby [She touched her belly with a smile].

According to Emilia's interpretation of the U.S. Embassy's visa regulations,[6] a mother of a young child is considered to return more willingly than a person without the intimate ties that would bind him or her to the country of origin. This is why she speaks of a duplication of hope: Emilia expects not only her first child, but also to increase her visa eligibility through this key biographical shift, which would transform her personal status and enhance her chances considerably. Interestingly, during my stay in Cape Verde, this nexus between a newborn baby and the probability of a successful visa application was confirmed several times. Another woman told me that it makes sense if a mother applies for a visa in the early phase of her pregnancy, as the bureaucratic procedure will take some time and the child should not become too old. An older child, she told me, would not be understood as forcing a Cape Verdean mother to return within a few weeks. One woman tried to translate the perspective of the consulate official for me:

> They want to know the reasons, good reasons for our return. It is important for them that we do not stay when we enter their territory as tourists. And these people working here at the embassy, they know that a woman, in Cape Verde, wouldn't hesitate to leave her children behind if they are older. Simply having a child is a weak reason for return. But if she has a small, a very small baby which remains at home, the mother is expected to return within a couple of weeks. The people at the embassy say that a mother would be too irresponsible if she stayed away. For Cape Verdean mothers this is a bit different, but they do not understand.

Both Emilia and this informant connected their reading of migration law to an assumed interpretation of their visa claims by 'them'—i.e., state bureaucrats, who employ 'moral categories' of deservingness when making their decisions. Such a bureaucratic interpretation refers to the discretionary powers of consular officials who are empowered to apply legal regulations in order to defend their country's interests. Several authors have elaborated on the 'culture of suspicion' (Alpes and Spire 2014) among street-level bureaucrats who are committed to combating fraud (Griffith 2012; Hoag 2010). In his work on state power at the U.S.–Mexico border, Josiah Heyman (2001, 129) highlights bureaucratic classification as *'public acts of cognition* of selves and others' (emphasis in original) and asks 'how categorical statuses attach to people so that they stick: how they are publicly broadcasted, widely acknowledged, and internalized into actions' (2001, 129). He introduces the term 'thought-work' (131) to describe the perspectives of immigration officers, who employ conceptual schemas through which abstract regulations are translated into the evaluation of specific cases. In his model of 'classificatory performances', the decision to admit or reject refers not only to a legal superstructure but also to 'covert classifications', which serve to classify and evaluate an applicant's moral worth (Heyman 2001, 131).

As the classificatory performances of migration law promise the eligibility for cross-border mobility for certain categories of person, people try to make themselves fit into these categories. Comparable to the person mentioned in the paragraph above, who tried to copy the bureaucratic steps undertaken by his friend in order to uncover the 'hidden secrets' of visa application, many Cape Verdeans compare their own 'classificatory features' with other applicants who have been successful or have failed before. Among those intending to follow the same path, parallels and similarities are closely observed in order to glean the alleged key information. The arbitrariness resulting from covert classifications has an impact on the attitude of visa applicants, who feel obliged to interpret the officers' thought processes and identify the perfect 'classificatory void' into which they might fit.

Obviously, a person's characteristics—age, financial or employment status, social conditions, and situation of dependency—change over the life course. Scholars such as Fassin and D'Halluin (2005), Kastner (2010) and Ticktin (2006) have examined these classificatory transformations, when pregnancies, marriages, personal threat, disease, or other events change a person's eligibility for a visa or citizenship. I discussed Emilia's peculiar idea—that a pregnancy or a newborn baby might facilitate the mother's visa application—with one of the consular officials at the American Embassy in Cape Verde's capital, Praia. She confirmed that many comparable types of rumor exist and that she and her colleagues were aware of misunderstandings resulting from the positive admission of a person in a certain 'category', which then is taken as an example to be followed by others. This officer, in an interview at the U.S. American Embassy in January 2007, commented:

> The problem is that the characteristics and features of one successful case cannot simply be copied. Our decisions rely on a very complex assemblage of impressions, forms, individual accounts, additional information that the applicant eventually is not aware of. But we can't change this. This can cause unforeseen misunderstandings, as in this case, and this is surely unfortunate, but we can't change this.

In addition to their individual interpretations of covert classifications, visa applicants focus on their expected dialogical encounter with a consular official. When Emilia repeatedly stated that she does not have 'much to offer' she revealed a particular understanding of this administrative procedure. As an applicant, she tried to learn the rules of the game and submit herself to some kind of bargaining situation in which she would have to offer a certain value in order to receive admission.

After the longed-for invitation to an interview, hope flourishes again. A person who is invited to the consulate tries to learn from other people's prior experiences and invests much time and energy in discussing the appropriate dress code, the expected conduct, and the variety of answers from which they might chose. Several interviewees told me that they needed to maintain a positive attitude and sympathy towards the bureaucrat, in order to face the tension of this particular moment. Emilia, who had been invited to present herself at the consulate for the first time in her life, was extremely anxious about this event, which she perceived as having an enormous potential impact on her future. During one of our meetings, she calculated the approximate time span between her child's birth and the interview date and said:

> I might have a big belly in this week. If it's a woman, she might be nice, she might think that a mother is a good person and needs support. A man, if it's an old man especially, you never know. I think I can handle the situation. But I am very nervous; I am even scared, yes, sure.

Imagining 'the bureaucratic other's gender and age, and thinking of her or him as a person having a humanist attitude or simply 'a good day', and his/her space for decision-making, helps would-be migrants to transform the yet unknown into a more predictable situation. Several interviewees considered the applicant's ability to remain confident and trusting as being crucial to withstanding the pressure of this stressful encounter. Therefore, visa applicants also try to measure and eventually adjust the plausibility and credibility of their own biographies and migration interests before the real encounter with the administration. During my fieldwork, I heard several stories about bureaucrats who were known for detecting discrepancies or missing information and who had used the personal encounter to demonstrate their own cleverness. In most of these stories, the migration official is imagined as an evil, mistrusting human being who focuses on 'minor' errors such as misspelled names or the blushing of a candidate.

As several ethnographical studies on encounters in bureaucratic contexts have brought to light, both service applicants and officials are obliged to negotiate their particular sense of 'truth' or 'honesty' and handle impressions of uncertainty, contradiction, and disagreement (Fassin and d'Halluin 2005; Griffith 2012). Heath Cabot, working in a refugee center on the EU border of Greece, concentrates on the limited forms of agency emerging within systems of aid and protection:

> [. . .] aid candidates and service providers are also deeply engaged in seeking to respond to and make sense of each other, through highly personal, contextualized, and unpredictable sets of encounters. These intersubjective dynamics and the social aesthetics through which they unfold reflect, invoke, but also sometimes undermine normative frameworks of assessment.
>
> (Cabot 2013, 453)

In this phase of the process, the applicant's ability to believe in the positive outcome of the process of visa application not only depends on bureaucratic facts but is once more nourished by multiple aspects ranging from the moral backing of friends and relatives to the capacity to organize the formal requirements, the ability to have a positive, sympathetic attitude towards the bureaucrat, and the will to repeatedly overcome structural barriers. What becomes obvious here is the fact that not only is hope a social resource, but that institutions—such as states' visa regimes, and also consulates and other kinds of migration broker—foster and distribute hope as a crucial resource.

At certain moments, the moral support necessary to persevere even needs to be activated through 'external', i.e., transcendent, spheres. On the day on which Emilia had packed her bag to travel to Praia and to present herself at the consulate, she sat uneasily in her kitchen, sipping her tea and listening to her father's seemingly endless advice. Then one of her mother's good friends entered and passed her a small picture of the Virgin Mary, which she suggested that Emilia should carry on her way. In Cape Verde, offering a blessing on the day of a traveler's departure is a typical way of expressing solidarity and empathy in precarious moments, when hope runs the risk of losing its strength.

## An Open Ending: When Hope Travels Abroad

In this chapter I have elaborated on the uneven and bumpy trajectories of visa applications and the hopes that accompany or fuel this process. Comparing the cases of Emily, Mauricio, and Laura, three young Cape Verdeans who shared similar visions at a certain point in their common lifetime but who experienced different outcomes, I have tried to show that the confidence an applicant feels in obtaining a positive outcome to her or his migration plan usually passes through changing conditions and experiences. Referring to Phillip Mar's suggestion that we understand hope as a method for approaching processes of knowledge formation, I isolated three socio-cultural dimensions through which hope is generated.

First, those aspiring to migrate depend on *social networks*, which support their transition from aspiration to realization. This personal backing differs according to the key characteristics of the would-be migrant, i.e., his or her gender, age, income, or profession as well as the individual capacity to prevail. Within social networks, hope can remain at a utopian, open-ended level. Among the three individuals, Mauricio is an example of a person whose hope never managed to transcend the social dimensions. In contrast to his stagnating position, would-be migrants have to turn their hope into a 'goal-centered', more individual way of longing, and of being successful in visa applications. In this phase, the moral, financial, and organizational support provided by relatives and friends is crucial in reaching the second dimension, namely the *organization of knowledge*: Putting things into practice requires accessing the requisite information, organizing papers such as passports and visas, and filling in forms (in the correct way), as well as gaining advance knowledge about the personal encounter at the embassy—necessary in order to resist frustrations and overcome formal obstacles. Emilia, who understood her pregnancy as a key moment enabling her to eventually be granted a tourist visa, found herself in just this particular open phase of hoping. And finally, the discretionary and contingent character of visa applications offers the necessary space for imagining the 'fit' between a person's own classificatory category and the visa requirements. Those aspiring to migrate need to understand the inner social logics and *bureaucratic performances of visa application*, and to face the imagined 'covert spheres' in the minds of the 'bureaucratic other' through an optimistic, sympathetic attitude. This institutional dimension of hope was accessed by Laura, the third individual presented in this chapter, who was able to rely on a particularly stable social network, which provided her with the information necessary to interpret these bureaucratic encounters appropriately.

According to my interpretation, the ability to learn, adapt, and achieve one's aims not only depends on individual skills, capacities, or resources, but also needs to be understood as a collective and affective process, as an attitude fostered not only in social networks, but also through institutions that 'govern through hope' (Turner 2015). As a continuous outcome of social mediation, hope binds together the visions, emotions, and actions of multiple actors, who contribute actively to an open and contingent migration-related livelihood. I finally want to point out that my clear chronological distinction between these three dimensions does not necessarily correspond to the empirical facts. Hope does not accompany the visa application process in a clear-cut and linear way but, rather, as Kleist also mentioned in the introduction to this volume, it has an elastic quality, moving back and forth, shrinking and prospering in irregular curves between societal, social, and individual phases of hoping.

These collective, institutional, and affective dimensions of hope do not end at the border. Visa applicants who have successfully negotiated this long trajectory of interpretation, networking, submission, dialogue, and trust, who have acquired a visa and managed to transform themselves into international beings, will again be accompanied by the hope of others who stay behind. Through staying in touch, calling, sending remittances, or visiting, migrants provide the imaginative space for hope to prosper among those who intend to leave their country of origin sooner or later. Migrants not only serve as projection screens, but are also expected to act as informants, supporters, and sponsors, in order that others can persevere on the long trajectory of hope which is the visa application process.

However, after gaining access to cross-border mobility and reaching those longed-for places abroad, many migrants realize the consequences of an often 'liminal legality' (Menjívar 2006). Depending on their conditions of entry and residency, many have to understand their personal capacity to stabilize their lives and to accept how much their particular legal status affects their right to political and economic participation, their position within their personal networks, and their contacts with family members left behind. Some also have to carefully balance their contact with bureaucratic structures and state representatives and interpret the limiting body of the law, which impinges on the vital parts of their private lives. Finally, migrants have to accept that they are submitting themselves, again, to a long and bumpy learning process during which the ability to persevere is crucial, not only for themselves, but for everyone projecting their hopes onto their successful trajectories.

## Acknowledgments

This chapter is based on anthropological fieldwork in Cape Verde, which was financed by the German Academic Exchange Service (DAAD) in the form of a post-doctoral scholarship. Additional time for writing was generously provided by a fellowship at the Research Center 'Work and the Life Course in Global Perspective' (Re:Work) at Humboldt University, Berlin (2011/2012) as well as the Freiburg Institute of Advanced Studies (FRIAS) (2015). My thanks go to Nauja Kleist and Dorte Thorsen, who invited me to become part of this book project, as well as to the two anonymous reviewers, who provided precious comments and feedback.

## Notes

1. All personal names have been anonymized by being replaced by common Cape Verdean names in order to protect the individual's identity.
2. Emilia used the creole version of the English term here.
3. Interviews in this article have been translated from either Portuguese or Cape Verdean *kriolu* to English.
4. Due to bilateral agreements and their membership of the *Comunidade Económica dos Estados da África Ocidental* (CEDEAO), Cape Verdeans can travel without a visa to a relatively large number of African countries. However, as the living conditions in Cape Verde are generally considered better on the islands, these routes are mainly used by traders and other types of business people.
5. For Cape Verdeans, the legal conditions for international travel have changed constantly in the course of history, depending on the relevant political regimes, types of destination, and the kinds of traveller. For good overviews, see Góis (2006); Halter (1993); Sánchez (1998).
6. The respective paragraph can be found on the website of the American Embassy: 'US law requires that your eligibility for a non-immigrant visitor's visa be determined on the basis of strong, well-established ties to a residence outside the United States, as well as on the basis of reasonable, credible plans for your visit to the United States', http://praia.usembassy.gov/non-immigrant_visas.html, accessed 13 September 2015.

## References

Åkesson, L. 2004. *Making a life: Meanings of migration in Cape Verde*. Göteborg: Göteborg University, Department of Social Anthropology.
Alpes, M. J., and A. Spire. 2014. Dealing with law in migration control: The powers of street-level bureaucrats at French consulates. *Social and Legal Studies* 23 (2): 261–274.
Batalha, L. 2004. *The Cape Verdean diaspora in Portugal: Colonial subjects in a postcolonial world*. Lanham, Boulder and New York: Lexington.
Bauböck, R. 1991. *Immigration and the boundaries of citizenship*. Warwick: Centre for Research in Ethnic Relations.

Bigman, L. 1993. *History and hunger in West Africa: Food production and entitlement in Guinea-Bissau and Cape Verde.* Westport, CT and London: Greenwood.

Bosniak, L. S. 1991. Human rights, state sovereignty and the protection of undocumented migrants. *International Migration Review* 25 (4): 737–770.

Cabot, H. 2013. The social aesthetics of eligibility: NGO aid and indeterminacy in the Greek asylum process. *American Ethnologist* 40 (3): 452–466.

Carling, J. (2001). Aspiration and ability in international migration. Cape Verdean experiences of mobility and immobility. *Department of Sociology and Human Geography.* Master thesis, University of Oslo. https://www.duo.uio.no/bitstream/handle/10852/32655/1/dt2001.05.carling.pdf.

Carling, J. 2002. Migration in the age of involuntary immobility: Theoretical reflections and Cape Verdean experiences. *Journal of Ethnic and Migration Studies* 28 (1): 5–42.

Carling, J. 2008. The human dynamics of migrant transnationalism. *Ethnic and Racial Studies* 31 (8): 1452–1477.

Carling, J., and L. Åkesson. 2009. Mobility at the heart of a nation: Patterns and meanings of Cape Verdean migration. *International Migration* 47 (3): 123–156.

Carling, J., and L. Batalha. 2008. Cape Verdean migration and diaspora. In *Transnational archipelago: Perspectives in Cape Verdean migration and diaspora,* eds. L. Batalha and J. Carling, 14–35. Amsterdam: Amsterdam University Press.

Chavez, L. R. 1992. *Shadowed lives: Undocumented immigrants in American society.* Fort Worth, TX: Harcourt, Brace and Jovanovich.

Dauvergne, C. 2004. Sovereignty, migration and the rule of law in global times. *The Modern Law Review* 67 (4): 588–615.

Donnan, H., and T. M. Wilson. 2010. *Borderlands: Ethnographic approaches to security, power, and identity.* Lanham and Boulder: University Press of America.

Drotbohm, H. 2009. Horizons of long-distance intimacies: Reciprocity, contribution and disjuncture in Cape Verde. *The History of the Family: An International Quarterly* 14 (2): 132–149.

Drotbohm, H. 2016. Celebrating asymmetries: Creole stratification and the regrounding of home in Cape Verdean migrant return visits. In *The Upper Guinea Coast in Global Perspective,* eds. J. Knörr and C. Kohl, 135–153. London: Berghahn.

Fassin, D. and E. D'Halluin. 2005. The truth from the body: Medical certificates as ultimate evidence for asylum seekers. *American Anthropologist* 107 (4): 597–608.

Feldman, G. 2012. *The migration apparatus: Security, labor, and policymaking in the European Union.* Stanford: Stanford University Press.

Gaibazzi, P. 2014. Visa problem: Certification, kinship, and the production of 'ineligibility' in the Gambia. *Journal of the Royal Anthropological Institute* 20 (1): 38–55.

Góis, P. 2006. *Emigracão Cabo-Verdiana para (e na) Europa e a sua inserção em mercados de trabalho locais: Lisboa, Milão, Roterdão.* Lisbon: Alto-Comissariado para a Imigracao e Minorias Étnicas.

Griffith, M. 2012. Vile liars and truth distorters: Truth, trust and the asylum system. *Anthropology Today* 28 (5): 8–12.

Guyer, J. 2004. *Marginal gains: Monetary transactions in Atlantic Africa.* Chicago: University of Chicago Press.

Halter, M. 1993. *Between race and ethnicity: Cape Verdean American immigrants, 1860–1965.* Chicago: University of Illinois Press.

Heyman, J. C. 2001. Class and classification at the US–Mexico border. *Human Organization* 60 (2): 128–140.

Heyman, J. M. 2009. Trust, privilege and discretion in the governance of the US borderlands with Mexico. *Canadian Journal of Law and Society/Revue Canadienne de Droit et Société* 24 (3): 367–390.
Hoag, C. 2010. The magic of the populace: An ethnography of illegibility in the South African immigration bureaucracy. *PoLAR: Political and Legal Anthropology Review* 33 (1): 6–25.
Hyndman, J. 2000. *Managing displacement: Refugees and the politics of humanitarianism*. Minneapolis: University of Minnesota Press.
Jansen, S. 2009. After the red passport: Towards an anthropology of the everyday geopolitics of entrapment in the EU's immediate outside. *Journal of the Royal Anthropological Institute* 15 (4): 815–832.
Kastner, K. 2010. Moving relationships: Family ties of Nigerian migrants on their way to Europe. *African and Black Diaspora: An International Journal* 3 (1): 17–34.
Khoo, S.-E. 2004. Sponsorship of relatives for migration and immigrant settlement intention. *International Migration* 41 (5): 177–199.
Lindquist, J. 2012. The elementary school teacher, the thug and his grandmother: Informal brokers and transnational migration from Indonesia. *Pacific Affairs* 85 (1): 69–89.
Mar, P. 2005. Unsettling potentialities: Topographies of hope in transnational migration. *Journal of Intercultural Studies* 26 (4): 361–378.
Menjívar, C. 2006. Liminal legality: Salvadoran and Guatemalan immigrants' lives in the United States. *American Journal of Sociology* 111 (4): 999–1037.
Miyazaki, H. 2003. Economy of dreams: The production of hope in anthropology and finance. *Cultural Anthropology* 21 (2): 147–172.
Monsutti, A. 2007. Migration as a rite of passage: Young Afghans building masculinity and adulthood in Iran. *Iranian Studies* 40 (2): 167–185.
Morris, L. 2002. *Managing migration: Civic stratification and migrants' rights*. London and New York: Routledge.
Obadare, E., and W. Adebanwi. 2010. The visa god: Would-be migrants and the instrumentalization of religion. In *Religion crossing boundaries: Transnational religious and social dynamics in Africa and the new African diaspora*, eds. A. Adogame and J. V. Spickard, 31–48. Leiden: Brill.
Piot, C. 2010. *Nostalgia for the future: West Africa after the Cold War*. Chicago: Chicago University Press.
Salter, M. 2006. The global visa regime and the political technologies of the international self: Borders, bodies, biopolitics. *Alternatives* 31 (2): 167–189.
Sánchez, G. 1998. Between Kriolu and Merkanu: Capeverdean diaspora identities. *Cimboa* 5 (5): 22–25.
Sassen, S. 2006. *Territory, authority, rights: From medieval to global assemblages*. Princeton and Oxford: Princeton University Press.
Ticktin, M. 2006. Where ethics and politics meet: The violence of humanitarianism in France. *American Ethnologist* 33 (1): 33–49.
Turner, S. 2015. 'We wait for miracles': Ideas of hope and future among clandestine Burundian refugees in Nairobi. In *Ethnographies of uncertainty in Africa*, eds. E. Cooper and D. Pratten, 173–192. Basingstoke: Palgrave Macmillan.
Van Gennep, A. 1909. *Les rites de passage: Etude systématique des rites de la porte et du seuil, de l'hospitalité, de l'adoption, de la grossesse et de l'accouchement, de la naissance, de l'enfance, de la puberté, de l'initiation, de l'ordination, du couronnement, des fiançailles et du mariage, de funérailles, des saisons, etc*. Paris: Nourry.

# 3 Sticking to God

## Brokers of Hope in Senegalese Migration to Argentina

*Ida Marie Vammen*

### Introduction

In recent years it has become exceedingly difficult for African migrants to enter the European Union. The EU and its member-states have made further restrictions on national asylum and migration policies and have *de facto* outsourced its border control by establishing agreements with transit migration countries in Africa. This development and the economic recession have together limited the possibilities for successful migration to Europe. For African migrants who, despite the odds, do manage to enter Europe, life often becomes a struggle at the margins of society (Jackson 2013; Lucht 2011; Vigh 2009).

Concurrently, on the other side of the Atlantic Ocean, Argentina has emerged as a destination for West African migrants, especially since the middle of the 2000s. Argentina is a country with no former colonial ties, or direct diplomatic or socio-economic links to West Africa. When the opportunities to enter Europe are reduced, it seems that hope for a better future is redirected towards new destinations and emerging economies in the Global South (see, for example, Bertoncello and Bredeloup 2009; Haugen 2012; Pelican and Tatah 2009). The current political landscape in Latin America appears to give migrants more leeway. The Argentinian state has, for example, introduced new liberal initiatives that depart from restricted and securitized European and North American immigration models by introducing reforms that highlight, *inter alia*, the protection of migrants' universal human rights (Ceriani 2011; Freier 2013).

In this chapter, I examine a regularization program for undocumented migrants in Argentina, implemented at the beginning of 2013, in order to explore how the affected group of migrants perceived the opportunity to transcend their irregular status and the process of law-making. By focusing on this event, I seek to show how hope is shaped and reworked among Senegalese migrants in Argentina. I focus particularly on the role of what I refer to as 'brokers of hope' in this process. Theoretically, I argue that hope, as an analytical lens for migrant mobility, can capture phenomenological aspects of how imaginaries frame and affect livelihood strategies, mobility, and notions of the future. But this lens can also be extended beyond the

DOI: 10.4324/9781315659916-3

subjective expressions of hope by drawing our attention to how visions of hope are linked and shaped by political, economic, and other social domains.

Empirically, the chapter draws on a total of eight months of fieldwork in Argentina and Senegal. The main part of the fieldwork was conducted from November 2012 to May 2013. I followed a group of male and female hawkers from different parts of Senegal, mainly in two areas of Buenos Aires: *Once*, a commercial zone with a high density of informal hawkers, and *Retiro* train and bus station. During those seven months I carried out participant observation and interviews with the Senegalese migrants and the people who formed part of their everyday life. I also interviewed the Senegalese diaspora association, NGOs, and lawyers working on migrants' rights in Argentina, and the Argentinian migration authorities. In April 2014, over the course of three weeks, I conducted interviews with family members of nine migrants whom I knew from Buenos Aires in the towns of Dakar, Mboro, Tivaouane, Gay, Thiés, Touba, Mbacke, and M'bour. I also interviewed Senegalese migration scholars and officials at the Brazilian Embassy in Dakar. Apart from spending time with the migrants and their families, I have kept in regular contact with key informants on Skype and Facebook since my return to Denmark.

## Brokerage in the Political Economy of Hope

In this chapter I narrow my analytical gaze on hope. In so doing, it is not my intent to disregard the structural constraints that shape migrants' trajectories. Rather, I want both to direct our attention to how hope is part of the political economy in Argentina and to use this analytical lens to try to understand how the migrants I met in Argentina, often to my amazement, kept pushing forward and creating new alternatives when faced with constraints. Hope was not a passive activity of waiting for a better tomorrow; it was an active stance that seemed to expand their ways of orientating themselves and acting in the world. I am particularly interested in exploring the role of alternative horizons of experiences and logics—in this case religious ones—which, in my case, played an important role in this process.

To further anchor the concept of hope theoretically, I draw on the late German philosopher Ernst Bloch and his major work on hope to try to grasp the individual's capacity to push forward in adverse circumstances. I also draw on the ideas of the Lebanese-Australian anthropologist Ghassan Hage regarding the capacity of states to distribute hope in society. Instead of seeing their work as contradictory, I want to use them as two complementary lenses. Where Bloch's perspective of hope can provide us with an understanding of how hope as affect and emotion directs the migrant, Hage shows how hope is part of a political economy, where it becomes a capital form that can be distributed unevenly in society.

For Bloch (1986), hope is embedded in concrete historical conditions and struggles. He is not interested in the known and already experienced but in the latency of the world as it is unfolding in the 'not yet' and in the capacity to think differently about what is possible. Hope does not dwell on the already existing but is a future-orientated attitude (Bloch 1998 in Miyazaki 2004, 69). Bloch's interpretation of hope seems, at times, to be an almost mystical force that makes a human being able to transcend the often brutal facts of everyday life and gloomy prospects for the future.

In *The Principle of Hope* (1986), Bloch's starting point is the subjective experience of dissatisfaction and lack and the drive to fill this void. Hope is not only linked to escapism and daydreams but also to tendencies in the material world which emerge from time to time. It can be a rebellious hope that is provocative in its non-acceptance and discontentment with negative circumstances. It is a hope that does not accept renunciation and is not confined to individual ponder but can be learned and is teachable. Bloch (1986, 3) describes hope as:

> ... in love with success rather than failure. Hope, superior to fear, is neither passive like the latter, nor locked in nothingness. The emotion of hope goes out of itself and makes people broad instead of confining them.

Wishing for something better is what Bloch calls a 'driving method'. The more vividly the goal is imagined, the stronger the wanting is or, in other words, the active process of going towards the goal. This may lead us to think that hope is a kind of over-confidence in the positive nature of the future. However, what has not yet become manifest is projecting neither the positive nor the negative but holding the latent state of a momentum of change. Disappointment is thus enclosed in hope because hope has not yet been defeated—even though it has not yet won either (Bloch 1998 in Miyazaki 2004, 69). Hope in a Blochian sense can thus, as Hirokazu Miyazaki (2006, 157) has emphasized, be seen as a social method or practice, as a way of reimagining the present from the perspective of the end. So, for Bloch, hope is not leading to passivity or resignation but is linked to action.

Bloch's perspective on hope can guide our understanding of the ways in which the migrants experience and practice hope but, as mentioned above, to complement this perspective I link the concept of hope to tendencies in the political economy. Ghassan Hage (2003) explores this aspect in his analysis of how societal hope within late capitalism is distributed in the political economy. He starts at a different scale to Bloch's more existential outset by emphasizing that

> ... societies are mechanisms for the distribution of hope, and that the kind of affective attachment (worrying and caring) that a society creates among its citizens is intimately connected to the capacity to distribute hope.
>
> (2003, 3)

The distribution of hope is linked to the distribution of social being and Hage, here, draws on Bourdieu's notion of capital in that hope, like any other capital form, is not evenly distributed within a given social field (interview with Ghassan Hage in Zournazi 2002). One example of this is the rise of a neo-liberal economic policy agenda that has led Western nation-states to fail in infusing hopefulness and social opportunities in their citizens, consequently leading to a societal crisis. Societies thus become limited in their capacity to distribute hope to all the subjects within their territory and therefore exclude weak groups like refugees or migrants from hope.

I use these theoretical perspectives to explore how hope is distributed by the Argentinian state, and, at the meso level, how hope is brokered for migrants. In this regard I introduce the concept of 'brokers of hope' to try to capture how different actors, both political and religious, become intermediaries in the migrants' future-making in Argentina. 'Brokers of hope', like 'regular brokers' in the migration industry, play a vital role in the migration process by shaping alternative and viable routes of potentiality when other options seem closed, out of reach, or simply not worth investing in. The concept illuminates the unfolding of things from a meso-level perspective and thus sheds light on how brokerage is entangled in both macro-political ambitions and in the aspiration of the individual migrants. Hope brokers thus mediate the ongoing exploration of possibilities for further mobility and economic gain that characterize many of the Senegalese migrants' trajectories in Argentina and beyond.

Brokers, connection- or middlemen are not, of course, novel characters in the migration literature. In the recent literature on the migration industry, they are characterized as part of the parcel of actors who facilitate migrants' mobility in licit or illicit ways through a range of services (Gammeltoft-Hansen and Sørensen 2013; Spaan and Hillmann 2013). Such brokers can form part of the informal sector that acts between the state and the migrant (Alpes 2013) and often circumvent the legal barriers that hinder mobility. Migrants' dependency on migration brokers seems to increase as legal migration becomes more curbed and securitized (see, for example, Lucht 2011). Yet the literature often tends to overlook the imaginary potential of these actors. They not only have the ability to broker documents or facilitate travels from A to B for economic gain but also, I argue, broker hope by producing ideas of potential futures that drive migrants' trajectories beyond structural constraints. To analytically proceed beyond the individual migrant's aspirations, we need to include those who partake in both distributing, shaping, and brokering hope in the migration process. I define a broker of hope as one who, through the act of brokerage, negotiates, sustains, directs, and, in some cases, governs people's hope. With this definition, the scope of the actors involved becomes more multifaceted and not merely linked to concrete licit or illicit remedies to facilitate mobility. Depending on the given context, other actors such as religious leaders, migrants, family members, diaspora organizations, and political actors can also broker hope.

Brokers are part and parcel of the creative ways in which migrants try to build momentum by manipulating and keeping their options open through some form of intermediary agent. They are thus a key to our understanding of the migration process and the way in which migrants perceive their possibilities for mobility in a world characterized by uneven and restricted access to social and physical mobility (Carling 2002; Ferguson 2008).

The following analysis of the regularization program shows how different actors are involved in the process of hope brokerage. To understand not only who it is who brokers hope for the migrants but also the power struggles involved, I focus on the exchange and expectations involved in the process. The case will show that the transaction between the migrant and the broker of hope is not an economic one but resembles the logics of gift-giving. To explore this process further I draw on Marcel Mauss's ([1954]2002) classical work on the gift.

## Brokering Societal Hope in the Argentinian Political System

At the beginning of January 2013, the area around Retiro, one of the busiest railway and bus stations in Buenos Aires, was transformed. Standing out from the thousands of daily passengers in transit, Senegalese migrants—many in their best clothes, carrying briefcases and paper folders—became visible in the crowds. A Congolese refugee commented with thick irony in his voice 'If you didn't know better, you would think that they were on their way to a formal job interview', referring to the unlikely event that an African migrant in Argentina would get the opportunity to work at a white-collar job. But it was not job openings that made the Senegalese migrants pass through the station, it was the opportunity of entering into a temporary regularization program for undocumented Senegalese nationals in Argentina.[1] Many stopped to ask directions from their compatriots who, like most Senegalese men and women in Buenos Aires, were selling all kinds of *bijouterie*, imitations of popular designer watches, wallets, and leather belts. They formed part of the large informal economy of hawkers, an economic activity they shared with other migrants from neighboring countries and Argentinian nationals. After having exchanged the formal respectful handshake and greetings, asking about the well-being of family members and the latest news from Senegal, they were directed towards the old harbor, where the office of the migration authorities is located in a large white building. More than a century ago, the same premises were used as an immigrant asylum for the large number of European migrants who had crossed the Atlantic Ocean in search of greener pastures.

The regularization program was the culmination of long and persistent negotiations between the Argentinian authorities, the Senegalese diaspora organizations, and Argentinian human-rights lawyers and NGOs. They had used the liberal framework of the national migration policy for migrants from the MercoSur zone,[2] initiated in 2004 (Ceriani 2011; Novick 2012;

Pacecca and Courtis 2008), to push for similar rights for non-MercoSur migrants in Argentina. The final regularization program was not the initial solution to the irregular situation of the Senegalese migrants in Argentina. To create a more durable solution, different scenarios had been discussed. Among these the diaspora organization had lobbied for a bilateral agreement between Senegal and Argentina. The NGOs had tried to include all non-MercoSur migrants in the program but without success. In the end the special initiative was directed only at Senegalese and Dominican migrants because the authorities reasoned that they belonged to a category of particularly precarious and vulnerable migrants.

Despite the fact that it was not an ideal solution, Abba Goudiaby, the president of the Senegalese diaspora association, was very content when I met him one hot afternoon at the end of January 2013. 'It is the biggest victory in our history and the result of years of negotiations. This would not happen in Europe today and especially not for African migrants', he told me. Solving their undocumented status and securing legal residency for his compatriots had been one of the diaspora association's main priorities. He explained that, although the liberty of an undocumented migrant in Argentinian, to his knowledge, did not exist in any other place, it was of utmost importance to secure migrant rights. 'Argentina is not like the countries in Europe where they reject your asylum application and then return you. But you never know when a crisis will arrive and they start looking for you and deport you', he explained. The new possibility of modifying the legal status of the majority of the Senegalese migrants was a milestone that he hoped would not go unnoticed by the Senegalese community in Argentina. They might finally recognize the importance of the association and start participating more actively in its meetings, in which, in general, there was a very low level of participation.

Abba and the Argentinian lawyers and NGOs had managed to broker societal hope for the undocumented Senegalese (and Dominican) migrants. They had acted as mediators between the state and the migrants by pushing the state to distribute hope in the form of recognition and legal rights. Their brokerage had made the authorities launch the program that, at least on paper, would give the migrants easier access to formal labor, housing, social services, and education, as well as the prospect of obtaining permanent residency within three years and access to Argentinian citizenship.

In the following section I further explore not only who brokered hope for the migrants but also the expectations at play among the different actors involved. Brokers in the migration industry most often have an economic interest in mind. Yet the form of brokering and the relationship between giver and receiver at play in this case appears to be closer to Maussian notions of exchange and the three obligations within reciprocity: giving, receiving, and repaying (Mauss [1954]2002, 50). Consequently, the regularization and the subsequent access to the new National Identity Document or DNI *did* come with expectations of some kind of reciprocity from the migrants in terms of repaying 'the gift' of rights or, in other words, the societal hope which the document seemed to offer.

## Reciprocating the 'Gift of Societal Hope'

The actors involved in the creation and launch of the regularization program all had different expectations of some kind of reciprocity. As indicated above, the diaspora association hoped for reciprocity in the form of recognition, leading the Senegalese migrants to value the association and engage more actively in its meetings and work. Yet the state had different expectations of reciprocity for their act of distributing hope.

A few days after the program was launched, Martin Duval, the director of the Argentinian migration authorities, appeared on national television CN23. He explained that the program was part of a political aim of granting people access to rights, presented as a win–win scenario. The new DNI would allow the migrants to access their rights and step out from the shadows of society. He also presented the program as a remedy against the trafficking of migrants (with special reference to Dominican migrants who were perceived as being trafficked to work in the sex industry). The state, on the other hand, benefited from knowing the people living on Argentinian territory—a prerequisite for planning and realizing any public policy. Concerning the reason why the Senegalese migrants had gained this opportunity, Duval commented:

> The Senegalese community has integrated very well in our society. It is very tranquil and peaceful and there have been no cases of Senegalese or Senegalese organizations involved in criminal activities. The state had to come up with a solution. Their deeds have shown that these people have the will to stay in our country and do not want to return.
> (Interview 17 January 2013, CN23, my translation)

In sum the official narrative presented an image of a responsible and responsive state that cared for its people, especially migrants in a vulnerable situation and those showing good character and moral behavior. The hope distributed to the migrants can be characterized, in the way it cares and worries about them, as a form of societal hope (Hage 2003). The government had been pushed to distribute this hope and used the rhetoric of affective attachment to justify its actions. Thus, the moral configurations (Fassin 2011) emphasized by the state were, in the Senegalese case, one of empathy and a caring relationship to the good well-behaved subjects.

Interestingly, this societal hope seemed to both open up new possibilities and also to confine the migrants. While granting formal access to legal and social rights, as well as legal mobility within the MercoSur Zone, the regularization program also subjected them to new forms of responsibility towards the state. It was, for example, a prerequisite for obtaining the DNI that one had to be *monotributista* (a person working on his/her own account, or freelance). As *monotributistas*, the migrants would have to pay a fixed monthly tax and a small amount for their pension and social services, all in all around 300 pesos—approximately 45 euros a month. If the migrant failed to pay this fee, he/she could lose their right to residency upon renewal. Thus, the gift not only contained the value of the document and the subsequent rights but came with the obligation of being part of the order and logics of the Argentinian state-governed system of benefits and taxes. The 'gift' was, in that sense, not free but had a 'burden attached' for the receiver (Mauss [1954]2002, 53).

The Senegalese migrants I talked to were very well aware that the documents came with obligations.[3] However, they saw little reason why they should invest in securing themselves a future in a country where they, in sharp contrast to Duval's expectation, did not expect to reside for a long period of time. They accepted the gift but did not seem interested in reciprocating it through investing in their future in Argentina, and they were reluctant to subordinate themselves to the state logic of reciprocity. Nor did they seem interested in becoming active members of the diaspora association, despite the fact that some of the migrants actually recognized the association's efforts. Using Bourdieu's metaphor of the game, they seemed disinterested in partaking in the *illusio* or game involved, partly because it offered very few probabilities for fulfilling their expectations for the future (Bourdieu 2000). In order to further explain their ambivalence towards the state and the brokerage of the diaspora association, the following two sections first describe some of the structural constraints that shaped the migrants' expectations and, second, explore the alternative and unofficial account of how the regularization came into being. As we shall see, a radically different description flourished on the streets of Buenos Aires, a version where power relations were flipped upside down and the role of the state and the diaspora association were almost neglected.

## 'It Will Not Change a Thing': Contextualizing the Document

Despite the fact that the migrants chose to enroll in the regularization program, many, to my initial surprise, seemed almost indifferent about their new status. Abdoulaye, a man in his late twenties, explained: 'The document will not make a difference. You can't send money home with this document; it will not change a thing'. Or, in the words of Alla, a Senegalese street hawker selling next to Abdoulaye: 'Right now things are very complicated here. The document will not change much, even the Argentinians here are poor like us'. Alla and Abdoulaye pointed to the fact that life as a migrant in Argentina was, indeed, complicated. A number of structural barriers and contingencies that influenced their everyday life were not about to vanish with the introduction of a new document.

With very few exceptions, the migrants I talked to had come to Argentina with high hopes but were disillusioned when they became aware of the

Argentinian reality. They had expected much more. Migration brokers in Senegal not only facilitated visa applications but also planted the ideation of a new destination. In Senegal, in the region of Thiés, a *marabout* who 'facilitated' young men's travel to Latin America explained that 'getting people successfully to Europe is too difficult these days. I don't offer people that anymore. Today it is all about Latin America, where people can make something of themselves'. In a similar vein, migrants told me about the stories of successful migration they had heard in Senegal before embarking on their own journey. The imaginary playing field seemed vast and uncontested, as only a few bits of news about migrants in Latin America reached Senegal. One example was the stories of the heydays when the Argentinian *peso* was one to one with the U.S. dollar. Many considered it recent history—an epoch they just had missed. In those days you could easily earn money and help the family, they claimed. 'People could construct a house at home (in Senegal) after only a year in Argentina', one woman told me. However, in reality such narratives referred back to a period where there were only very few pioneer migrants from Senegal in Argentina. The '*uno a uno*' monetary regime collapsed at the end of the year 2000 and was followed by a profound economic and political crisis. Despite the fact that the current economic context was more stable, it was still marked by flux and inflation. In other words, it was far from the long-awaited favorable exchange between *peso* and *CFA-franc* for which many had hoped.

Another cause of disillusionment was the limited access to the formal labor market. Many of the young men had come to Argentina to find 'proper' work in construction or the agricultural sector. However, other migrants from neighboring countries already occupied these sectors and had the advantage of being proficient Spanish-speakers in comparison to the mostly Wolof-speaking Senegalese migrants. Consequently, most of these latter ended up hawking in the street, forming part of the large informal economy that characterizes the Argentinian labor market (Maurizio 2012).[4]

Despite the fact that the migrants saw hawking as a fast and fairly easy way to start generating an income in Argentina, it was not without difficulties. Depending on the area, most vendors gave some sort of weekly bribe to the local police officer to ease their mutual relationship. Yet, from time to time, the police would confiscate the migrants' goods and chase them around the city. There were also more alarming cases, where the police entered migrants' houses, claiming to look for drugs, and then 'confiscated' all items of value. Another immediate risk to migrants' livelihoods was the efforts by the autonomous government of Buenos Aires to clean the city of hawkers. Hawkers were seen as a threat to small-scale shop-owners and as 'matter out of place' that filled up and blocked the pavements in many areas of Buenos Aires. In sum, a range of structural barriers hindered the migrants' efforts to secure a stable income, obstacles that would not be alleviated by the granting of a new legal status.

Another pertinent issue was the *quasi*-impossibility of sending remittances. For most Senegalese migrants in Argentina, it was essential for the fulfillment of their migration project to be able to remit money cheaply and easily to their families in Senegal. Yet, the Argentine government had put restrictions on such transactions through a series of measures designed to avoid capital flight. To obstruct the efforts of upper-class Argentinians to secure their wealth by exchanging U.S. dollars and placing their savings abroad, the government put a number of limitations on access to foreign currency and the possibility of remitting money. While these initiatives were targeted towards the domestic upper and middle classes, they had a significant impact on the migrants, who had to go to a Peruvian remittance firm charging very high commission rates and similarly low exchange rates. The migrants, as well as the Argentinians, were troubled by the decreasing value of the Argentinean *peso*. For those remitting money to their families in Senegal, it was a question of how much money would reach their pockets in the end. One of my interlocutors, a woman from Casamance, told me that 'The *peso* is like a fart; you can only smell it for a very short while and its smell often can't reach Senegal'. This unpredictable economic situation was holding migrants back and making it almost impossible for them to gain momentum, and many therefore considered going elsewhere or moving back to Senegal.

Exploring new possibilities in new territories was one thing that the DNI document could facilitate because it allowed for mobility within the MercoSur Zone and facilitated legal mobility between Argentina and Senegal. Mustafa, a young man from Thiés, was dreaming of going to Brazil or even to the United States. 'There is nothing here, I came with the promise that there was something and there is nothing. People tell me that you can get a proper job in Brazil and that they have a much stronger economy', he told me. The promises of onward migration to Brazil were repeated again and again among the street hawkers, building up a collective hope that things might be different in another geographical context. The new document and their expectations of what the FIFA World Cup in 2014 and the Olympic Games in 2016 could generate in the way of commerce and other possibilities seemed to inspire onward migration.

Migrants in Brazil or people who circulated between the two countries thus also brokered hope, connecting the new document more with its capacity to facilitate legal mobility than rights in Argentina. It offered them the opportunity to explore new possibilities and find a place where their livelihood might be less uncertain. However, Senegalese migrants showed little interest in becoming long-term settlers and forming a citizen-like relationship with the Argentinian state. Mauss emphasizes that the act of accepting a gift is a way of forming a social relationship and committing oneself to the giver (Mauss [1954]2002). But why should the migrants form such a social relationship if the gift exchanged had very little value? Due to the gravity of the structural barriers, the migrants did not acknowledge the potentiality and value of the gift, as it was not transformative for their current situation. Or, simply put, they had obtained recognition from the government but the legal papers did not alter the daily challenges on the ground. Hence, why should they form a committed relationship to the giver if the gift failed to infuse any substantial societal hope, other than facilitating onward spatial mobility? To trigger the dynamics of obligation between the giver and the recipient, the gift needs to be considered of value. Hence, the diaspora association's act of brokering hope was acknowledged but not valued.

The above analysis has shown the importance not only of paying attention to how states distribute hope and to whom but also of following how the affected groups respond to such gestures. The next section demonstrates that the societal hope distributed by the Argentinian state was disenchanting in a Weberian sense. The hope and transformation which the document created did not stem from the state but was embedded in a religious horizon. I will show that the migrants' reluctance can also be explained by the fact that many perceived the 'victory' of the regularization process to be caused by a figure outside the Argentinian political system. As we shall see, the 'gift' had a much greater impact in infusing hope in the migrants from this perspective.

## Carving the Future by Committing to a Spiritual Master and a Moral Practice

For many migrants, the real broker of hope was a particular spiritual master, rather than the state or the diaspora association. Unofficial versions of how the new regularization came into being flourished on the streets. I heard on several occasions that the community's good fortune was closely linked to the migrants' collective behavior and moral conduct as good Muslims. More importantly, it was through the powers and blessings of a visiting *marabout* that the program came into being, I was told. Thus the *marabout*, not the diaspora association, was seen as the broker of hope. As a friend of God, he could untie the knots of hindrances on the migrants' path and was a man with a special visual faculty—he could see into the future. In other words he could, through God, make divinations of the future and manipulate it to the migrants' advantage. He was known as a man who had a talent for solving document issues and, on his previous visit the year before, he had offered up special prayers for a solution to the migrants' irregular situation in Argentina. On this occasion he had emphasized that his prayers alone could not do it. The community's fortune would also be determined by their correct moral behavior and he had urged them to be peaceful law-abiding subjects comporting themselves as good Muslims. In other words, the legal barrier that the migrants faced would only be overcome through commitment to their faith.

Such alternative supra-legal accounts are authoritative in their own manner. They show how agency and future-making are perceived by some of the migrants in Argentina. This alternative version of the birth of the regularization program re-worked and overturned the power relation between minority and majority. Completely shifting the horizon from the secular to the religious sphere, it was not political actors, at least not directly, who had facilitated change. Rather change came from God through the brokering of the *marabout* (through his clairvoyance and ritual action) on the community's behalf, in conjuncture with the migrants' moral practice. In this shift of agency, the gift was also seen in a different light. From being a gift of societal hope in the form of individual rights it became, apart from the actual document, a sign of confirmation that one had the blessings of God and was on the right moral path—not only as an individual but also as a collective. Rather than the actual potentiality of the document, the whole event became a symbol of hope and empowerment for the future. Through using the *marabout* as an intermediary and by practicing good conduct, the migrant could partially contribute to the carving out of his or her own future. The document, in other words, not only solved a problem of legality here and now, but also pointed towards a particular way of collective being, a moral being bestowed with blessings and agency.

The spiritual realm thus offered an enchanted potential hope. It seemed to expand the migrants' world rather than confine it. The anthropologist Michael Jackson has eloquently observed that people who do not feel that they are offered any hope or care from society withdraw their investment in it and seek alternative fields of recognition. In these alternative fields, such as religion, marginalized people can find re-enhancement often by looking inward and working with themselves (Jackson 2005, xxv). In other words, investing in and subjecting oneself to religious practices can recreate a sense of agency. Yet the unknown nature of life was still present for the migrants but became somewhat tamed by engaging with a religious horizon. As Phillip Mar emphasizes, '. . . on a practical and dispositional level, hope is germane to the capacities to wait, to defer, discipline and even transform oneself in anticipation of some object that cannot be obtained in the present' (2005, 365). Reliance on a spiritual guide and proper conduct thus constituted a way of disciplining the present towards a future goal, creating a sense of direction and hope.

The *marabout*'s act of brokerage was by no means extraordinary for the migrants, but was closely linked to the Senegalese religious–cultural space. A range of scholars have emphasized the role of religious Murid networks and *marabouts* in the migration process (see, for example, Gemmeke 2013; Kane 2011; Riccio 2003). Most migrants regularly consulted *marabouts* in Senegal to solve and transform the problems they were facing or potentially might encounter, both prior to and after migration. Apart from solving problems, the *marabout* was also seen as a broker who could carve out the pathway to the fulfillment of their desires. Like the transaction between the migration broker and the migrant, there was usually an economic exchange involved, although many migrants emphasized that it was not an obligation. The migrant expected some sort of advancement in social, economic, and/or spiritual terms in return for this economic exchange. In other words, the event of the regularization was not extraordinary in itself but rather confirmed the tangibility and strength of a religious path. Yet it also confirmed the capacities and powers of this particular *marabout*. While he was in Argentina for a short visit before going to Brazil in 2013, the queue of migrants seeking his advice and wanting his blessings was long.

Hence, rather than granting state recognition and legal papers, the regularization program reaffirmed and infused an affective hope of the possibility of overcoming hardship through a good relationship with God, a spiritual master, and a collective discipline. In the final analytical section I put the migrants' understandings of regularization in perspective by dwelling on how their belief in transcendental interference was essential if they were to avoid falling into despair under the challenging circumstances in Argentina.

## Securing the Future through Endurance

Issa was 18 years old when he arrived in Argentina from his home town of Dakar after a failed attempt to get scouted as a football player in Europe. When I met him, he was trying to navigate between his own ambitions of making it as a professional footballer in Argentina and his mother's expectations that he send home enough money to start a small business in Senegal. He spent most of his time training in a park where Argentinian (mostly) football players waiting to be discovered played and trained together. At the same time he had a small stand at the above-mentioned Retiro train station which he paid a local Argentinian girl to man during his hours of workout, which cut considerably into his profits. Time was running out, he was getting older day by day in a context where youth was crucial to being scouted as the next new football talent. After I returned to Denmark, we continued our conversations on Facebook and Skype. One night Issa wrote:

> The only error I made in my life was to go to Argentina. *Los Latinos* are poor like us. They are good for nothing. I don't know what we are doing here. What we can earn here isn't worth the trouble. I know it is like that all over today—there is nothing. You know what we should do, we children of Senegal? We should go home to our belovèd country and try to earn a proper living there. It is what we ultimately should do but nobody is going to do it.
>
> My children will never travel, never. I have the experience now and that is what I will teach them. I am here now and it is not easy to go back in the state I am in. I am talking about the future. I lost almost three years of my life here—I don't want that to happen to my children or anyone I know. Only God knows the way now. Argentina is not a country for migration, it is the most discriminatory country in the world. I would prefer getting deported than to live like this. It is a country that doesn't give work to foreigners and does not let us send money home. It is becoming more and more complicated . . .[5]

In times like this, the sacrifice that Issa was willing to make seemed fragmented from the expected renewal and transformation (Jackson 2013). It made him question his migration to Argentina and, with that, his current existence and identity as a migrant. Time was not leading to progress but, rather, was wasted and alienated him further from who he was striving to become. Argentina was not turning out to be a place for migration or *chercher la fortune*; rather, spatial mobility had robbed Issa of precious years of his life instead of enhancing it. Like Guinean migrants in Lisbon, the realization that it 'was the same shit in a different continent' (Vigh 2009, 104) created a sense of disillusion and despair. The feeling of being stuck in a disadvantaged position, robbed of the possibilities of transcendence, made it clear for Issa that he could not look for a life in Argentina. Like Senegal, the country was placed at the periphery of economic development. In his disillusion the only remedy for overcoming despair and renew the directionality in his life was through relying on God. In *Sickness until Death*, Kierkegaard observed in a Christian context that it only becomes possible to 'embrace despair as the passageway to faith' and thus overcome the contingencies of the self through a reorientation of the self towards God ([1849]1941, 74–75). In his having faith and surrendering to God, we can thus see Issa's struggle as a way to regain a form of intermediated agency and resume the potentiality of hope. Whereas Issa turned to God for comfort and hope, he also embraced his 'belovèd country' as the ultimate possible arena for social becoming for himself, his compatriots, and the future generations embodied in his unborn children. Although being stuck physically in mobility without the possibility of returning home, Issa's imagination was not stuck. Hope traveled in the sense that he was projecting a future where migration and the sacrifices that come with it were not the answer for future generations.

The realization that Argentina was not an arena for social transformations was shared by many of the other Senegalese migrants I talked to there. One of them was my close interviewee Abdou who, despite his efforts over the previous three years, had not been able to realize his dream of returning home with enough money to settle down with his young wife and set up a solid business. Nevertheless, despite what appeared to be a state of stagnation, Abdou appeared optimistic and calm.

> They say money is the key to the world. I don't have that kind of money yet but I know tomorrow will be better. Not tomorrow like this Monday or the next day. But I have a strong faith that tomorrow will be better, I just know it. As long as I live a good life and don't do bad things, I know that, sooner or later, God will recognize my actions. It is like an investment—sooner or later it has to pay off. If not now, then in Paradise.

The certainty of knowing that he could become closer to God's blessings through his patient hope and practice reassured him again and again that things would eventually work in his favor, despite the rather gloomy present.

Abdou was not passive in his waiting but faithfully set up his small stand with sunglasses and watches every day and stayed there until late before packing up. Every day, seven days a week, except for when it was raining or the police or the municipality obstructed the hawkers' work. Like Issa, he turned to God. It is agency through the act of surrendering to an all-compassing cosmology of reward through hard work, morality, and submission that characterizes Murid practice (Cruise O'Brian 1971; Kane 2011). By refocusing his efforts on working on his inner state, rather than on the chaotic outer reality, Abdou seemed to regain a sense of control. If he did what he was supposed to, it was just a question of endurance and patience before God would reciprocate his actions. During the time between the action and the awaited reward, the migrants often said: '*Hay que aguantar*'—'One must endure'. They were enduring their lives in Argentina in a state of hopeful expectation.

Faith and discipline thus constituted essential ways in which migrants like Issa and Abdou also brokered hope in their everyday lives. It was a driving force for the migrants, a way of maintaining the possibility for an alternative future—that life, after all, could be different. By not dwelling on the present, they could gather the strength to endure and keep going without surrendering completely to despair and disillusion. However, it was a driving force that did not have a clearly defined goal (Bloch 1986). The reciprocal relationship between God and the migrant was never transparent and the future reward for their efforts lay hidden in God's secure unknown.

## Conclusion: Sticking to God

In this chapter I have analyzed the events of a recent regularization program, showing how Senegalese migrants perceived the opportunity to transcend their irregular status in Argentina. The case illuminates how Senegalese migrants navigate in a fairly new destination and how they try to gain momentum by relying on their known path of spirituality, but seem less interested in becoming new citizens within a state-governed framework of rights and obligations.

By introducing the concept of 'brokers of hope', I have tried to capture both structural and phenomenological aspects of hope-in-the-making. The concept can enhance our understanding of the wide scope of brokers involved in the migration process and the multifaceted ways in which they intervene in the migrants' lives and imaginaries beyond mediating concrete remedies to facilitate mobility. The chapter also exemplifies how the hope and promise brokered by middlemen in Senegal can rapidly be transformed into despair when the migrants are confronted with the contingent Argentinian reality. In this particular case, different political and religious actors constituted brokers of hope for the migrants' future in Argentina. However, the case also reflects the notion that hope is only brokered if it is linked to some kind of transformative potential for the recipients. By highlighting the transactions involved in brokerage, my analysis demonstrates that, not surprisingly, the gesture by the Argentinian state involves obligations for the migrants. Yet the Senegalese men and women seem reluctant to fulfill such obligations because they ascribe the legal document with very little transformative potential in terms of alleviating the structural barriers that limit their livelihood possibilities in Argentina.

Rather than accepting the gift and forming a new committed relationship to the Argentinian political system and/or the Senegalese diaspora association, many migrants saw the event from the perspective of a known religious path of agency and imagination. From this perspective, the power relation between state and migrant is reversed. The regularization had only become manifest due to a visiting *marabout*'s power and providence and the community's continuous good moral conduct. The *marabout* was thus the real broker of hope—a hope that transcended the event itself, because it was closely linked to how the migrants already kept the world open by believing in God and through exercising moral discipline in their everyday practices. In this way their seemingly disadvantaged position could be transformed and give them a sense of agency and a direction in their lives. The religious horizon offered them a map by which to navigate which was open to mobility and change and not controlled by nation-states' changing caprices. A space where the individual had some degree of control through his or her actions. Sticking to God was thus a way of keeping the world open rather than being weighed down by global stratification factors, where race and geographical placement do not favor Senegalese migrants.

## Notes

1. El Régimen Especial de Regularización de Extranjeros de Nacionalidad Senegalesa.
2. *Mercado Común del Sur*, the Southern Common Market—an economic and political agreement between the member-states of Argentina, Brazil, Paraguay, Uruguay, Venezuela, and Bolivia for promoting free trade and the movement of goods, people, and currency.
3. The 'gift' was not masked by a common collective repression of the objective nature of give and take that Bourdieu (1998) has suggested.
4. In 2006 it was estimated that 46.8 per cent of the labor force was active in the informal sector (Maurizio 2012, 11).
5. Chat text omitted for legibility.

## References

Alpes, M. J. 2013. *Migration brokerage, illegality and the state in anglophone Cameroon*. Copenhagen: Dansk Institut for Internationale Studier, DIIS Working Paper 2013:07.
Bertoncello, B. and S. Bredeloup. 2009. Chine–Afrique ou la valse des entrepreneurs-migrants. *Revue Européenne des Migrations Internationales* 25 (1): 45–70.
Bloch, E. 1986. *The principle of hope*. Cambridge, MA: MIT Press.
Bloch, E. 1998. *Literary essays*. Stanford: Stanford University Press (W. Hamacher and D. E. Wellbery, eds.; Andrew Joron *et al.*, trans.).

Bourdieu, P. 1998. *Practical reason*. Cambridge: Blackwell.
Bourdieu, P. 2000. *Pascalian meditations*. Cambridge: Blackwell.
Carling, J. 2002. Migration in the age of involuntary immobility: Theoretical reflections and Cape Verdean experiences. *Journal of Ethnic and Migration Studies* 28 (1): 5–42.
Ceriani, P. 2011. *Argentina avances y asignaturas pendientes en la consolidación de una política migratoria basada en los derechos humanos*. Buenos Aires: Centro de Estudios Legales y Sociales (CELS).
Cruise O'Brian, D. 1971. *The Mourides of Senegal: The politics and economic organization of an Islamic brotherhood*. Oxford: Clarendon Press.
Fassin, D. 2011. *Humanitarian reason: A moral history of the present*. Berkeley: University of California Press.
Ferguson, J. 2008. Global disconnect: Abjection and the aftermath of modernism. In *Readings in modernity in Africa*, eds. P. Geschiere, B. Meyer and P. Pels, 8–16. London: International Africa Institute.
Freier, L. F. 2013. *Open doors (for almost all): Visa policies and ethnic selectivity in Ecuador*. La Jolla: Center for Comparative Immigration Studies (CCIS), Working Paper 188.
Gammeltoft-Hansen, T. and N. N. Sørensen. 2013. *The migration industry and the commercialization of international migration*. London: Routledge.
Gemmeke, A. 2013. Marabouts and migrations: Senegalese between Dakar and diaspora. In *Long journeys: African migrants on the road*, eds. A. Triulzi and R. McKenzie, 113–134. Leiden: Brill.
Hage, G. 2003. *Against paranoid nationalism: Searching for hope in a shrinking society*. Annandale, NSW: Pluto Press.
Haugen, H. Ø. 2012. Nigerians in China: A second state of immobility. *International Migration* 50 (2): 65–80.
Jackson, M. 2005. *Existential anthropology: Event, exigencies and effects*. New York: Berghahn.
Jackson, M. 2013. *The wherewithal of life: Ethics, migration, and the question of well-being*. Berkeley: University of California Press.
Kane, O. 2011. *The homeland is the arena: Religion, transnationalism, and the integration of Senegalese immigrants in America*. Oxford: Oxford University Press.
Kierkegaard, S. [1849]1941. *Sickness until death*. Princeton, NJ: Princeton University Press.
Lucht, H. 2011. *Darkness before daybreak: African migrants living on the margins in Southern Italy today*. Berkeley: University of California Press.
Mar, P. 2005. Unsettling potentialities: Topographies of hope in transnational migration. *Journal of Intercultural Studies* 26 (4): 361–378.
Maurizio, R. 2012. *Labour informality in Latin America: The case of Argentina, Chile, Brazil and Peru*. Manchester: University of Manchester, Brooks World Poverty Institute Working Paper 165.
Mauss, M. [1954]2002. *The gift, the form and reason for exchange in archaic societies*. London: Routledge.
Miyazaki, H. 2004. *The method of hope: Anthropology, philosophy, and Fijian knowledge*. Stanford: Stanford University Press.
Miyazaki, H. 2006. Economy of dreams: Hope in global capitalism and its critiques. *Cultural Anthropology* 21 (2): 147–172.
Novick, S. 2012. *Migraciones y políticas públicas. Nuevos escenarios y desafíos*. Buenos Aires: Editorial Catálogos—Universidad de Buenos Aires.

Pacecca, M. I. and C. Courtis. 2008. *Inmigración contemporánea en Argentina: Dinámicas y políticas*. Santiago de Chile: Cepal.
Pelican, M. and P. Tatah. 2009. Migration to the Gulf States and China: Local perspectives from Cameroon. *African Diaspora* 2 (2): 229–245.
Riccio, B. 2003. More than a trade diaspora. Senegalese transnational experiences in Emilia-Romagna (Italy). In *New African Diasporas*, ed. K. Koser, 95–110. London: Routledge.
Spaan, E. and E. Hillmann. 2013. Migration trajectories and the migration industry: Theoretical reflections and empirical examples from Asia. In *The migration industry and the commercialization of international migration*, eds. T. Gammeltoft-Hansen and N. Nyberg Sørensen, 64–86. London: Routledge.
Vigh, H. 2009. Wayward migration: On imagined futures and technological voids. *Ethnos* 74 (1): 91–109.
Zournazi, M. 2002. *Hope: New philosophies for change*. Annandale: Pluto Press Australia.

# 4 Zouglou Music and Youth in Urban Burkina Faso
## Displacement and the Social Performance of Hope

*Jesper Bjarnesen*

### Introduction

One of the most striking consequences of the recent armed conflict in Côte d'Ivoire is the forced displacement of Burkinabé labor migrants and their families from Côte d'Ivoire to Burkina Faso over the decade 2000–10. It is estimated that at least 500,000—and probably more than 1 million—Burkinabé living in Côte d'Ivoire were forced to leave the country during this time (Boswell 2010; Reister 2011), and yet these displacements have received relatively little attention from researchers and humanitarian actors alike.

Burkina Faso and Côte d'Ivoire emerged during the colonial era as closely tied and mutually interdependent parts of a regional mobility regime that fueled the Ivorian miracle economy in the decades after independence. Burkinabé labor migrants thereby provided an essential part of the workforce for Côte d'Ivoire's plantation economy—the world's largest cocoa producer (Beauchemin 2005; Cordell *et al.* 1996). This same interdependence eventually fueled the xenophobic rhetoric and ethnicized politics at the heart of the Ivorian armed conflict, as shifting regimes in Côte d'Ivoire drew ever-tighter boundaries around the notion of Ivorian autochthony in order to exclude northerners and people of immigrant descent from political influence (Dembélé 2002; 2003).[1]

This chapter analyzes the practices and aspirations of young Burkinabé migrants arriving as refugees in Burkina Faso for the first time during the Ivorian crisis,[2] usually accompanying their parents, who had been forced to abandon their migrant careers in Côte d'Ivoire. Born and raised in Côte d'Ivoire, these young migrants faced an entirely different challenge to that of their parents in integrating into a socio-cultural context with which they were unfamiliar and which held specific ideas about and prejudice against the children of the Burkinabé diaspora in Côte d'Ivoire. Through the concepts of hope and displacement, the chapter reflects on how Ivorian Zouglou music became an important cultural vehicle for these young migrants, intent on performing their otherness and quite successful in exploiting that difference in competition with non-migrant youths over access to employment

DOI: 10.4324/9781315659916-4

and other privileges. Zouglou music was a predominant genre in Ivorian popular culture in the 1990s but gained new life in Burkina Faso a decade later, in the context of the Ivorian armed conflict.

In exploring the meanings and uses of Zouglou music in this context, the analysis suggests that this particular musical style served to articulate multiple modes of hope. In relation to their non-migrant peers, the social performance of Ivorian youth culture by young migrants served to evoke a cosmopolitan youth identity that represents the hopes and dreams of many Burkinabé youths—to migrate to the regional metropolis of Abidjan and take part in global flows of urban youth culture, consumption, and privilege. On a more personal level, the lyrics of Zouglou music, together with its shared consumption, inspired a sense of hopefulness and confidence in its listeners in the face of their social exclusion as immigrants in the city.

## Displacement and the Social Performance of Hope

As noted by most scholars reflecting on hope, the notion is difficult to pin down and therefore challenging to use as an analytical concept. However, rather than despair at the concept's complexity, it may be more useful to consider several *modes of hoping* (Webb 2007; Zournazi 2002) in conjunction and reflect on their characteristics and implications. As a point of departure, we may say that hope generally relates to, or even springs from, a sense of uncertainty or ambiguity (cf. Cole and Durham 2008; Crapanzano 2004; Hage 2003; Harvey 2000; Miyazaki 2004). Hoping for something means wishing for a particular outcome of undetermined circumstances and the uncertainty thus implied may relate to both the source and the likelihood of that outcome. As a prelude to delimiting the different modes of hoping relevant to my purposes here, let me briefly consider how uncertainty may be seen as a fundamental consequence of social displacement.

As a number of anthropological studies of forced displacement have shown, the distinction between forced and economically motivated migration is rarely clear-cut. Rather than movement *per se*, displacement has been related analytically to the disruption of subjective senses of belonging (Agier 2011; Bjarnesen 2013; Jackson 2002; Jansen 2008; Lubkemann 2008a). The notion of displacement, from this perspective, has been applied when researching empirically how processes of life-making or belonging may be disrupted or challenged by other actors or by larger structural forces (Lubkemann 2008b, 193; see also Gill *et al.* 2011, 301–302). Approaching displacement as a life-rupturing form of mobility (cf. Barrett 2009, 95) invites a detailed empirical investigation of specific histories and experiences of (im)mobility without the need for overall categorizations of migrants or their movements—in other words, a shift in focus from 'the displaced' as a population towards *processes* of displacement. This perspective also calls attention to migrant aspirations and the outlooks of refugees, even when the goal of such decisions may be difficult to envisage or articulate (Piot 2010, 20). In this way, the uncertainty created by displacement has been argued to hold the potential for productive as well as detrimental effects (e.g., Hammar 2014). Involuntary moves or 'stuckedness' may have unexpected consequences, leading to new opportunities.

The ambiguity entailed by displacement leads us back to the relation between hope and uncertainty. Inspired by John Dewey's pragmatist philosophy, Susan Reynolds Whyte locates hope in the space between uncertainty and possibility or, as she phrases it, in *subjunctivity*—in the conditional: '. . . it is not just doubt, but hope for a better future that hangs on the ifs and maybes' (Reynolds Whyte 2002, 177; see also Weiss 2004, 14). The mode of hope evoked by the idea of subjunctivity may be said to rely on a sense of optimism in the face of an uncertain future (Hage 2003, 24). Behind this seemingly innately personal capacity, however, lies a fundamental structural condition that is important for an anthropological analysis of hope: '. . . [H]ope depends on some other agency—a god, fate, chance, an other—for its fulfilment . . . [H]ope presupposes a metaphysics' (Crapanzano 2003, 6). In political terms, hope's reliance on the agency of another presupposes an unequal power relationship: some external source of agency is needed to fulfil hope and, whether that source is perceived to be metaphysical or not, this reliance expresses a hierarchical relation between the one(s) hoping and the one(s) granting those hopes. Here, some analysts evoke hope as a resource that is distributed unequally within a population (Ghassan Hage in Zournazi 2002, 155). For example, Arjun Appadurai speaks of 'the capacity to aspire' as a 'navigational capacity' accumulated by those with the privilege of more opportunities to exercise it (Appadurai 2004, 69). In this fairly neoliberal vision, wealth generates wealth, whereas the disadvantaged are left searching for ways to expand their '. . . more brittle horizon of aspirations' (2004, 69).

It seems to me that the social distribution of hope evokes the stratification of a relative dependence on external agency. Those who hope would probably rather not be in such a position of dependency. Here it is important to distinguish between two different modes of hope: hope as a personal disposition and hope as a social predicament. On the one hand, a sense of well-founded optimism may be seen as a resource—what Hage refers to as 'dispositional hopefulness'. '[H]opefulness', he argues, 'is above all a disposition to be confident in the face of the future, to be open to it and welcoming to what it will bring, even if one does not know for sure what it will bring' (Hage 2003, 24). Such a confidence may certainly be nourished by past experiences of success or achievement, as Appadurai suggests. On the other hand, hope may be the last resort in the face of profound uncertainty. The uncertainty caused by displacement may also be seen to be unequally distributed—in refugee research, it is consistently emphasized that neither war nor natural disaster strikes the civilian population on a social *tabula rasa*, but rather accentuates existing inequalities and stratifications (see, eg., Allen 1996; Hoffman and Oliver-Smith 2002; Jansen and Löfving 2009). Being reduced to a state of hoping for the intervention of external agency, whether in the form of humanitarian or of supernatural forces, is anything but a desirable position to be in (Bjarnesen 2009). The predicament of hope reflects social stratification as much as it reflects the accumulation of dispositional hopefulness.

Hope may, in other words, be both an expression of a personal faculty of resourcefulness and a social condition resulting from uncertainty, for example, in the context of forced displacement. However, even the former, more positive, mode of hope—or hopefulness—is an ambiguous state of being. Just as we must understand the external agency evoked by different modes of hope in specific social contexts and particular situations, we must examine analytically how hopes are inspired and articulated by larger social discourses and institutions. Hopefulness may seem to the individual to be an innate capacity, independent of outside intervention but, as Hage (2003) shows, a central function of a society or a nation-state may be said to be that of inspiring 'social hope' in its citizens, by which he means a sense of 'existential mobility', of 'going somewhere' (Hage 2007). Hope, from this perspective, is laced with power and potentially with structural violence, rather than simply being a synonym for optimism: '[W]e have to note how capitalism hegemonises the ideological content of hope so it becomes almost universally equated with dreams of better-paid jobs, better lifestyles, more commodities, etc.' (Hage 2003, 14). Although I would argue that it remains to be empirically tested in each instance, it is significant to relate the passivity implied by this kind of hope to capitalist ideology, since '[t]he power of these hopes is such that most people will live their lives believing in the possibility of upward social mobility without actually experiencing it' (Hage 2003, 14).

This warning is critical to our analysis of the experiences of young Africans, who may be said to generally face some of the poorest odds for achieving such aspirations. In most studies of young Africans, youth agency makes little sense without a consideration of the hierarchical orders that young people take part in. The social position of youth implies that young people direct their efforts towards expanding their social networks and accumulate social recognition by all possible means (Christiansen *et al.* 2006; Durham 2004, 2008; Honwana and De Boeck 2005), leading some to evoke their youthfulness in a context where such a social role is perceived as an asset, and others to emphasize their sense of responsibility and moderation to a different audience.

In relation to the aspirations of Burkinabé labor migrants, the overall dream of upward social mobility and an idea of a globalized middle-class consumer lifestyle were certainly present in the narratives of those still hoping to leave Burkina Faso for Côte d'Ivoire and of those who had been forced to return. However, capitalism takes specific structural and discursive forms in specific contexts and, in the relationship between Burkina Faso and Côte d'Ivoire, it has been shaped by the colonial division of labor, by which the former has been constituted as a reserve of cheap manual labor for the plantation industry of the latter (Amin 1967; Cordell *et al.* 1996). In this particular case, the hopes of aspiring migrants in Burkina Faso have been inspired by the successful returns of several generations of migrants, who were able to acquire the right to cultivate land in Côte d'Ivoire and accumulate enough wealth to retire back home. In this way, the narratives of aspiring migrants during my fieldwork in 2009–10 articulated the hopes of stepping in the footsteps of past generations of migrants—what Miyazaki characterizes as an 'inherited hope' (2004, 139). In Miyazaki's understanding, hope works as a driver of social action; a *method* for inspiring agency, and this method '... is predicated on the inheritance of a past hope and its performative replication in the present' (2004, 139). The inherited hope of aspiring Burkinabé migrants was based on the history of Côte d'Ivoire's social, cultural, and economic superiority in the eyes of aspiring Burkinabé labor migrants. The standardized contents of the narratives of aspiring migrants in Burkina Faso, then, did not stem from a global homogenizing force of capitalism, but from the specific institution of circular labor migration between Burkina Faso and Côte d'Ivoire, developed and maintained in its fundamental structure since the early twentieth century.

These introductory remarks on hope and displacement have served to outline several aspects, or modes, of hope that will be relevant for understanding how Zouglou music and its adherents in urban Burkina Faso coped with uncertainty. For young adult involuntary migrants in Bobo-Dioulasso, Burkina Faso's second-largest city, uncertainty arose primarily from their persistent sense of displacement—a predicament that had followed them on their travels from Côte d'Ivoire to Burkina Faso during the Ivorian armed conflict. The following section traces the origins and shifting sociopolitical affiliations of Zouglou music. After this brief historical contextualization, the chapter continues by analyzing the modes of hope evoked by Zouglou lyrics, and by the shared consumption of Zouglou by young urban refugees in Bobo-Dioulasso.

## Generation Zouglou

Originating in the academic circles of Cocody University in Abidjan, Zouglou emerged as a musical genre around 1990, in the context of Ivorian President Félix Houphouët-Boigny's last years in power and the political transition from a one-party state to multiparty democracy (Blé 2006, 170). The often satirical prose of the lyrics was initially an expression by university students of their dissatisfaction with the political elite and the experience of exclusion and marginalization by the well-educated youth (Konate 2002, 784–785). In this way, Zouglou served its originators as both a source of insight into the societal transformations taking place in Côte d'Ivoire and a source of belonging mobilized by a sense of shared struggles and identity

(Blé 2006, 170). The name Zouglou itself is usually said to stem from its meaning in the Ivorian Baoulé language, designating a shapeless mass but used as a derivative for a garbage heap or trash can (Adom 2013, 32). Another interpretation refers to the Bété phrase *zou glou*, meaning 'bury us' or 'reject us'—both linguistic references connoting abjection and marginality from the establishment and a rhetorical sense of hopelessness.

During the 1990s, the messages of Zouglou lyrics developed from being primarily concerned with the hardships of life as a student to reflect on larger issues of being an urban resident and on the escalating political crisis and armed conflict in Côte d'Ivoire. In this way, as I explore in more detail below, its emergence is intimately linked with the advent of a new urban slang and its accompanying urban youth culture in Abidjan during the same period (Konate 2002, 783; Newell 2012). From its highly localized point of departure, in other words, the messages of Zouglou gradually encompassed the frustrations and desires of a whole generation of young Ivorians (Blé 2006, 176).

Zouglou's image of being the voice of Ivorian youth (see also Konate 2002, 792) appealed to political actors on both sides of the divide that gradually widened during the 1990s between the proponents of Ivorian autochthony and its various opponents. Zouglou's origins among university students in Abidjan included the involvement of the influential FESCI student union, whose figureheads during the 1990s included men who would become dominant in Ivorian politics a decade later—on opposing sides of the political divide (Konate 2003). Charles Blé Goudé, as President Laurent Gbagbo's 'street general'[3] and mobilizer of the *Jeunes Patriotes* youth militias throughout the troubled decade of 2000–10, became a known patron of and investor in the production of Zouglou (Koffi 2013). Even the reconciliatory messages—evoking an end to armed conflict and the shared responsibility of power holders on both sides of the political divide—of some Zouglou artists in the latter years of the Gbagbo regime were promoted on national TV and radio in an attempt to diffuse the resentment of the youth of the opposition (Blé 2006, 180).

Despite its affiliation with the Gbagbo regime and the *Jeunes Patriotes*, then, Zouglou in Côte d'Ivoire gradually came to be seen as the voice of the disenfranchised, yet politically aware, Ivorian youth, evoking a shared sense of national belonging and injustice rather than a specific political allegiance. In the remainder of this chapter, I illustrate how Zouglou was re-appropriated by young Burkinabé citizens who were forced to leave Côte d'Ivoire during the armed conflict and had settled in Bobo-Dioulasso. Given its former affiliation with the xenophobic *Jeunes Patriotes* militias, it may seem paradoxical that this particular musical genre became a rallying point for these young migrants but the analysis shows that Zouglou in Burkina Faso became associated with a cosmopolitan youth culture rather than a localized political message by virtue of Abidjan's standing as the preferred destination for aspiring Burkinabé migrants, and its image as a gateway to globalized popular culture and connectivity.

## Displacement, Uncertainty and Hope in Zouglou Lyrics

Musical performers in the booming Ivorian entertainment industry have come to represent a combination of cosmopolitanism and modernity to their audiences across the French-speaking countries of West Africa. In music videos by Ivorian artists, the most prestigious sites of global modernity—Paris, New York, London, Tokyo or Dubai—have become familiar backdrops to the choreography of the performers. The hopes of many young Ivorians are nourished by such displays of participation in global flows of mobility and consumption.

One Zouglou group in particular incarnated this hope of global cosmopolitanism by naming themselves '*Espoir 2000*' ('Hope 2000')! Once they were successful enough to become featured on Ivorian television, their own hopes had already been realized and the name came to be interpreted as representing the hopes and dreams of young Ivorians in a more general sense (Adom 2013, 103). The mode of hoping represented by the group *Espoir 2000* is, first and foremost, an expression of the social distribution of hope. Hope, here, is a resource that successful musicians redistribute to their audiences through their lyrics, music videos, and, in rare cases, band names. The underlying power imbalance, of course, consists in the very slim chances that members of their audience will experience a similar upward social mobility and, in this way, despite the best interests of the performers, the redistribution of the hope of success may be said to defuse tension and lull consumers of these messages into the passive 'waiting time of hope' (Crapanzano 2003, 5).

As noted in the previous section, however, Zouglou artists were not just concerned with displaying their own success; they also contributed to a social critique, originating in the circles of university students but eventually gaining traction among youths across the country. For example, Zouglou artist Soum Bill did not hesitate to berate the Gbagbo regime in the midst of armed conflict, lamenting, 'We no longer know who to count on, down with the politics of the belly'[4] in his 2004 song '*Nos problèmes*' ('Our Problems')—quoted in Adom (2013, 90). The expression 'politics of the belly'—whether inspired by Bayart's seminal work (Bayart 1993) or from the emic conceptualizations from which it is derived—implies a predatory and corrupt political rule wherein political elites feed on the resources of common citizens. The song thus berates the corruption of the political elite under Gbagbo's rule.

Befitting of social juniors in this context, however, most Zouglou artists have been somewhat vague in placing the blame for their generation's sense of despair. For example, *Espoir 2000*, in the song *Abidjan*, chose to appeal to their leaders rather than blame them for the predicaments of the young population, urging the political elite to fulfil the hopes to which God had not responded. Here, the shifting external agency affecting the circumstances of those hoping is spelled out: the hopers remain dependent on others to alleviate their misery but, having directed their hopes towards God in vain, they now address the power holders instead. The recognition of the authority of the power holders as social seniors in relation to the musicians who evoke the role of social juniors, it should be noted, may be a fairly rhetorical maneuver, as it is shown to be in other confrontations between elders and their social juniors (see, e.g., Argenti 2007; Ottenberg 1971). In another song, the same group does not hesitate to impose its own clear-sightedness on the state of Ivorian politics, implying that politicians treat the population as sheep! Finally, the despairing sentiments towards divine intervention expressed in the song *Abidjan* do not prevent *Espoir 2000* from composing a celebratory hymn, thanking God for their own fortunes.

Reflecting a final mode of hoping, *Espoir 2000*'s song *Abidjan* is mainly concerned with a critique of the lack of employment opportunities and housing in the city, satirically changing the national motto '*Union, Discipline, Travail*' ('Unity, Discipline, Work') into '*Union, Discipline, Chômage*' ('Unity, Discipline, Unemployment'). These lyrics reflect the aspirations of many young people in Côte d'Ivoire, Burkina Faso, and beyond of being able to escape the social moratorium of youth (cf. Vigh 2006, 96) through employment and wage earning which, in turn, allows for the possibility of establishing oneself as a social adult. Remembering Hage's discussion of the relation between hope and capitalism, then, these aspirations are not utopian in the sense of being politically radical hopes for societal transformation or a structural redistribution of resources (cf. Argenti 2007, 246; Malkki 2001, 329) but, rather, conservative hopes of taking part in the privileges of a globalizing middle class—primarily through work, housing, consumption, and marriage. Zouglou is not decidedly, or even primarily, a social critique, although commentaries on the political leadership are part of the subject matter of the lyrics. The central image of Zouglou is to speak truthfully about life as a young person in Côte d'Ivoire and, by extension, about African youth. Having considered the shifting political affiliations of Zouglou in Côte d'Ivoire, and the diverse modes of hope evoked by a selection of its lyrics, the following section reflects on the role of Zouglou for young urban refugees in Burkina Faso.

## Zouglou and the Social Performance of Hope in Sarfalao

In the middle of the smoke-filled room where Youssouf, Félix, and a varying number of other young men sleep, Jo dances slowly with his eyes closed, while singing along to the lyrics that are pouring out of a stereo lit by a fluorescent blue backlight on the control panel. He has taken off his white t-shirt, and his body is glistening with sweat from the heavy heat of a Sunday afternoon in Sarfalao—an informal neighborhood in Bobo-Dioulasso which has attracted large numbers of self-settled refugees from the Ivorian civil war during the past decade (Bjarnesen 2014). Alassane explains to me that Jo is 'inspired' (*inspiré*) by the music, which describes a kind of trance where the listener is drawn into the music and forgets about his surroundings. He says that this is how a *zouglouman* draws hope and courage from Zouglou to endure the hardships of everyday life and face the world with his eyes open and his back straight.

In addition to their appreciation of Zouglou, these young men—all in their late twenties—shared an experience of having been born and raised by Burkinabé parents in Côte d'Ivoire. Their Ivorian upbringing was obvious to their Burkinabé neighbors in Sarfalao: they spoke French with a typically Ivorian accent, knew relatively little Dioula, the local *lingua franca*, and dressed in a style inspired by American hip hop, in this context associated with Ivorian urban youth culture. Although Alassane and his friends came to Burkina Faso with their families when they were forced to flee persecution during the armed conflict in Côte d'Ivoire, they quickly found each other in Sarfalao, where they were all coping with the social exclusion by their new neighbors. To the long-term residents of Sarfalao, the mass arrival of refugees from Côte d'Ivoire during the period 2000–05 put increased pressure on housing and livelihood opportunities, and local youths were provoked by the attitude of the migrant youths, whom they perceived as arrogant and flamboyant.

The attitude of local youths was, however, ambivalent, since the urban youth culture displayed by the new arrivals to the neighborhood represented the regional metropolis of Abidjan, Côte d'Ivoire's financial capital, to which many dreamed of migrating once the political situation in Côte d'Ivoire had stabilized.[5] The local youths perceived of the newcomers as '*diaspos*'—a term originating in the circles of university students in Ouagadougou as an abbreviation of 'children of or from the diaspora' (Zongo 2010, 35), referring to the tendency for Burkinabé migrants in Côte d'Ivoire to send their children to Burkina Faso to continue their education during the politically unstable decades of the 1980s and 1990s. In Sarfalao, the term was used to remind migrant youths of their otherness in two different social contexts, as both not quite Ivorian (in Côte d'Ivoire) and not quite Burkinabé (in Burkina Faso). Another term applied to migrant youths was '*ivorien vers*' (literally, 'Ivorian towards'), taken from the terminology of Burkinabé identity cards, where a person unable to state his or her precise date of birth would be listed as being born in an approximate year, stated in the identity papers as, say, *vers 1975*—literally 'towards', meaning 'around' or 'approximately' 1975. In other words, the term *diaspo* was intended by local youths to signify their neither/nor status as approximately, but not quite, Ivorian or Burkinabé.

It was in the face of this experience of being doubly excluded or persistently displaced that migrant youths found a sense of community with other migrants. Whereas migrant hometown associations typically center on more-delimited places of origin—sometimes specific towns, in other cases a more regional delimitation—migrant youths in Sarfalao paid little attention to the specific origins of other migrants. The common denominator for a sense of belonging to the group was, first and foremost, an experience of otherness and exclusion in relation to non-migrants in the city and, secondly, a familiarity with Ivorian urban youth culture, expressed through their dress, taste in music, and use of Ivorian *nouchi* slang. The sense of persistent displacement conveyed by the term *diaspo* resonated with the young migrants, who gradually came to embrace it and ascribe it with more positive connotations. This re-articulation of the connotations of the term *diaspo* sprang, to a great extent, from the sense of belonging and hopefulness that Zouglou inspired. For example, the popular song '*Quel est mon pays?*' ('Which is my country?'), by Ivorian Zouglou artists Yodé and Siro, explicitly addressed the sense of neither/nor experienced by the migrant youths, now self-identifying as *diaspos*: 'In Burkina they say "There's an Ivorian"; in Côte d'Ivoire, "There's a Burkinabé"'.

For the *diaspos*, the song's lyrics provided little by way of a social critique but simply stated that these experiences were made on a wrongful ascription of identity on the basis of appearances. Its force lay rather in its recognition of their own predicament, in the precise articulation of their own experience of persistent displacement. Other Zouglou songs dealt with themes that also resonated with the *diaspos*. Alassane told me that Zouglou was not dance music for parties but was intended to inspire reflection in the listener. Many songs were about hope, about not being corrupted by money, and about valuing friendship. These lyrics helped you to hold your head up high and be proud, Alassane explained. You could tell a *diaspo* from a Burkinabé by his taste in music, he claimed—if someone walked proudly, as if listening to Zouglou, he was bound to be a *diaspo*. He might even be dancing in the street in broad daylight—something you would never see a Burkinabé do. This was an attitude which the *diaspos* had brought with them from Abidjan, he said. In Abidjan there were plenty of *zougloumans*[6] and this was the style that Alassane and his friends had brought with them.

At one point Nico, who had arrived in Burkina Faso during the war and had made a career as a singer of Zouglou and other Ivorian musical styles, explained a song by saying that its message was that money changes a person and makes you forget what is important, such as friendship. He said the lyrics were meant to make us understand that the life of the rich—the politicians and 'the bosses'—was not worth striving for. I asked who the 'we' referred to in this context and he said that it was for 'us, the weak'. He said that Zouglou was about getting good advice from people who knew how it was to be 'small'. He translated the following song, about a man who leaves his car at the site of an accident in Paris, despite having the law on his side in placing the blame for the collision. Nico explained the message as being that, if you go to Paris (or some other place) without papers, you do not have rights and you would be thrown out of the country by the authorities if you stay. This was a fitting example of how the Zouglou songs also provided advice on situations that people like Nico knew nothing about but which represented their aspirations. They were songs to make you think and retain your focus. They were songs that inspired hope. Hope, in this way, evokes

Hage's notion of dispositional hopefulness: through the shared consumption of Zouglou, the *diaspos* inspired each other with optimism and faith in the future by creating a space of inclusion in the face of persistent displacement.

Nico had come to embrace the role of *diaspo* as a cultural style—a role that he had only become aware of through his stigmatization in Burkina Faso. In Côte d'Ivoire, listening to Zouglou and speaking *nouchi* slang had been a popular youth cultural style, even in the town of San Pedro, where he grew up—informed by music videos and by friends and acquaintances with access to Abidjan. In Burkina Faso, Nico's speech, mannerisms, and musical preferences stood out and, through sharing these tastes and dispositions with other young migrants, he gradually came to perceive his labeling as a *diaspo* as a source of pride and distinction, rather than as a derogatory label assigned to him by envious and narrow-minded non-migrant neighbors. As a re-defined social marker, *diaspo* came to represent a cosmopolitan youth cultural style, brimming with energy, satire, and wit (Bjarnesen 2014).

A social performance (cf. Goffman 1959, 77; see also Argenti 2007, 11), in this way, is not about pretending but about embodying a social role. As Alassane expressed it above, the embodiment of *diaspo* youth culture in Sarfalao was intimately linked to the internalization of Zouglou, starting from its consumption in an enclosed space where the listener is gradually 'inspired' by letting the music and its lyrics fill him. As Alassane describes it, the music is carried with him out onto the streets, where his posture and attitude make him look as though he is (still) listening to Zouglou. By embodying the spirit of Zouglou, the *diaspos* performed an attitude of confidence and hopefulness that gradually came to define their sense of community and resourcefulness, in contradistinction to the local 'Burkinabé' youths. In this way, the *diaspos* practiced what Miyazaki calls 'the method of hope', replicating the inherited hopes of generations of Burkinabé labor migrants through their social performances (Miyazaki 2004, 139).

As a self-conscious promotion of a social role, performing *diaspo* youth culture may be understood, in this way, to be relying on the same playful performances that Sasha Newell has described as 'the bluff' in his work on the *nouchi* youth culture in Abidjan (Newell 2009, 380). In Côte d'Ivoire, *nouchi* slang had been developed as a subversive language of the youth, serving as a coded language with which to critique the power holders through satire. Originally, this use had lent itself to Zouglou as well, allowing artists to express opinions that might otherwise have been censored by the authorities (Adom 2013, 56). In Sarfalao, however, whereas *nouchi* slang served exclusively as a tool of counter-exclusion—a coded language designed to leave the uninitiated guessing as to what was really being said—the role of Zouglou eventually became more than just a subcultural signifier, shared by the *diaspos* in opposition to non-migrant youths. In fact, Zouglou became the first of a series of subcultural styles that found its way into local communities, serving more as a bridge between the *diaspos* and their neighbors than as a vehicle for exclusion or stigma.

Nico was involved in a musical group consisting entirely of *diaspos*, who would meet and play music around a shared pot of mint tea in the afternoons. The group's musical skills soon caught the attention of a neighbor, who was arranging for the celebration of his newborn son's baptism and who eventually hired Nico and the others to play at the party. The group thus rose to local fame and would play at weddings, funerals, baptisms, and other social events in the neighborhood, thereby earning both a livelihood and a legitimate place in the community. In a similar way, *diaspo* youths gradually became attractive to local radio stations because of their cosmopolitan French vocabulary, whereas the outgoing and fun-loving attitude associated with the *diaspo* social performance proved useful for local politicians in need of a visible and dynamic youth wing at political rallies and important meetings. During President Blaise Compaoré's electoral campaign in 2010, Nico and his friends could be seen riding around in the back of an open truck, singing songs in support of the same man who, in a speech following a series of riots at the university campus in Ouagadougou in 2005, blamed young migrants from Côte d'Ivoire for the increasing disorderliness of university students!

The relative success of *diaspo* youths in acquiring access to local elite networks and livelihood options in these different ways confirmed to the *diaspos* that their otherness could be used as an asset and further inspired the consolidation of a self-aware social performance of *diaspo* youth culture. During the last few months of my fieldwork, new steps were being taken to form an NGO named *Diaspora et développement* (Diaspora and Development), inspired by the success of *diaspos* in using their otherness to get ahead in the competition over scarce livelihood options. In this way, the performance of the defiant hopefulness at the heart of *diaspo* youth culture gradually became a key livelihood strategy, reflecting the *diaspos*' overall hopes for a secure income. This, in turn, would provide them with a way out of the informal neighborhood and into more gentrified areas of the city, with prospects for consumer goods such as a television set, a refrigerator, a motorcycle, and fashionable clothing, and, finally, with the possibility of getting married and raising a family. Zouglou, in this way, became one of the vehicles through which *diaspo* youth culture was gradually re-defined as a vibrant and cosmopolitan social performance in Bobo-Dioulasso. More than any other musical style originating in Côte d'Ivoire, Zouglou came to define the *diaspo* subculture in Bobo-Dioulasso, and, most importantly, to symbolize at one and the same time its singularity and its adaptability to the social life of the neighborhood.

## Conclusion

This chapter has argued that Zouglou music became a central source of hopefulness for young adult migrants in Bobo Dioulasso, in the face of social exclusion and in spite of an uncertain future. Through their shared consumption of this music, *diaspo* youths found a space in which to articulate and reshape a new collective identity against their persistent displacement. Nevertheless, Zouglou did not serve to mobilize the *diaspos* socially or politically in the way that rock music is said to have been a driver of social critique in the cultural youth revolution in the Europe and America of the 1960s (cf. Hobsbawm 1995, 325–327). Zouglou had served as a social mobilizer in a different context—first in the university circles of Abidjan and, later, as part of a larger pro-Gbagboist movement of articulating 'true Ivorianness' (*ivoirité*), juxtaposed with the unauthentic urbanites from the hinterland and from countries like Burkina Faso and Mali (Newell 2012). The paradox of why this very same style of music would become the flagship in the refashioning of *diaspo* youth culture in Bobo-Dioulasso has been shown here to relate to several modes of hoping. For the *diaspos*, Zouglou inspired their social performance of hope, which proved to be a useful strategy in catching the attention of the local elite and enabling access to their networks in the city.

Zouglou music became an important vehicle for simultaneously distinguishing and integrating *diaspo* youths in their new neighborhood in Bobo-Dioulasso. Despite Zouglou's paradoxical political roles in Côte d'Ivoire, young migrants in Burkina Faso who had experienced the increasingly violent xenophobia of the Gbagbo regime first-hand developed a special bond to this particular musical genre for several reasons. Firstly, Zouglou was, to the *diaspos*, a favorite style during their upbringing in Côte d'Ivoire in the 1990s—before the *ivoirité* rhetoric targeted them as 'strangers' and, in a sense, turned Zouglou against them. In this way, Zouglou became associated with a pre-displacement nostalgia for life in Côte d'Ivoire prior to the armed conflict which eventually led to their forced 'return' to their parents' country of origin. Secondly, the shifting political affiliations of Zouglou in Côte d'Ivoire were understood by the *diaspos* as an expression of the unavoidable obligation of social juniors to align with authority figures—an expression of the *débrouillardise*, or social navigation, that all youths must engage in (see, e.g., Christiansen *et al.* 2006). Furthermore, although Zouglou became affiliated with the Gbagbo regime in Côte d'Ivoire, its lyrics still carried universalist aspirations of instilling hopefulness in young people, and was famously vague in its commentaries on the political situation in Côte d'Ivoire. The distinction between the interpretative possibilities of the music in its own right and its use in social mobilization is essential for appreciating how Zouglou became so important to youths displaced by its proponents among the political leadership in Côte d'Ivoire. Third, in Burkina Faso, Zouglou carried the inherited hope of generations of Burkinabé labor migrants of seeking their fortune in Côte d'Ivoire. The *diaspos* thus exploited their otherness by evoking the cosmopolitanism associated with Ivorian urban youth culture—as a 'stepping stone to modernity' (Newell 2012, 42)—regardless of the fact that *nouchi* youth culture in Abidjan was explicitly articulated in contradistinction to the figure of the uncultivated youth from the village and its extension to the poorer neighbors of Burkina Faso, Mali, and Guinea.

In this endeavor, the consumption of Zouglou was not only a social performance directed at non-*diaspo* youths but also a collective practice that brought *diaspos* together and inspired hope in the listeners through the act of sharing their appreciation, as well as through the messages of the lyrics. The consumption of Zouglou thereby illustrates the general point that the performance of *diaspo* youth culture—as any social performance, in Goffman's understanding—cannot be reduced to the self-conscious impression management of the actor but is a multi-faceted social practice that may provide a deeply felt sense of belonging and hope while simultaneously serving as an identity-marker of other social roles.

Mobilizing *diaspo* youth culture in Sarfalao, in this way, may be seen as one among several strategies in the pursuit of social recognition and access to networks of privilege. Despite oppressive social hierarchies and debilitating material conditions, these social practices are oriented towards possible futures within their structural limitations. By conceptualizing the actions and expectations of *diaspo* youths as enactments of hopefulness, we might avoid the idealizing tendency of the concept of youth agency (cf. Durham 2008) and move towards an approach that treats the hopes and dreams of the people we study as central to social dynamics and processes of social change.

This expression of youth agency should not be seen as revolutionary. Most young people seek ways in which to benefit from and fit into existing orders, rather than turn them upside down (Durham 2008). The concept of hope, in this context, allows us to appreciate two aspects of youth agency that may otherwise be neglected: first, that youth aspirations, to a great extent, rely on external agency—social seniors for the most part—and, second, as Hage argues, that the relatively standardized discourses of these aspirations warrant consideration of the larger structural forces that influence and shape young people's hopes of partaking in a globalized vision of middle-class prosperity.

This understanding of youth agency and the conservative nature of hope are also expressed in the roles and lyrics of Zouglou. Zouglou's main message is not that authority can be challenged or overturned—it is as subservient as it is subversive—but that there is room for reflection; that the immense uncertainty of youth in Côte d'Ivoire and elsewhere can be articulated and scrutinized. This articulation inspires hopefulness: a sense of control and oversight in an otherwise uncertain and disorienting social terrain that enables the envisioning of potential futures. The main appeal of Zouglou lyrics is not to inspire hope for structural transformations or even for individual fortune but, rather, to instill hopefulness in the disenfranchised—'us, the weak', as Nico phrased it.

## Acknowledgements

The author is grateful to Mattia Fumanti and Sylvie Bredeloup for their valuable comments on earlier versions of this text. Two anonymous reviewers pointed out important shortcomings in a more recent draft and provided useful suggestions for their amendment. Finally, the editors of this volume have provided insightful, generous, and constructive feedback throughout the editorial process. Any inaccuracies or shortcomings in the text remain, of course, the author's responsibility.

## Notes

1. Of course, these identity boundaries were notoriously hard to define, given the centuries-long history of population movement that renders most residents in present-day Côte d'Ivoire the descendants of migrants (Geschiere 2009).
2. The term refugee is used here to emphasize the involuntary and war-related circumstances of this movement, in a context where similar routes have been traveled by labor migrants for generations. Throughout this chapter, the term is not used with the intention of raising debate about the legal status of these migrants in relation to international humanitarian law.
3. Charles Blé Goudé and Laurent Gbagbo are both currently indicted by the International Criminal Court for crimes against humanity (AFP 2014).
4. 'On sait plus sur qui compter ô'/'A bas la politique du ventre'.
5. During the time of my fieldwork, Côte d'Ivoire was preparing for the presidential elections which were held in October–November 2010. The dramatic aftermath of the elections, in which the two main candidates—Laurent Gbagbo and Alassane Ouattara—both claimed victory, led to renewed instability and the displacement of several hundreds of thousands of people during the period December 2010–April 2011 (see Banégas 2011; Bassett 2011; Strauss 2011). The hesitation by aspiring migrants in Bobo-Dioulasso to initiate new journeys to Côte d'Ivoire, at a time when a peace agreement had officially been in place since 2007, proved well-warranted.
6. '*Zougloumans*' is the French plural of '*zouglouman*', as used by my informants.

## References

Adom, M. C. 2013. *Mélanges autour du zouglou: Anthropolectures d'un genre néo urbain de Côte d'Ivoire*. Abidjan: Nodus sciendi.
AFP. 2014. Côte d'Ivoire: Charles Blé Goudé rejoint Laurent Gbagbo à la CPI. *Jeune Afrique* (Paris), 22 March. Online at: http://www.jeuneafrique.com/Article/DEPAFP20140322160604/, accessed 03 October 2015.
Agier, M. 2011. *Managing the undesirables: Refugee camps and humanitarian government*. Cambridge: Polity.
Allen, T. 1996. *In search of cool ground: War, flight and homecoming in Northeast Africa*. London and Trenton: James Currey.
Amin, S. 1967. *Le développement du capitalisme en Côte d'Ivoire: Grands documents*. Paris: Les Éditions de Minuit.
Appadurai, A. 2004. The capacity to aspire: Culture and the terms of recognition. In *Cultural and public action*, eds. V. Rao and M. Walton, 59–84. Stanford: Stanford University Press.
Argenti, J. 2007. *The intestines of the state: Youth, violence, and belated histories in the Cameroon grassfields*. Chicago and London: The Universtiy of Chicago Press.
Banégas, R. 2011. Post-election crisis in Côte d'Ivoire: The *Gbonhi* War. *African Affairs* 110 (440): 457–468.
Barrett, M. 2009. The social significance of crossing state borders: Home, mobility and life paths in the Angolan-Zambian borderland. In *Struggles for home:*

*Violence, hope and the movement of people*, eds. S. Jansen and S. Löfving, 85–108. New York and Oxford: Berghahn.
Bassett, T. J. 2011. Winning coalition, sore loser: Côte d'Ivoire's 2010 presidential elections. *African Affairs* 110 (440): 469–479.
Bayart, J.-F. 1993. *The state in Africa: The politics of the belly*. London and New York: Longman.
Beauchemin, C. 2005. Les migrations et l'effritement du modèle ivoirien: Chronique d'une guerre annoncée? *Critique internationale* 28 (3): 9–20.
Bjarnesen, J. 2009. A mobile life story. Tracing hopefulness in the life and dreams of a young Ivorian migrant. *Migration Letters* 6 (2): 119–129.
Bjarnesen, J. 2013. *Diaspora at home? Wartime mobilities in the Burkina Faso–Côte d'Ivoire transnational space*. Uppsala: Acta Universitatis Upsalienses.
Bjarnesen, J. 2014. Social branding in urban Burkina Faso. *Nordic Journal of African Studies* 23 (2): 83–99.
Bjarnesen, J. 2016. Between Labor Migration and Forced Displacement. Wartime Mobilities in the Burkina Faso-Côte d'Ivoire Transnational Space. *Conflict & Society* 2 (1): 52–67.
Blé, R. G. 2006. Zouglou et réalités sociales des jeunes en Côte d'Ivoire. *Africa Development* 31 (1): 168–184.
Boswell, K. V. 2010. *Migration, war, and repatriation from Côte d'Ivoire to Burkina Faso, West Africa*. PhD thesis, Indiana University.
Christiansen, C., M. Utas and H. E. Vigh, eds. 2006. *Navigating youth: Generating adulthood: Social becoming in an African context*. Uppsala: Nordic Africa Institute.
Cole, J., and D. Durham. 2008. Introduction. Globalization and the temporality of children and youth. In *Figuring the future: Globalization and the temporalities of children and youth*, eds. J. Cole and D. Durham, 3–24. Santa Fe: SAR Press.
Cordell, D. D., J. W. Gregory and V. Piché. 1996. *Hoe and wage: A social history of a circular migration system in West Africa*. Boulder, CO: Westview Press.
Crapanzano, V. 2003. Reflections on hope as a category of social and psychological analysis. *Cultural Anthropology* 18 (1): 3–32.
Crapanzano, V. 2004. *Imaginative horizons: An essay in literary-philosophical anthropology*. Chicago, IL: Chicago University Press.
Dembélé, O. 2002. La construction économique et politique de la catégorie 'étranger' en Côte d'Ivoire. In *Côte d'Ivoire: L'année terrible 1999–2000*, eds. M. Le Pape and C. Vidal, 123–172. Paris: Karthala.
Dembélé, O. 2003. Côte d'Ivoire: La fracture communautaire. *Politique Africaine* 89 (1): 34–48.
Durham, D. 2004. Disappearing youth: Youth as social shifter in Botswana. *American Ethnologist* 31 (4): 589–605.
Durham, D. 2008. Apathy and agency: The romance of agency and youth in Botswana. In *Figuring the future: Globalization and the temporalities of children and youth*, eds. D. Durham and J. Cole, 151–178. Paris: SAR Press.
Geschiere, P. 2009. *The perils of belonging: Autochthony, citizenship, and exclusion in Africa and Europe*. Chicago: University of Chicago Press.
Gill, N., J. Caletrío and V. Mason. 2011. Introduction: Mobilities and forced migration. *Mobilities* 6 (3): 301–316.
Goffman, E. 1959. *The presentation of self in everyday life*. London: Penguin.
Hage, G. 2003. *Against paranoid nationalism: Searching for hope in a shrinking society*. Annandale, NSW and London: Pluto Press and Merlin.

*Ghassan Hage and the weight of words.* 2008. Up Close, episode 43. Melbourne: The University of Melbourne. Radio broadcast. http://upclose.unimelb.edu.au/episode/43-ghassan-hage-and-weight-words.

Hammar, A. ed. 2014. *Displacement economies in Africa: Paradoxes of crisis and creativity.* London and New York: Zed Books and Nordic Africa Institute.

Harvey, D. 2000. *Spaces of hope.* Edinburgh: Edinburgh University Press.

Hobsbawm, E. J. 1995. *Age of extremes: The short twentieth century, 1914–1991.* London: Abacus.

Hoffman, S., and A. Oliver-Smith, eds. 2002. *Catastrophe and culture: The anthropology of disaster.* Santa Fe, NM and Oxford: School of American Research Press and J. Currey.

Honwana, A., and F. De Boeck, eds. 2005. *Makers and breakers: Children and youth in postcolonial Africa.* Oxford: James Curry.

Jackson, M. D. 2002. *The politics of storytelling: Violence, transgression, and intersubjectivity.* Copenhagen: Museum Tusculanum Press.

Jansen, S. 2008. Misplaced masculinities: Status loss and the location of gendered subjectivities amongst 'non-transnational' Bosnian refugees. *Anthropological Theory* 8 (2): 181–200.

Jansen, S., and S. Löfving. 2009. *Struggles for home: Violence, hope and the movement of people.* New York: Berghahn.

Koffi, C. 2013. En 20 ans, le zouglou est devenu la bande-son de la jeunesse ivoirienne. *Akwaba.biz.* Online at: http://www.akwaba-ci.net/index2.php?page=cont&n=324, accessed 06 October 2015.

Konate, Y. 2002. Génération zouglou. *Cahiers d'Etudes Africaines* 168 (42/4): 777–796.

Konate, Y. 2003. Les enfants de la balle. De la fesci aux movements de patroites. *Politique Africaine* 89: 49–70.

Lubkemann, S. C. 2008a. Involuntary immobility: On a theoretical invisibility in forced migration studies. *Journal of Refugee Studies* 21 (4): 454–475.

Lubkemann, S. C. 2008b. *Culture in chaos: An anthropology of the social condition in war.* Chicago: University of Chicago Press.

Lubkemann, S. C. forthcoming. The meanings of the move? From "predicaments of mobility" to "potentialities in displacement". *Conflict and Society* 2 (1): 16–36.

Malkki, L. 2001. Figures of the future: Dystopia and subjectivity in the social imagination of the future. In *History in person: Enduring struggles, contentious practice, intimate identities,* eds. D. Holland and J. Lave, 325–349. Santa Fe and Oxford: School of American Research Press and James Currey.

Miyazaki, H. 2004. *The method of hope: Anthropology, philosophy, and Fijian knowledge.* Palo Alto, CA: Stanford University Press.

Newell, S. 2009. Godrap girls, Draou boys, and the sexual economy of the bluff in Abidjan, Côte d'Ivoire. *Ethnos* 74 (3): 379–402.

Newell, S. 2012. *The modernity bluff: Crime, consumption, and citizenship in Côte d'Ivoire.* Chicago and London: The University of Chicago Press.

Ottenberg, S. 1971. *Leadership and authority in an African society: The Afikpo village-group.* Seattle and London: University of Washington Press.

Piot, C. 2010. *Nostalgia for the future: West Africa after the cold war.* Chicago and London: The University of Chicago Press.

Reister, A. 2011. *Migration and conflict: The integration of Burkinabe migrants displaced from Côte d'Ivoire.* Cologne: Rüdiger Köppe Verlag.

Reynolds Whyte, S. 2002. Subjectivity and subjunctivity. Hoping for health in Eastern Uganda. In *Postcolonial subjectivities in Africa*, ed. R. Werbner, 171–190. London and New York: Zed Books.
Strauss, S. 2011. 'It's sheer horror here': Patterns of violence during the first four months of Côte d'Ivoire's post-electoral crisis. *African Affairs* 110 (440): 481–489.
Vigh, H. E. 2006. *Navigating terrains of war: Youth and soldiering in Guinea-Bissau*. New York and Oxford: Berghahn.
Webb, D. 2007. Modes of hoping. *History of the Human Sciences* 20 (3): 65–83.
Weiss, B. 2004. Contentious futures: Past and present. In *Producing African futures: Ritual and reproduction in a neoliberal age*, ed. B. Weiss, 1–20. Leiden: Brill.
Zongo, M. 2010. Migration, diaspora et développement au Burkina Faso. In *Les enjeux autour de la diaspora burkinabè: Burkinabè à l'étranger, étrangers au Burkina Faso*, ed. M. Zongo, 15–44. Paris: L'Harmattan.
Zournazi, M. 2002. *Hope: New philosophies for change*. New York: Routledge.

# 5 The Lack of Liberty Drove Us There

Spatialized Instantiations of Hope and Contested Diasporan Identity in the Liberian–American Transnational Field (1810–2010)

*Stephen C. Lubkemann*

### Empirical and Conceptual Re-Orientations to 'Hope' and 'Diaspora'

This chapter examines two episodes in the long history of transatlantic movements between America and Liberia in an effort to posit that hope may be spatially, rather than only temporally, constituted, and to explore how a spatialized constitution of hope factors into the production of at least some forms of diasporan identity. More specifically, I want to suggest that, under conditions of extreme social exclusion, diasporicity might be usefully conceived as a particular instantiation of hope which is constructed through processes of social imagination that rely upon spatialization.

In introducing spatialization as potentially the lead ingredient in the constitution of a variant of hope—and through my discussion of how that variant compares to, and may even be brought into contention with, other variants of this form of social imaginary (Taylor 2004)—I aim to extend and complicate contemporary theoretical formulations of hope. These formulations have tended to presume that temporalization factors as the primary requisite imaginary mechanism in the social construction of hope. Thus, foundational references for the new theorists of hope, including Jurgen Moltmann (1967) and Ernst Bloch (1986), cast hope as a form of temporalized difference—namely that between (currently) lived experience and the promise of a potential (hence future) alternative to that experience. Other theorists who have more recently grappled with the concept (Browne 2005; Crapanzano 2003; Miyazaki 2004; 2006) have generally followed suit in presuming temporality to be the central axis along which are drawn the key contrasts that are signified in—and ultimately constitutive of—hope as a particular form of sentiment or social imaginary.[1] Zigon (2009, 267), for example, describes hope as a social process in which 'the intentional and creative uses of the past and the future—allows for intentional and ethical action'.

Here, I propose that temporalization need not be the primary—and under certain conditions may even prove to be an entirely insufficient—mechanism for producing and sustaining credible alternative social imaginaries to those currently being experienced, and thus for constituting hope. In particular,

DOI: 10.4324/9781315659916-5

when conditions of structural violence (such as those of racially violent nineteenth-century North America which I examine in the first part of this chapter) are so extreme and historically sustained, I argue that notions that the passage of time alone might bring better alternatives into being may become increasingly implausible—and eventually even come to be deemed (at least for some) entirely impossible.

Under such circumstances, temporalization alone may prove incapable of constituting hope—in the sense defined by Jarrett Zigon as '[the temporal structure of] the background attitude that allows for living a sane life in a specific social world . . . [of moral breakdown]' (2009, 267) . . . that is 'born out of the socio-historic-cultural, as well as the personal, conditions of struggle' (2009, 262). Zigon's formulation is somewhat distinct in conceptualizing 'hope' not so much as a map for future action but as a form of social imaginary that allows those under duress to contend with, and in, the here-and-now. Following Zigon's focus on hope as a posture for navigating the present as 'an active agent in the attempt to live acceptably for oneself and for others . . . within the world in which one finds herself . . .' (2009, 259), I depart from him, however, to argue that the 'creative use of the past and present' alone (i.e., a social imaginary constituted primarily through temporalization) may prove incapable of underwriting and sustaining a 'sane life' in the most extreme situations of 'moral breakdown' (as Zigon terms it) or of 'structural violence' (as I term it).

I develop this part of my argument through a discussion of the emergence of the nineteenth-century 'back-to-Africa' movement which ultimately gave birth to Liberia. I demonstrate that, for those for whom no light seems to beckon at the end of the temporal tunnel, the spatialization of an aspirational alternative to the lived here-and-now may more aptly sustain faith in the possibility of its eventual realization. In such cases spatialization, rather than temporalization, thus becomes the central—and indeed an indispensable—narrative mechanism through which a variant of hope comes to be socially imagined.

In the course of this discussion I further posit that one particular form of identity narrative—'diasporicity'—may represent an embodiment of this variant of hope in that it relies upon spatializing strategies for rendering alternative social imaginaries credible under conditions of structural violence. Diasporicity—as a form of identity narrative—relies upon and is organized around origin mythologies that locate the source of group- and self-authentication in a social milieu that is different to that in which protagonists currently live (Lubkemann 2015). This alternative milieu, from which attributes originate in the past, may exist in the 'now', but is most certainly not the 'here' in which protagonists live.

In suggesting that hope's spatialization—and its enshrinement in a particular social identity form ('diasporicity')—may emerge primarily in reaction to structurally violent conditions in the 'here-and-now', this argument turns at least one conventional theoretical notion about the production and reproduction of diasporan identity somewhat on its head. Although differing in other respects, predominant theories about diasporas presume that the retention of social attachments to others who remain in the place of imputed origin are either a requisite or a primary determinant in the social production and reproduction of diasporan identity. Demonstrating how a diasporan identity emerged and gained social subscription when no such social attachments had been retained, I argue that this form of identity narrative—and the very myths of origin around which it is organized—may be generated as a reaction to particularly extreme experiences of social exclusion and discrimination in the lived 'here'. As a form of identity in which a spatialized variant of hope is expressed, diasporicity is particularly likely to be 'invented' (Hobsbawm and Ranger 1983) in this fashion under circumstances in which entitlements believed to be legitimate have not only been denied in the past and in the present of a lived in social milieu but are also seen as certain to continue being denied in its foreseeable future. In such instances, diasporan mythologies of social origin may garner social subscription because they sustain a belief in the realizability of aspirations in the face of evidence—past, present and, in future, foreseeable—by locating that realizability elsewhere. In so doing they sustain a belief that a more desirable alternative to the currently lived experience and a more entitled self are still possible—even if not so in either the 'now' or the foreseeable future of the lived 'here.'

I grapple with the re-theorization of both of these concepts—'hope' and 'diasporicity'—through a comparative examination of diasporan identity formation across historical time within the transnational field that has linked Liberia and the United States for over 250 years. Originating in the transatlantic slave trade that brought Africans to North American shores throughout the seventeenth, eighteenth, and nineteenth centuries, and reproduced most recently by refugees fleeing Liberia's long civil war (1990–2003), this transnational 'social world' (Marx 1990) currently links residents of Liberia with relatives and compatriots dispersed throughout Africa, Europe, and North America. My discussion draws upon both the work of several prominent scholars of nineteenth-century Liberia and African-America and my own ethnographic, historical, and demographic research conducted since 1999 in multiple locations (the United States, Ghana, and Liberia) within that social field.

As a point of departure I take the specific theoretical formulation for 'diaspora' that Klimt and I proposed in earlier work (Klimt and Lubkemann 2002) and that I have elaborated upon further more recently (Lubkemann 2015). This approach posits that 'diasporicity' should be considered as a particular form of identity discourse in which the social self is 'imagined' (Anderson 1983) and publicly 'presented' (Goffman 1959) through particular types of claim[2] about group origins.

What is the most distinctive about diasporicity as a form of identity narrative is that, whereas it always makes reference to a history of population dispersal, from an analytical perspective such histories are the most usefully viewed as mythological. From this perspective, the critical question about how diasporan identities are produced or sustained is not about population dispersal *per se* but, rather, about how, under what conditions, and for whom particular narratives that define group boundaries in relation to a narrative of dispersal emerge and gain (or, alternatively, lose) social subscribers. This approach insists that any relationship between mobility (as a social process) and diasporicity (as a social identity) must be empirically ascertained rather than theoretically assumed. Thus, rather than being the self-evident product of mobility, this form of identity is merely a possibility—one that can be, and often is, contested or even rejected, even amongst those who share similar migratory experiences.

In the course of this chapter I discuss two specific examples—one historical and another contemporary—of migrants and their descendants in the Liberian–American transnational field who pursued self-identification strategies that varied immensely in this regard, ranging from those who publicly proclaimed themselves to be sojourners from an African homeland of origin, to others who chose—sometimes quietly and privately but at times publicly and vociferously—to de-emphasize any African connections imputed to them and who, in this sense, can be viewed as having 'opted out of diaspora' altogether.

By exploring how various forms of social difference influenced subscription to (or, conversely, rejection of) diasporan identity at these two different historical moments of social disagreement, I bring into sharper relief those conditions that tend to underwrite the spatialized constitution of hope, while also exploring the sorts of choice which such spatialization implies. I suggest that, in contrast to variants of hope that rely solely upon temporalization, strategies that also focus centrally upon spatialization cleave the past, the present, and the future in two and then assign social potentiality to one side of that spatialized divide while precluding it from the other.

I then examine the consequences of embodying such a spatial distribution of hope in (diasporan) identity narratives in which the social milieu that authenticates the self and to which potentiality is assigned is located elsewhere, and in which potentiality is precluded from the present as well as the future of the social milieu of lived experience. I suggest that, in some cases, diasporan identity narratives thus come to imply that the journey of the self from an undesirable condition of structural violence to a desirable alternative in which authenticity is realized cannot occur without spatial relocation. My discussion of social differentiation in subscription to diasporan identity in both the historical and the contemporary Liberian transnational field demonstrates how such a proposition may threaten and undermine other variants of hope that remain predicated on temporalization.

## The Historic Back-to-Africa Movement: The Spatialized Instantiation of Hope

Liberia was one of the very earliest and has certainly served as the most historically sustained symbolic rallying point for the idea of black 'return' to an 'Africa-of-origin' from North America. The Liberian Republic came into being as a result of three major waves of black migration from the United States and resettlement in West Africa that spanned much of the nineteenth century, and which ultimately led, in 1847, to the declaration of Liberian independence (Beyan 1991).

However, it is important to understand that, from the very outset, subscription to an identity that mythologized Africa as an original and yearned-for homeland was never a foregone conclusion for the black Americans to whom this notion was proposed. In fact, the very idea of Liberia required a great act of social imagination and a re-forging of identity that ran against broader currents of thought and opinion—not least of all the mainstream of thought amongst black Americans themselves. At the time, most black Americans firmly believed that Africa was part of North America's black population's past rather than its future—and felicitously so. This belief had been nurtured by the actual apologists of American slavery themselves, who had long labored in the public forum to re-cast the relationship between slave-owner and slave as one of familial patronage rather than of mere bondage, de-emphasizing the abuses of power and the slave's legal status as mere (and, in fact, easily alienable) property. Central to that argument was a perverse recasting of enslavement itself as a form of divine redemption through which 'savage Africans' had been ushered out of the heathen dark and into the civilizing benefits of Christian light. This discourse left no question that African slaves 'belonged'—not just by might but by divine right—in the Americas and thus proposed that any and all black attachments to Africa itself had been severed by the grace of God—and, of course, the legal rights of property-owners (Barnes 2004; Clegg 2004; Tyler-McGraw 2007).

The fact that black Americans often reworked Christian allusions to recast slavery as a social journey through trial and tribulation did not mean that a return to Africa was envisioned by most of them as the way forward, nor did many harbor an attachment to Africa as a 'homeland'. In fact the overwhelming majority of the American black leaders of the day vociferously opposed the American Colonization Society (ACS)—the organization that was founded at the beginning of the nineteenth century and that propagated and financed 'return voyages' to Liberia—and publicly decried the idea of the back-to-Africa movement that it represented. In dozens of meetings that brought together hundreds and, in some cases, even thousands of freed blacks, the objectives of the American Colonization Society were publicly denounced and resolutions were passed which explicitly rejected any idea that blacks in America naturally belonged back in Africa. Convening many of the leaders and notables of the free black community, the 1848 Colored National Convention minced no words in denouncing Liberia in the year after it had declared itself an independent republic:

> That among the many oppressive schemes against the colored people in the United States we view the American Colonization Society as the

most deceptive and hypocritical—clothed with the very livery of heaven to serve the devil himself in. . . .

(Clegg 2004, 16)

Many of these critics were well aware of the objectives that animated some of the most prominent founders and ardent supporters of the ACS—amongst *whom were featured several well-known slaveholders and some of the most prominent public defenders of the institution of slavery*! These included the prominent U.S. Senator Henry Clay of Kentucky, who saw in the Liberia project an opportunity to strengthen the institution of slavery by ridding the South of the growing number of emancipated blacks, who were loathed and feared by Southern whites. Similarly, Bushrod Washington (The first U.S. president's nephew and a major slaveholder in his own right) served as the ACS's first president. Even many of the white abolitionist Quakers, who also figured prominently in the ACS, are documented to have been as motivated by segregationist impulses as by religious conviction. Thus, for example, the Quaker stronghold of Philadelphia was amongst the strongest financial backers of the colonization-to-Liberia movement largely because they were reluctant to have freed black co-religionists resettle in their midst (Clegg 2004).

Ultimately, only a very small minority of black Americans subscribed to the idea of Liberia or migrated there (Beyan 1991; Campbell 2006; McDaniels 1995). However, the motivations of that small minority may be explained by any interest in maintaining or preserving already existing social attachments in Africa, given that almost all were generations removed from the experience of the Middle Passage. Instead, the choice to migrate to Liberia had far more to do with the social and political struggles and racial violence of Antebellum America than it did with long-atrophied social attachments to Africa. Notably, patterns of interest in, and ultimately subscription to, this identity narrative thus tended to correlate with and—to a certain extent, reflect—greater degrees of exposure to structural violence. Thus, whereas most free blacks in the North vociferously opposed the 'back-to-Africa movement', the idea of returning to Africa found much greater resonance amongst blacks who were still enslaved in the Southern United States—such as the Hillsboro, North Carolina slave Cledwell Whitted, who asserted that 'There is no place in the World I should like to go as much as to Leberra' (Clegg 2004, 183). Similarly, in his study of the development of the Negro Spiritual genre—which evolved amongst the enslaved in the South (and only later migrated to free black congregations in the North)—Fisher noted that many of the referents that have been interpreted to refer to heavenly transcendence (such as the referent to 'home' in the famous song *Swing Lo Sweet Chariot*) may have been veiled referents to Liberia and Africa more generally. The possibility of claiming a form of identity emphasizing attachment to Africa also resonated more strongly within free black communities in Southern slaveholding states, which were particularly besieged by racial violence which was always far more overt than was the case in Northern states[3] (Barnes 2004; Clegg 2004; Tyler-McGraw 2007).

It is equally notable that, once migration to Liberia did begin to occur, those contacts and social attachments that were retained between blacks in America and the initial black settlers to Liberia tended to dissuade rather than encourage further return migration and the accompanying identity claims that expressed such aspirations. The discouraging news sent by the earliest settlers in Liberia to friends and relatives back in America about the insalubrious and harsh conditions that prevailed in that colony and that produced its atrocious mortality rates (Clegg 2004; McDaniels 1995) played a significant role in the subsiding of the first wave of black-American migration to Liberia. Certainly, startling cases such as that documented in A Bill for the Relief of Emily Hooper of Liberia 1858, a young woman who sought to re-enter bondage back in America rather than remain 'free' in Liberia, must thus have proved potently dissuasive:

> That Emily Hooper, a negro and citizen of Liberia, be and she is hereby permitted, voluntarily, to return into a state of slavery, as slave of her former owner, Miss Sarah Mallet of Chapel Hill, North Carolina.
> (quoted in Clegg 2004, 187)

In fact, the overall trend in both the private and public reports from the first settlers was deemed so damaging to the ACS's objective of fostering black interest in migration to Liberia that the organization felt compelled to commission and disseminate its own (unsurprisingly favorable) 'independent' account in 1853, drawn up by the Reverend Peterson in order to counter this threat. In short, even when it became possible to realize (rather than merely imagine) social attachments to Africa, these tended to undermine subscription to diasporan identity narratives.

After the initial settlement wave subsided, black migration from the United States to Liberia occurred again only in small numbers and brief bursts—each one driven by particularly horrifying surges in the white brutalization of blacks, particularly throughout the American South—rather than by any developments in Liberia itself. The earliest of these waves occurred prior to the American Civil War, when free blacks throughout the slaveholding South were murderously targeted by frenzied whites after the 1831 Turner rebellion. Two decades later, in 1850, the passage of the Fugitive Slave Act facilitated the process whereby whites could claim ownership and sue for the possession of blacks they claimed had once been their slaves, even within states that had abolished slavery. The fear occasioned by this law motivated a modest revitalization of interest in the Liberian option over the decade that preceded the American Civil War. Short-lived interest in migration to Liberia re-emerged yet again a quarter of a century later, when anti-black violence peaked during southern reconstruction after the Civil War and slavery's abolishment, when whites in the South mobilized violently to oppose the perceived threat of black enfranchisement (Barnes 2004; Clegg 2004; Tyler-McGraw 2007).

What is most noteworthy is that, in each of these historical instances, the primary factors underwriting renewed subscription to this 'diasporan identity' (and, by extension, interest in the 'return-to-Africa' project) were always the deepening problematics of racial exclusion confronted in America, rather than pre-existing social attachments in Africa. In this sense, rather than being the producers of diasporan identity formation, sentiments of attachment to Africa were very much the products of deepening despair at the accentuation of structural violence in America.

The emergence of diasporan identity narratives in this historical case is thus not well explained by prevailing theories[4] which tend to identify and/or privilege (the preservation of) 'social attachment' as the primary 'independent/causal variable' in the formation, persistence, (and even demise) of diasporan identity. The decisions of those nineteenth-century black Americans who opted to embrace Africa as their homeland and to migrate 'back' cannot be attributed to such social attachments—for no such prior social attachments had been retained. Rather, it was the strength and nature of historically specific forms of social exclusion and discrimination that were confronted by slaves, former slaves, and free-born blacks in their everyday lives in nineteenth-century America that underwrote the emergence of this form of identity, in which origin was aspirationally claimed elsewhere (in Africa).

The sentiments of deprivation engendered by these experiences can be described as the products of structural violence. Against an array of competing 'objectivist' definitions of 'structural violence' (Farmer 1997; Galtung 1969; Uvin 1998), I have argued elsewhere (Lubkemann 2008a) for a definition that emphasizes the sentiments of frustration that are generated by the gap between subjective expectations about one's entitlements and the capacity to realize these as dictated by structural conditions. It is precisely this type of gap that, I would argue, underwrote the interest in the original Liberian option—as a mechanism for achieving an emancipated status to which so many of those who confronted racial violence and exclusion aspired but saw little prospects for ever realizing in America. In short, under conditions of extreme social exclusion that belie the possibility for future change in the lived in 'here', I want to suggest that diasporicity might be usefully conceived of as a particular instantiation of hope—however, as a variant of that form of social imaginary that relies first and foremost on spatialization, rather than only, or primarily, upon the processes of temporalization that tend to be emphasized by the leading contemporary theorists of hope. Stripped down to its analytical essence, I would thus suggest that we can think (analytically) of hope as the *sustenance of the possibility of a (desired)[5] alternative to a (currently lived) reality*. A differentiation between an undesirable experienced state and a desired/aspirational one may, in fact, be constituted through the forms of temporalization that tend to be emphasized as the central mechanism in the production of hope (Crapanzano 2003; Miyazaki

2006; Moltmann 1967; Yurchak 2003); however, in other cases I would suggest that this differentiation may be more effectively constituted through other processes such as spatialization.

Indeed, in certain societal situations in which oppressive structural violence is particularly virulent and profoundly entrenched, spatialization may provide a degree of potency for underwriting the credibility of alternative possibilities—and thus for 'a sane life' (Zigon 2009)—which temporalization alone is incapable of providing. In the historical Liberian case, it is precisely such forms of spatialization of an aspirational alternative that located the authentic and potential self in an 'elsewhere'—in reaction to a structurally violent 'here' in which lived experience was realized—that I suggest was the central dynamic informing the production of the nineteenth-century diasporan identity and that led some black Americans to claim attachments with Africa—and to migrate to Liberia.

## Disputing Diasporicity in the Historical Past: Spatial Versus Temporal Strategies for Constituting Hope

A theoretical understanding of some of the implications of reliance upon spatial—rather than temporal—instantiation in the constitution of hope may help to explain socially differentiated interests, reactions, and subscription to diasporan identity narratives that we witness in both the historical and the contemporary Liberian transnational field. As I have already briefly alluded to, in the historical case a diasporan identity that embodied and expressed spatialized variants of hope ultimately appealed to only a small minority of nineteenth-century black Americans—most particularly to those who found themselves the most oppressed.

By way of contrast, free black communities and their leaders—particularly those in the northern states where slavery had been abolished—were the most active and publicly vociferous in rejecting this new form of identity that emphasized their African origins. They rejected this identity because they realized that, hand-in-hand with its explicit claims that their natural entitlement to Africa should be recognized, yet another idea was also implied: that they were not entitled to stay in America. For this reason, leading black intellectuals of the time, despite pursuing often quite different social and political projects and goals, tended to find common ground against the ACS and the notion that blacks were 'really African' (and therefore not 'American') and should return (or be returned) to Africa. Thus, the early black separatist Martin Delaney decried Liberia as an unwelcome scheme to 'exterminate the free colored of the American continent' (Clegg 2004, 181–182), whereas others such as the abolitionist Frederick Douglass fervently denounced the ACS as the 'arch enemy of the free colored citizens of the United States' that aimed to ultimately strengthen and insulate slavery by hauling away its most glaring contradiction—the free black man.

In short, whereas a diasporan identity may have offered an effective strategy for sustaining the credibility in the possibility of a better alternative for those nineteenth-century black Americans who saw no possible improvement in America—by spatially assigning all the potential for that realizability to an 'elsewhere'—that very same assignment also implied the preclusion of any such potentiality in the lived 'here'. The denial of any potentiality for imagining improvement in the lived 'here' constituted a profound affront and violation of the expectations, social projects, and ambitions of those nineteenth-century black Americans who continued to envision, and strive for, change and betterment in America itself. Their focus on the possibility of improving lives in America itself was readily evident in the many resolutions (such as that passed at a Bethel African Methodist Episcopal Church of Philadelphia in 1817 and quoted below) that were passed in city after city by free blacks during their efforts to denounce the ACS and discredit the deportation ambitions of its white leadership:

> Relieved from the miseries of slavery, many of us by your aid, possessing the benefits which industry and integrity in this prosperous country assures to all its inhabitants, enjoying the blessings of religion, opportunities of worshipping the only true God, under the light of Christianity, each of us according to his own understanding; and having afforded us and our children the means of education and improvement; we have no wish to separate from our present home, for any purposes whatever. Content with our present situation and condition, we are desirous of increasing the prosperity by honest efforts, and by the use of the opportunities, for their improvement, which the Constitution and laws allow ... Any measure or system of measure, having a tendency to banish us would not only be cruel, but in direct violation of those principles which have been the boast of this republic.
> (Mehlinger 1916, 278, quoted in Sawyer 1992, 35)

To those invested in the project of changing racial inequality in America, the very idea of 'Liberia' galvanized a sense of indignant entitlement to America itself and a vociferous rejection of black resettlement to Africa—which most leading black intellectuals decried as nothing more than a nefarious new strategy aimed at depriving them, through deportation, of the right to participate in a country that was, in the most literal of senses, the fruit of their labor. For those for whom social conditions had not overwhelmed the credibility of the claim that social change was possible in America, hope continued to operate in a predominantly temporal register. They therefore rejected an identity that embodied a distinctively spatial instantiation of hope, because that instantiation precluded and denied the possibility of believing in or pursuing improvement in the social milieu in which they lived.

86  *Stephen C. Lubkemann*

## Disputing Diaspora in the Present: Gender and Class Differentiation

Problematics of social exclusion have played no less a role in shaping the constitution of, and socially differentiated patterns of subscription to, diasporicity within the contemporary Liberian transnational field. Over the last 30 years, that field has been dramatically transformed by political upheaval and civil war. Exclusion from meaningful participation in the political process and educational opportunity, as well as from the economic benefits of the nation, were significant factors which allowed student protests to converge with popular outrage at price increases and spark a military coup in 1979. The assassination of President Tolbert, the subsequent military trial and public execution of prominent Americo-Liberian government officials, and the assumption of power of Liberia's first 'indigenous' president (and coup co-leader), Master Sergeant Samuel Doe, signaled the demise of over a century of Americo-Liberian privilege and dominance.

These events also generated the first contemporary wave of migrants—mostly of Americo-Liberians—back across the Atlantic to the United States. Successive waves of different social composition followed over the next quarter of a century. A second wave arrived in the mid-1980s after Doe's violent crackdown against the Gio and Mano ethnic groups in the wake of a failed putsch. A third outflow followed Doe's overthrow and assassination in 1990 and continued throughout the country's notorious descent into seven years of brutal civil war (Adebajo 2002; Ellis 1999; Levitt 2005). Out-migration peaked again at the turn of the millennium, as new insurgencies challenged the warlord-turned-president, Charles Taylor, until an UN-brokered peace settlement resulted in his exile in 2003 (Levitt 2005; Moran 2006).

Liberia has since undergone a challenging transition to democratic governance, safeguarded by one of the UN's largest armed missions in Africa and creating the possibility of return for the hundreds of thousands of Liberians displaced throughout West Africa and further afield in North America and Europe. Yet not everyone who left Liberia has chosen to return. Much as blacks in Antebellum America confronted alternative identity choices, so, too, did Liberians in the United States confront a similar question: ['Will I be] "Liberian" or "[African] American"?'

For some, the answer to that question is clearly an affirmation of a diasporicity that simultaneously locates their origin and displaces their aspirations elsewhere: locating their self-potentiality in Liberia. Much as in the historical epoch during which Liberia emerged, experiences of social exclusion and frustrated expectations in contemporary America have underwritten and sustained this new diasporicity. For many Liberians who arrived after 1980, America did not turn out to be the promised land which they once envisaged. Thus, whereas some have obtained permanent residency or U.S. citizenship, a significant number are technically illegal immigrants who overstayed their visitor visas. Many others have Temporary Protective

(TPS) or Deferred Enforced Departure (DED) status, which is subject to annual renewal by executive order and could end at any time (as has already befallen Salvadoreños and Sierra Leoneans). This insecure status tends to limit employment prospects for many—forcing them to work multiple shifts at menial jobs even if they have professional training or backgrounds. These conditions are accentuated by the challenges that confront most Liberians who made it to the United States during the war, who generally struggle to pay bills while also supporting relatives back in Liberia. Such conditions only accentuate the discriminating effects of racism that powerfully shape the American socio-economic landscape. Moreover, Liberians in the United States also often experience additional exclusion and hostility from an African-American community that sometimes interprets their disinterest in locally oriented civic and political activism as evidence of a deficient commitment to anti-racist agendas in the United States (Habecker 2009; Lubkemann 2008b; Waters 2001).

The convergence of these different strands of social exclusion has played a significant role in motivating subscription to a new Liberian-oriented identity narrative amongst many of those who found wartime refuge in the United States. Many emphasize their 'Liberianness' in pointed distinction to other (potential) social identities (particularly 'African American') which are often assigned to them by a broader American public, who take their phenotype (rather than their nationality) as the primary indicator of ethnic identity. Ascriptions as 'African Americans' are often challenged in multiple ways by those who think of themselves as 'Liberian diasporans', including explicit pre-emptions or corrections in everyday social interaction ('No, you see, I am Liberian [not African American] . . .') or a preference for social fora with large Liberian membership, such as Liberian associations, churches, etc.

The performance of 'Liberianness' to internal audiences within the Liberian immigrant community is particularly important for those who claim a diasporan identity, and takes place in socially and culturally specific registers. Thus, as I have documented elsewhere (Lubkemann 2008b), sending remittances and maintaining contact with relatives in Liberia—and making this known publicly to other Liberians—can be as much about maintaining status and performing Liberian identity in U.S. compatriot social circles as it is about maintaining attachments with the recipients of funds or of phone calls to those who reside back in Liberia.

Ultimately, more than merely affirming attachments elsewhere, such performances of 'Liberianness', whether to internal or to external audiences, often signal a form of detachment from, and a critique of, the (often disappointing) here, and the now that is lived through every day in America. In affirming their 'Liberianness' these migrants actively claim (and ultimately privilege) their stake in a social reality alternative to the one in which the identity is being invoked. This identity thus signposts a possible different world in which an individual's true social worth is recognized, talents are fully utilized, and legitimate social standing is acknowledged. By deploying this identity narrative, a former government official in Minneapolis thus reasserts a 'rightful' status that is not recognized by his current degrading menial job, whereas a nursing assistant in Maryland signals her potential to be a county health department director 'back home' and an adjunct college instructor harbors hopes of recognition as a major national political leader and contender for political office in Liberia.

However, subscription to this contemporary diasporic identity is no more universal amongst Liberian migrants at the dawn of the twenty-first century than was the case amongst black Americans who considered and bitterly argued about the merits of the initial Liberia option throughout the nineteenth century. Notwithstanding the status of Ellen Johnson-Sirleaf (Liberia's and Africa's first elected female president) as an icon for progress in gender equality, many Liberian women whom I have interviewed in the United States remain deeply ambivalent about the prospect of returning to Liberia because they fear the loss of the forms of autonomy, power, and opportunity many have come to enjoy in the United States. Such fears are particularly pronounced amongst women whose higher-education credentials and professional experience would suggest that they might be attractive recruits for government posts or NGOs back in the 'New Liberia', where gender equality is one of the most trumpeted refrains of the international donor community. Many of these women are well aware, however, that, whereas education may afford them access to status, maintaining that status in culturally prescribed ways is likely to place enormous pressure on them to eventually forgo the professional activities which they currently pursue.

Thus, much as documented by Moran (1990) over three decades ago, status for women at the highest social levels in Liberia is still largely mediated by marriage. Whereas their education may open the door for professional Liberian women to marriages with men of higher social status, Liberian social conventions about how that status is to be maintained and enacted often highly constrain or preclude women from certain forms of professional, economic, and political activity. Confronted with a Liberian social ideology that continues to render social status antithetical to, or at the very least highly restrictive of, certain forms of professional activity and personal autonomy, many educated Liberian women resettled in the United States thus prefer to remain abroad, where many social objectives are more mutually conducive rather than socially contradictory.

By way of contrast, men—and particularly those who once held elite status in Liberia—are arguably amongst the most eager to return to post-war Liberia and the most vocal in claiming and performing their Liberian identity. In part, this eagerness may be explained by the fact that sentiments of abjection are particularly pronounced within this group, in light of the fact that their educational qualifications have often failed to be recognized in the United States, nor has political or socio-economic status once held in Liberia translated into commensurate standing in their country of refuge. Many also angrily decry the presumptions of the institutional refugee resettlement system that requires them, nevertheless, to seek employment but only offers them positions for which they feel overqualified and that fail to offer pay or status commensurate with that which they once enjoyed and feel entitled to. The predominance of such individuals in the myriad Liberian community associations throughout the country—and particularly in the fierce politicking therein—is readily noticeable, as is the extent to which they voice much greater interest in returning 'home' than is the case for many others.

## Conclusion: The Differentiation of Discontentment in Social Subscription to Spatialized Instantiations of Hope

I have argued elsewhere (Lubkemann 2015) that diasporicity is an identity frame that relies upon an implicit invocation, juxtaposition, and comparison of alternative possible contexts of social experience that are differentiated in space. Lived experiences in one location are implicitly compared with experiences in an 'elsewhere'—one to which links are claimed through a social process of memory about migration and displacement that comes to be enshrined as a charter myth for social-group identity. Through an explicit claim about the self's most genuine attachment to a 'social elsewhere' (of an individual's claimed origin), diasporicity is capable of providing a powerful critique of degrading social conditions that are confronted in the lived here-and-now. Thus, embedded within the central diasporan claim of 'Elsewhere is a place to which I most truly belong' lurks the unstated critical recognition that 'Here is a place in which I am not allowed to fully/satisfactorily belong'.

In this case study, I have suggested that conditions of extreme social alienation may underwrite the production of and subscription to—and sometimes even the outright social invention of—those narratives and notions of social attachment and orientation to the 'elsewhere' (i.e., an imputed homeland of origin) that features as the central organizing referent for diasporan identities. In this vein, the diasporicity that emerged in Antebellum America and that underwrote the initial back-to-Africa movement can be seen as a desperate social effort to sustain the credibility of alternatives in a context of extreme structural violence in which, at least for some, temporal projection alone was insufficient to that task of social imagination. For those so oppressed in this particular context of 'moral breakdown' that the future of the social milieu in which they lived looked unchangeable, the perseverance of a 'sane life' (Zigon 2009) required a spatialized strategy for differentiating and protecting aspirational potentiality from experienced reality.

However, in relying on spatialized strategies for constituting hope, diasporan identity narratives implicitly assign spatial criteria to potentiality, requiring relocation as a requisite for the realization of aspirations while precluding any potential for realizing aspirations in the lived 'here'. In this sense, spatialized strategies for constituting hope may be mutually exclusive of—or at least come into contention with—those that rely primarily upon social processes of temporalization. I would argue that it is precisely this peculiar effect of hope's spatialized instantiation that renders diasporicity at once a particularly potent narrative for contending with seemingly hopelessly entrenched structural violence while, at the same time, making it a socially contested ascription. As illustrated by both the historical resistance to the back-to-Africa movement by most nineteenth-century free black Americans and by the highly gender-differentiated views and anxieties about the desirability of 'return' amongst contemporary Liberian refugees in America, the notion that relocation is an inherent pre-condition for realizing the aspirational self may thus be highly contested.

In short, if the social appeal of diasporicity as an identity option lies in its capacity to protect aspirational potentiality and self-authenticity by projecting these in space, social variation in the subscription to this identity is likely to depend on whether such spatial assignment is seen as offering social recourse or, conversely, as undermining it. Answers to this question may depend in large part on how exposure to structural violence in the here-and-now is mediated by socio-economic differences (such as those between free and enslaved black Americans in the nineteenth century). Responses may also depend on the forms of alternative structural violence which agents foresee as likely, should the spatial aspirations expressed in diasporan identity come to be realized (such as those foreseen by many educated Liberian women who are so reluctant to return to war-torn Liberia today). In short, the implications of hope's spatial instantiation rarely resonate in the same way for all social agents. Rather, subscription to (or rejection of) identities that instantiate hope and address discontent through spatial strategies that locate potentiality 'elsewhere' is likely to be mediated by how socio-economic and socio-political differences shape agents' views on the future possibilities for addressing that discontentment 'here.' In this sense, spatialized strategies for constituting hope are the most likely for those whose experiences with sustained moral breakdown and extreme structural violence underwrite mounting skepticism about the possibility of ever realizing positive social change within the social milieus which they subordinately inhabit.

## Notes

1. For an important exception see Phillip Mar (2005), who discusses how migrants construct social imaginaries in which different aspects of the lives they aspire to are mapped onto different destinations. Inasmuch as such distributions present migrants with a zero-sum choice between the different types of aspiration (for example, social and economic objectives) when these can only be realized in different places, Mar's formulation implies a particularly powerful conundrum for migrants. In particular, it infuses the constitution of any aspirations for resolving this contradiction with enormous uncertainty, if not (I would argue) a certain sense of resignation and perhaps even 'hopelessness'. Mar does not delve into the conditions that potentially underwrite—or even require (as I suggest in this article)—the spatialization of aspirations in order to sustain hope, nor does he explore the implications of organizing social identities around such imaginaries—both central questions in this discussion.

2. More specifically, Klimt and I argued that identity narratives qualify analytically as 'diasporic' (rather than as 'ethnic', 'racial' or 'class') if they engage with a series of core propositions that include an orientation to a place of origin from which a dispersal was remembered, a sense of affinity with others dispersed from that place of origin to other locations, a sense of attachment to both the place of attributed origin and the current place of residence—but in which the former was recognized as the more authoritative source for the legitimization of social practice in determining the authenticity of cultural forms, in delimiting the boundaries of moral community, and in establishing boundaries for groupness (Klimt and Lubkemann 2002, 148). Other theorists who have offered conceptualizations of diaspora as a form of identity narrative include Axel (2002; 2004), Brah (1996), Kleist (2008; 2010) and Werbner (2002).
3. This is not to suggest that racist discrimination and violence were not also rampant in the North—notwithstanding the technical demise of the institution of slavery itself by the turn of the eighteenth to the nineteenth century. On this, see, for example, Anne Farrow *et al.* (2005).
4. Thus, while differing in many other respects, both assimilationist and transnational analytical frameworks emphasize the central role that social attachments between migrants and those in their claimed homelands of origin assume in sustaining diasporan identities and communities (Alba and Nee 2003; Basch *et al.* 1994; Fouron and Glick Schiller 2002; Gans 1992; Glick Schiller and Fouron 2001; Gordon 1964; Haines 1997; Levitt 2001; Levitt and Glick Schiller 2004; Rapport and Dawson 1998; Rumbaut 2002; Sheffer 2003; Waters 1990). Assimilationist frameworks, in particular, go on to explain the demise of diasporan identity (i.e., 'assimilation' if and when it ultimately occurs) as a result of the atrophy of such ties and their replacement by others in the society of resettlement, whether over biographical or, more often, generational, time.
5. The opposite of 'hope' in this sense might be 'dread', thought of as the sustenance of the possibility of an *undesired* alternative.

# References

Adebajo, A. 2002. *Liberia's civil war*. Boulder, CO: Lynne Rienner.
Alba, R. D., and V. Nee. 2003. *Remaking the American mainstream: Assimilation and contemporary immigration*. Cambridge, MA: Harvard University Press.
Anderson, B. 1983. *Imagined communities: Reflections on the origins and spread of Nationalism*. London: Verso.
Axel, B. K. 2002. The diasporic imaginary. *Public Culture* 14 (2): 411–428.
Axel, B. 2004. The context of diaspora. *Cultural Anthropology* 19 (1): 26–60.
Barnes, K. C. 2004. *Journey of hope: The back to Africa movement in Arkansas in the late 1800s*. Chapel Hill: University of North Carolina Press.
Basch, L., N. Glick Schiller and C. Szanton Blanc. 1994. *Nations unbound: Transnational projects, postcolonial predicaments, and de-territorialized nation-states*. Amsterdam: Gordon and Breach.
Beyan, A. J. 1991. *The American colonization society and the creation of the Liberian state*. New York: University Press of America.
Bloch, E. 1986. *The principle of hope*. Cambridge: MIT Press.
Brah, A. 1996. *Cartographies of diaspora*. London: Routledge.
Browne, C. 2005. Hope, critique, and utopia. *Critical Horizons* 5 (1): 64–86.
Campbell, J. T. 2006. *Idle passages: African-American journeys to Africa 1787–2005*. New York: Penguin.

Clegg, C. 2004. *The price of liberty: African Americans and the making of Liberia.* Chapel Hill: University of North Carolina Press.

Crapanzano, V. 2003. Reflections on hope as a category of social and psychological analysis. *Cultural Anthropology* 18 (1): 3–32.

Ellis, S. 1999. *The mask of anarchy: The destruction of Liberia and the religious dimension of an African civil war.* New York: New York University Press.

Farmer, P. 1997. On suffering and structural violence: A view from below. In *Social suffering*, eds. A. Kleinmann, V. Das and M. Lock, 261–283. Berkeley: University of California Press.

Farrow, A., J. Lang and J. Frank. 2005. *Complicity: How the North promoted, prolonged, and profited from slavery.* New York: Balantine Books.

Fouron, G., and N. Glick Schiller. 2002. The generation of identity: Redefining the second generation within the transnational field. In *The changing face of home*, eds. P. Levitt and M. Waters, 168–210. New York: Russell Sage Foundation.

Galtung, J. 1969. Violence, peace and peace research. *Journal of Peace Research* 27 (3): 291–305.

Gans, H. J. 1992. Second-generation decline: Scenarios for the economic and ethnic futures of the post-1965 American immigrants. *Ethnic and Racial Studies* 15 (2): 173–192.

Glick Schiller, N., and G. Fouron. 2001. *Georges woke up laughing: Long-distance nationalism and the search for home.* Durham, NC: Duke University Press.

Goffman, E. 1959. *Presentation of self in everyday life.* New York: Doubleday and Anchor Books.

Gordon, M. 1964. *Assimilation in American life.* New York: Oxford University Press.

Habecker, M. L. 2009. *African immigrants in Washington DC: Seeking alternative identities in a racially divided city.* PhD dissertation, International Development Centre, Queen Elizabeth House, St. Antony's College, Oxford University.

Haines, D. W. ed. 1997. *Case studies in diversity: Refugees in America in the 1990s.* Westport, CT: Praeger.

Hobsbawm, E., and T. Ranger. 1983. *The invention of tradition.* London: Cambridge University Press.

Kleist, N. 2008. In the name of diaspora: Between struggles for recognition and political aspirations. *Journal of Ethnic and Migration Studies* 34 (7): 1127–1143.

Kleist, N. 2010. Negotiating respectable masculinity: Gender and recognition in the Somali diaspora. *African Diaspora* 3 (2): 185–206.

Klimt, A., and S. Lubkemann. 2002. Arguments across the Portuguese diaspora: A discursive approach to theorizing diasporas. *Diaspora* 11 (2): 145–162.

Levitt, J. I. 2005. *The evolution of deadly conflict in Liberia: From 'paternalism' to state collapse.* Durham, NC: Carolina Academic Press.

Levitt, P. 2001. *The transnational villagers.* Berkeley, CA: University of California Press.

Levitt, P., and N. Glick Schiller. 2004. Conceptualizing simultaneity: A transnational social field perspective on society. *International Migration Review* 38 (3): 1002–1039.

Lubkemann, S. 2008a. *Culture in chaos: An anthropology of the social condition in war.* Chicago, IL: University of Chicago Press.

Lubkemann, S. 2008b. Liberian remittance relief and not-only for profit entrepreneurship: Exploring the economic relevance of diasporas in post-conflict transitions. In *Diasporas and international development: Exploring the potential*, ed. J. Brinkerhoff, 45–66. Boulder, CO: Lynne Rienner.

Lubkemann, S. 2015. Diasporicity and its discontents: Generation and fragmented historicity in the Liberian transnational field. *Diaspora* 18 (1/2): 208–227.
Mar, P. 2005. Unsettling potentialities: Topographies of hope in transnational migration. *Journal of Intercultural Studies* 26 (4): 361–378.
Marx, E. 1990. The social world of the refugee: A conceptual framework. *Journal of Refugee Studies* 3 (1): 189–203.
McDaniels, A. 1995. *Swing low, sweet chariot: The mortality cost of colonizing Liberia in the nineteenth century*. Chicago, IL: University of Chicago Press.
Mehlinger, L. R. 1916. The attitude of the free negro towards African colonization. *Journal of Negro History* 1: 276–308.
Miyazaki, H. 2004. *The method of hope: Anthropology, philosophy and Fijan knowledge*. Stanford: Stanford University Press.
Miyazaki, H. 2006. Economy of dreams: Hope in global capitalism and its critiques. *Cultural Anthropology* 21 (2): 147–172.
Moltmann, J. 1967. *Theology of hope: On the ground and implications of a Christian eschatology*. London: SCM Press.
Moran, M. 1990. *Civilized women: Gender and prestige in southeastern Liberia*. Ithaca, NY: Cornell University Press.
Moran, M. 2006. *Liberia: The violence of democracy*. Philadelphia, PA: University of Pennsylvania Press.
Rapport, N., and A. Dawson. 1998. Home and movement: A polemic. In *Migrants of identity*, eds. N. Rapport and A. Dawson, 19–38. New York: Berg.
Rumbaut, R. G. 2002. Severed or sustained attachments? Language, identity, and imagined communities in the post-immigrant generation. In *The changing face of home*, eds. P. Levitt and M. Waters, 43–95. New York: Russell Sage Foundation.
Sawyer, A. 1992. *The emergence of autocracy in Liberia: Tragedy and challenge*. Oakland, CA: Institute of Contemporary Studies Press.
Sheffer, G. 2003. *Diaspora politics: At home abroad*. Cambridge: Cambridge University Press.
Taylor, C. 2004. *Modern social imaginaries*. Durham, NC: Duke University Press.
Tyler-McGraw, M. 2007. *An African republic: Black and white Virginians in the making of Liberia*. Durham, NC: University of North Carolina.
Uvin, P. 1998. *Aiding violence: The development enterprise in Rwanda*. New York: Kumarian Press.
Waters, M. 1990. *Ethnic options: Choosing identities in America*. Berkeley: University of California Press.
Waters, M. 2001. *Black identities: West Indian immigrant dreams and American realities*. Cambridge, MA: Harvard University Press.
Werbner, P. 2002. The place which is diaspora: Citizenship, religion and gender in the making of chaordic transnationalism. *Journal of Ethnic and Migration Studies* 28 (1): 119–134.
Yurchak, A. 2003. Soviet hegemony of form: Everything was forever until it was no more. *Comparative Studies in Society and History* 45 (3): 480–510.
Zigon, J. 2009. Hope dies last: Two aspects of hope in contemporary Moscow. *Anthropological Theory* 9 (3): 253–271.

# 6 Prospective Moments, Eternal Salvation

## The Production of Hope in Nigerian Pentecostal Churches in China

*Heidi Østbø Haugen*

Protected by prayer alone, undocumented African migrants leave their homes in the suburbs of Guangzhou to go to church. The police in this southern Chinese city may intercept them on the streets or on public transport. Incarceration, fines, and repatriation await those who are stopped and are without valid travel documents. The migrants each have a method for minimizing the likelihood of being intercepted: travel when the police are off for lunch and always move around alone. Once they reach the anonymous buildings that house the churches, they pray again, this time to give thanks for a safe journey and to request a successful service. Inside, the pastors promise prosperity—a main staple of Pentecostal churches worldwide—as well as uninhibited spatial mobility. 'You shall be a global citizen of supernatural influence', one pastor declared. 'It is not the will of God that you will be caged in one place. No matter where you are in your life this morning, there is divine increase and expansion coming up'.

The smothering feeling of encagement referred to above is well known to undocumented African migrants in China. Without a valid visa, they can neither move around freely nor return home. They have been pushed increasingly far away from the center of Guangzhou to live in areas that are less aggressively monitored. The policing of foreigners in and around the city has become increasingly tight over the past decade. African-run churches regularly lose members who are incarcerated for immigration offenses and forced to leave China. The Nigerian pastor quoted above had just seen one of the musicians from his church arrested. The sound of the incomplete ensemble served as a reminder of the risks facing all undocumented migrants. The ill-fated band member was obliged to pay his flight ticket and a fine of RMB 10,000 (USD 1,600) before he could be released and repatriated, but did not have the money to hand. A decade earlier, the church could be counted on for help in such situations. However, the sense of solidarity had been exhausted and no move was made to collect money for the release of the musician or other imprisoned congregants.

This chapter explores why undocumented migrants continue to attend activities in the African-led churches despite the risks this entails. As hinted at above, the churches have limited efficacy in providing migrants with

DOI: 10.4324/9781315659916-6

security and the means to incrementally improve their situation. I suggest that the prospective moments generated through worship are crucial to the congregants' continued commitment to the church. Hope is produced and reproduced and is shaped through religious practices and the congregants' experiences of mobility and immobility.

My analysis is based on fieldwork between 2009 and 2014 among Africans in Guangzhou and return migrants in Nigeria. In September 2009, Pastor Paul[1] granted me permission to do research in his church, The Tower of Salvation World Mission (The Tower, for short). Whereas more than half of the congregants were Nigerian, there were members from other parts of Africa, the global African diaspora, and Asia. I attended services weekly during two fieldwork periods (September–December 2009 and January–December 2014), with annual visits in between. The resulting data include notes from participant observation in The Tower, transcribed recordings of the sermons, and semi-structured interviews with congregants, pastors, and other African migrants. I also draw on notes from participant observation in two immigrant-dense neighborhoods in Guangzhou.

Hope is central in all strands of Christianity but in very different ways. The first section in this chapter reviews the literature on migrant Pentecostalism and the role of hope in Pentecostal theology. I discuss how the production of hope in Pentecostal contexts is associated with specific ontologies of time and with given spatial referents. In the second section, I contextualize my study by tracing the history of Nigerian migration to China. The ways of creating hope in the African Pentecostal churches in Guangzhou are inextricably linked to the modes of migration to China and the conditions facing migrants. Nigerians were the first Africans to establish churches in China, and I next describe how these are run in a secular regulatory environment. The three following sections draw upon my ethnographic material to examine the specific ways in which hope is produced in the migrant churches. First, their theology insists that hope has a moral dimension—hopefulness is portrayed as virtuous and despair as degenerate. Second, audacious hope is valued higher than plans for incremental improvements, and, third, the production of hope is an embodied exercise. The conclusion argues for a future-oriented stance when studying hopeful practices in Pentecostal churches.

## Pentecostalism and Hope

The topic of hope has been approached from two angles in the literature on African and migrant Pentecostalism. The first documents the ways in which religious engagement helps people to realize their desire to migrate and the hopes underpinning their migration projects. Such studies highlight the instrumental value of Pentecostal networks and theology at all stages in the migration process. Prospective migrants employ deliverance strategies to get protection during their travel (van Dijk 1997) and pastors offer both spiritual counsel and practical help to migrants *en route* to their destinations

(Hagan and Ebaugh 2003). Where the migrants settle down, Pentecostal churches provide services that facilitate life abroad: they challenge negative stereotypes of African migrants (Knibbe 2009); set up nurseries, kindergartens, and medical and counseling amenities (Hunt and Lightly 2001); facilitate access to overseas contacts, professional networks, and scholarships (Meagher 2010; Meyer 1998; Smith 2001); offer moral and material support (Adogame 2003; van der Meulen 2009); and provide opportunities to take on meaningful social responsibilities (Miller and Yamamori 2007). Pentecostal organizations thus act as stabilizing forces that narrow the gaps between expectations and realities.

The second approach to hope and Pentecostalism takes rupture as its starting point. This scholarship refers to the unsettling effects of radical economic and political uncertainty in the post-colony, where individual desires for material wealth are intense but largely frustrated. Pentecostal churches structure how people experience the world; they are 'narrative-machines as much as welfare societies and new economy interpellation devices' (Piot 2010, 56). The churches articulate the problems of living with fundamental uncertainty and offer strategies for overcoming the tribulations they cause (Marshall 2009; Piot 2010). These strategies include the instantaneous production of wealth through miracles at a time when most fortunes emerge without any evident basis (Mbembe 2004). Pentecostal theology also encourages withdrawal from communal obligations and kin, thus helping people to manage the tension between individual desires to prosper and social pressure to share wealth (Robbins 2004). Individualization is promoted through discourses that urge hand-to-hand combat with traditions and the ancestral past (Casanova 2001; Meyer 1998). Whereas Pentecostalism helps to manage some conflicting obligations, it creates new schisms: The Prosperity Gospel—the promise that God will grant believers this-worldly wealth—repeatedly fails to become manifest in the lives of most Born-Agains (Meyer 2004).

The juxtaposition of riches and material deprivation has elicited disparate theological responses in the Global South. In Latin America, liberation theology was developed from the 1950s onwards as a moral reaction to poverty and inequality. God was perceived to suffer with humanity, a creed elaborated by Jürgen Moltmann in his seminal 1967 book *Theology of hope*. Moltmann's work made Ernst Bloch's (1986) notion of 'not yet'-consciousness available to a wide Christian audience. It presents hope as a way of revolting against the deprivations in this world and working towards change. 'We hear of ineffable blessedness—but meantime we are here oppressed by infinite misery', Moltmann wrote (1967, 19). For liberation theologians, hope in eschatology ought to focus on alleviating misery on this side of eternity, 'in contradiction to our present experience of suffering, evil and death' (Moltmann 1967, 19).

The ways in which hope is practiced in Pentecostalism is radically different from the understandings put forward through liberation theology. This divergence is rooted in contrasting ontologies of time within the two theological traditions. As an activity pointed towards the future, hope is strongly conditioned by temporal conceptualizations. Whereas liberation theology advocates for collective action to change the *near future*, African Pentecostalism mainly works through two other time frames: the *immediate* and the *long-term*. Pentecostal churches emphasize immediate experience with God's presence. Services are understood as unique events rather than the re-enactment of rituals, with a dramaturgy that promotes direct encounters with God through the Holy Spirit. The long-term perspective points towards the Second Coming of the Messiah, when evil will be defeated and judgment passed on all human beings. Believers vigilantly look for signs of end times and prepare for them, never certain of how they will be judged. Utopian dreams permeated public discourse in Africa in the 1980s and 1990s, when the continent experienced strong Pentecostal growth. The policy rhetoric in Nigeria under structural adjustment and military rule invoked long-term vistas of progress, while most citizens struggled to get through the day (Guyer 2007). The suppression of the near future as a temporal frame in public life arguably deprived people of 'a set of practices and representations aimed towards active engagement in the social world' (Guyer 2007, 409).

The ontology of time in Pentecostal Christianity entails methodological challenges parallel to those associated with studying hope: how to approach practices to which temporal disjuncture—represented both in radical breaks with the past and prospective orientations towards the future—is integral. Hirokazu Miyazaki's (2006) treatise of hope in a Fijian context points towards ways of studying discontinuity and maintaining the prospective orientation of hope. 'The newness and freshness of the prospective moment that defines the moment as hopeful is lost as soon as hope is approached as the end point of a process', he writes (Miyazaki 2006, 8). Instead of treating hope as a subject of knowledge, Miyazaki proposes hope *as method* for comprehending a future-oriented way of being in the world. The hopeful moments in Fijian cultural performance are understood as ways of generating self-knowledge. Hope as method opens up opportunities for studying Pentecostal practices on their own terms, approaching the churches' fantastic promises of wealth as a reality still in a state of not-yet, and appreciating prophesies for the social momentum that they produce rather than their efficacy.

The not-yet is given *geographical referents* by Pentecostal churches. Images of success are intimately connected to the ability to transcend localness. The breaks with the past are also breaks with local cultures, but in ways that entail engagement through confrontation. The local is thus part and parcel of practices that envision positive change towards becoming global. Pentecostalism's engagement with the indigenous through combating it enables easy adaptation to local circumstances whereas the religion remains deterritorialized (Casanova 2001). From its inception more than a century ago, migration has been a main vehicle through which Pentecostalism has spread and taken on new forms.

## Nigerian Migration to China

The advent of Nigerian migration to China was conditioned by the two countries' colonial histories and their places in the global economy. In the 1990s, young Nigerian men who were unable to find jobs in the domestic manufacturing sector, which was brought to its knees by structural adjustment programs, turned towards East and Southeast Asia. Their first port of call was Hong Kong, where they were secured visa-free entry through Nigeria's membership of the Commonwealth of Nations. From the British colony they traveled to South Korea, Japan, the Philippines and other industrializing economies to take up factory employment. Many worked without formal documentation, and deportations to Hong Kong—the nearest territory which Nigerians could legally enter—were common.

A group of deportees formed the first Nigerian settlement in South China. Living costs in Hong Kong were exorbitant and, by moving across the border to mainland China, Nigerians could sustain themselves cheaply. They continued to provide services to visiting African traders in Hong Kong and waited for job opportunities in Asia. The first Nigerian to set up a business in China is said to be Ike Okane, a mechanic who became infirm after getting his arm trapped on an assembly line in South Korea. While visiting an Igbo friend in Guangzhou in 1997, Okane discovered a depot for seized motorcycles. He solicited the help of a compatriot graduate from a Chinese university to convince the depot management to sell him the vehicles for export. Soon, he brought unemployed Nigerians from Hong Kong to help dismantle the motorcycles, and the Nigerian population in Guangzhou counted 200 persons within a year. Okane and two other Igbo men secured the exclusive right to buy motorcycles from the depot, effectively forming a cartel. The Nigerian workers, who were excluded from the trade in motorcycle spare parts, invested their salaries in other products manufactured in China. They also helped African traders to procure goods directly from the mainland rather than via agents in Hong Kong. As more of these traders visited Guangzhou in person, Chinese and resident Africans set up accommodation, catering, and logistics services to cater to their needs.

Young men remain the main demographic group among Nigerian immigrants in China today. They leave Nigeria in search of the proverbial greener pastures. Increased economic interaction between the two countries has conjured up the impression that employment prospects in China are good: Chinese consumer goods are now ubiquitous in Nigerian markets and large amounts of Chinese investment capital flow into Nigeria. Whereas structural disparities represent an important underlying cause of migration, specific instances of departure from Nigeria are often precipitated by idiosyncratic events—an unwanted marriage, a failed football career, business bankruptcy. China is below Europe in a spatial hierarchy of destination countries but is considered an acceptable alternative, as opportunities to enter Europe are curbed. Some Nigerians in China have previous migration experience from

Europe that ended in deportation. Others highlight the physical danger of traveling to Europe by land and sea, and regard migration to Asia as a less perilous (and therefore morally superior) option.

The emerging infrastructure for visa brokerage to Asia contributed to the increase in Nigerians heading to China. Access to a credible broker offering to organize the journey to China has initiated migration for people who were not actively searching for opportunities to leave their home country (see Alpes 2011 for a discussion of this phenomenon in Cameroon). Brokers speed up the decision process. Potential migrants are forced to make a rushed decision about whether to accept a rare access to intercontinental mobility, and have few opportunities to learn more about the situation in China. Furthermore, many migrants in China did not think that more information prior to departure would necessarily prevent people from traveling. They described potential migrants, themselves included, as reluctant to assess their prospects of success based on other people's experiences. Consequently, they were reluctant to warn against others going to China. A song written by Ferdblack, an Igbo musician who regretted moving to Guangzhou, illustrates this mindset. In the lyrics of 'Let our hearts be strong', he describes the hardships which Africans encounter in China: going hungry, having no place to live, and being in want of a job. Yet, the ensuing text does not discourage others from trying to succeed in China. Instead, Ferdblack proposes that only God can tell people what to do and encourages fellow Nigerians to travel and pursue money 'because money is the head of this world' (Ferdblack 2009).

The relative ease with which Nigerians could initially enter China was not the result of deliberate policy choices. Until the turn of the millennium, there was no pressing need to regulate immigration at the national level because China received few intercontinental migrants (Pieke 2012). This changed as the presence of foreigners grew larger and more visible. In Guangzhou, riots staged by Nigerian migrants to protest at the deaths of compatriots in police custody and the disquiet expressed by Chinese inhabitants of areas with many undocumented foreigners prompted government concerns about immigration as a source of social unrest (Chinese People's Political Consultative Conference 2008; Yan 2012). Whereas *ad hoc* measures to restrict immigration were introduced on the ground, the central government decided to draft new immigration legislation. After a decade of preparations, China's first comprehensive immigration legislation—the Exit and Entry Administration Law—took full effect on 1 July 2013. The law embodies a tension between the need, on the one hand, to promote economic development and, on the other, to protect national security and social stability (Ministry of Public Security 2012). High-profile official campaigns, organized to crack down on 'illegal foreigners' in China's major cities, have accompanied these legislative changes (Lefkowitz 2014).

Legal permits to stay in China have always been more difficult to obtain than visas to enter the country. On arriving with a 30-day Chinese business visa, prospective Nigerian migrants are faced with a momentous decision: to return before their visa expires or stay on undocumented. Those opting for the latter must maneuver within an intricate legislative environment that was initially designed to manage internal migration in China through the household registration (*hukou*) system (Haugen 2012). Foreigners are required to register their place of residence within 24 hours and provide information about their visas in the process. Landlords face fines if their tenants are not registered or lack valid documents, and hotels are obliged to check their guests' papers. This drives up the price of housing for undocumented migrants. Local governments deliberately manipulate the residential pattern of foreigners by declining to register their housing in certain areas (Haugen 2015). Furthermore, the 2012 Exit–Entry Law obliges anyone aware of foreigners who have entered, who reside, or who work in China illegally to notify the Public Security Bureau.

Some of the difficulties which African migrants face in China can be illustrated by the story of Abel, a Nigerian who was brought to The Tower by a friend when he arrived in Guangzhou. As the youngest son in a politically well-connected family in Eastern Nigeria, Abel faced less pressure to provide for his relatives than most of his peers in China. When he grew up, his paternal grandfather wanted him to become a priest, but he landed a managerial job through family connections instead. Despite his comfortable life, Abel wanted to go abroad to prove that he could fend for himself and was, in his words, 'no longer a kid'. Migration was an adventure he desired in order to prove his ability (cf. Bredeloup 2008). He complained that his brother, who worked at a European embassy in Abuja, was 'too righteous' to assist him in getting a visa. One day, a man who courted Abel's sister offered to get him a Chinese visa through a connection. 'It's good to go somewhere else to gain more experience before going to Europe', Abel reasoned. The aspiring brother-in-law paid the visa agent US$2,000. Upon receiving the travel documents, Abel bought a plane ticket, called his mother to say goodbye, and left for China.

Abel reached Guangzhou shortly after the 2008 Beijing Olympics. He immediately realized that managing a state of illegality in China would be tough, and gave his passport to a new agent along with RMB 9,000 (US$1,440) to get his visa renewed. The agent disappeared with the money, but returned Abel's passport. The landlord allowed Abel to stay on without a visa, but asked him to move into an unofficial guesthouse in response to rumors of an upcoming police raid. As this is a common phenomenon for undocumented tenants, Abel did not suspect anything wrong at first, but the landlord never allowed him to move back and refused to refund the deposit. 'He knows I cannot go to the police because of the paper problem. That's why they can treat Nigerians like that', Abel said. Establishing a business also proved harder than he had expected. He rented a wholesale store in a trading mall frequented by Africans, but had to ask the Chinese wife of a friend to put the contract in her name and manage the store when police controls prevented him from being there.

The shame of having to hide was, for Abel, the most disturbing aspect of living as an undocumented migrant. 'I would not complain about the hardship here if it weren't for the harassment', he said upon recounting the various ways in which his status made him vulnerable. 'If you can live here, there's no place you can't stay. People here are too primitive. But I have learned a lot'. His comfortable financial situation and extensive social network helped Abel to manage the situation and eventually leave China. In December 2009, the Public Security Bureau announced the first and only amnesty in which exit visas were granted to foreigners who paid an RMB 2,100 fine for overstaying. Abel decided to use this opportunity to return home, and solicited my help as a Chinese speaker to complete the necessary formalities. When he was finally granted permission to leave China, Abel strode lightly and confidently out of the Exit and Entry Bureau, relieved to no longer hide from anyone. He was ready to celebrate Christmas in Nigeria before trying to go to Europe. 'You have been doing God's work', he told me as we parted, indicating not only that his freedom to leave China was the result of divine influence but also that my assistance did not place him in debt to me because I would be rewarded by God. In Pentecostal Christianity, 'doing God's work'—that is, giving Born-Again principles concrete application—is a means of accessing personal wealth and transnational connections (Marshall 2009), as we shall see below.

## African Churches in China: Spiritual Warfare in a Pugnaciously Secular Country

The early Nigerian migrants to Guangzhou established Christian fellowships that were run in much the same way as Chinese house churches: small groups of people gathered in apartments to pray and invoke the presence of the Holy Spirit. The first Nigerian pastors in China soon realized that the experientially oriented Pentecostal services appealed to a Chinese audience and they baptized new Chinese followers every month. But the limitations imposed by the secular Chinese state soon became apparent. Religious gatherings outside the state-sanctioned places of worship are prohibited for foreigners and Chinese nationals alike, but the subversive potential is seen as much greater when Chinese believers assemble and are led by a foreigner. In order to remain tolerated by the government, the Nigerian churches were forced to grow mainly through attracting African followers. Some set up smaller, discreetly run congregations exclusively for Chinese believers. The Chinese participation in the African churches was largely limited to the wives and children of their migrant members.

By 2014, there were around a dozen Nigerian-headed Pentecostal churches in Guangzhou, as well as congregations preaching in Lingala, French, Portuguese, and other languages spoken by Africans from across the continent. None were registered with China's Religious Affairs Bureau, which is a requirement if foreign churches are to operate legally. The authorities in

Guangzhou are well aware of the existence of the underground churches, and occasionally even communicate messages to undocumented migrants through the African pastors. The churches are tacitly tolerated as long as they do not become too visible or assertive. Church leaders rent spaces in office buildings, hotels, and restaurants, and are routinely forced to move by the police.

The Nigerian churches in China are either founded as branches of churches in Nigeria or set up independently by Nigerians living in China. The only Nigerian church in China that has welcomed media attention, the Royal Victory Church, was established in Guangzhou, and expanded from mainland China into Nigeria, as well as into Hong Kong, Cameroon, and the Philippines (RVC 2015). The names and aesthetics of the Nigerian churches parade their global connections and aspirations. In The Tower, the national flags of Israel, the United States, and Nigeria are placed on one side of the pulpit, with the flags of three other African countries on the other side. A mixture of Nigerian religious tunes and globally consumed Pentecostal songs fills the services, and the sermons are strewn with references to international travel and links with churches on other continents.

If The Tower had ever been effective as a network of support for vulnerable migrants, its capacity to assist congregants had been exhausted by 2009, when I joined the church. One congregant had stayed in prison for more than a year without receiving assistance to repatriate, while several others had been incarcerated for months. The size of the ministry fluctuated greatly. The Tower was established in 1998, and was at one point home to the largest African church in Guangzhou, attracting hundreds of people. However, many members abandoned the church following a dispute about money. By 2009, there were only a few dozen regular attendants, and Pastor Paul instructed congregants not to bother the remaining prosperous members of the congregation. The decline spurred tension. For example, Nigerian members criticized newly arrived Cameroonian congregants for expecting support from the church—'They use the church as insurance', one Nigerian complained.

Mobility, while celebrated during the church services, represents a challenge to the day-to-day running of the ministries. A high turnover of African migrants produces unstable congregations, often leaving positions of trust empty. The organizational volatility depletes the effectiveness of pastoral care. Without discounting the help occasionally extended between individuals in The Tower, the church barely qualified as a network of support for most migrants. Furthermore, many saw no advantage to conducting business with other church members and even deliberately avoided such transactions, as the ministry proved ineffective in negotiating in business disputes between congregants. In short, one must look beyond the practical utility of the Pentecostal churches in order to understand their appeal to African migrants in China. The churches are societies where hope is not only enabled, but constructed as a duty. It is to this hope that I now turn.

## Moral Value Assigned to Hope

Pentecostal theology insists that hope has a moral dimension. Hopefulness is portrayed as virtuous; despair is regarded as degenerate. In the Pentecostal moral universe, problems are not understood as structurally rooted or accidentally inflicted but, rather, cast in a narrative of good and evil. Overcoming trouble is equated with fighting the devil. In The Tower's Sunday services, Pastor Paul started to address the congregation's problems by naming them: the police forcing undocumented migrants to hide, shipments seized by customs officers, business partners in Africa 'eating your money', and the lack of resources enabling people to marry and establish a family. Sometimes, congregants testified publicly about overcoming such troubles and the pastor reinforced their testimonies by rephrasing them in ways that emphasized the importance of spiritual vigilance to secure worldly success. For example, the owner of a business called *Grace Logistics* testified about a fire that was quenched just before it reached his own warehouse. Pastor Paul then repeated the central elements of the story, praising the business man for his spiritual acumen. 'Grace Logistics was formed in The Tower and the devil cannot stop it from moving', he said, suggesting that the owner had saved his business by making the right spiritual choices.

Subsequent to the generic labeling of problems in the church services, congregants identified the sources of their specific afflictions. Problems were often traced back to their relationships with people who wished to inflict harm. The Tower, like many other African diaspora churches, retained a belief in wizards and witches who do the work of the devil and hinder people from achieving the success that God has in store for them. Evil spirits were combated through prayers and offerings, and the church services encouraged vigilance in everyday life against evil entities. The fight perceived to be going on between good and malicious forces affected migration and business decisions. For example, a church member who had traveled back and forth to China over a period of ten years said that he overstayed his one-month visa for fear of returning to his home town, where somebody was performing witchcraft on him. Another congregant canceled a business deal with a trader from Haïti because he believed she was a witch who would bring trouble if he took her money. In both cases, concrete business conflicts were assigned moral meaning which, in turn, affected how they were acted upon.

African migrants in China commonly face expectations for remittances that they are in no position to meet. By encouraging breaks with local cultures and kin, Pentecostal theology provides moral support to struggling migrants as well as business people who need to retain resources for reinvestment. Pastor Paul ended a prayer to free the congregation from ancestral spirits with a reminder that church has replaced family, calling out 'Mr Debt must die!' That particular service was missed by Prince, a young Nigerian who came to China to launch his football career and had disappointed his family by not sending them money. He later explained that he felt ashamed to go to church without any money to offer as 'seed'. For Prince, the emancipation from social obligations *vis-à-vis* relatives at home came at the expense of new debts to the church, which he was unable to honor. Furthermore, the comfort and familiarity offered by a Pentecostal spiritual universe with perpetual warfare between good and evil impedes integration into the host society. Whether or not the African ministries actively proselytize among the Chinese, individual believers are discursively positioned in a territory demarcated to be conquered for Jesus. Proselytization discourses in Pentecostalism have entailed a demonization of the object of conversion. As Ruth Marshall has put it, 'Underlying the bid to convert the other is the need to *convict* and *overcome* him, to identify him with the demonic that needs to be destroyed for salvation and redemption to occur' (2009, 14, emphasis in original). Both Christian and Muslim African migrants in Guangzhou cited the heathen nature of Chinese people as a reason for not learning the language or having a local girlfriend. By keeping the Chinese at a distance, they forewent resources that proved beneficial to the businesses and personal lives of their compatriots who were better integrated in China (Haugen 2013).

Once misfortune is inscribed with meaning, combating it becomes a moral obligation rather than a matter of choice. In The Tower, present problems were fought through the generation of prospective moments that pointed towards a utopian future. The production of hope was not just acts that *created* visions; the acts were also seen as the means to *actualize* these visions by enabling the work of the Holy Spirit. Yet, problems persisted in the lives of most congregants. In the face of such entrenched hardship, The Tower promoted patience and persistence through the notion that God 'works with time and season'. In other words, it is up to God to decide *when* to allow people to reach their goals. Phrases such as 'God's time is the best' were popular business mottos among Christian Nigerians in China. However, demonic influence could make congregants lose their faith in the possibility of turning things around for the better: 'Discouragement is Satan's best weapon against the believer', Pastor Paul preached. Reproducing hope, therefore, was equated with fighting with God against the devil.

The strong confidence in God's power to assist believers in reaching their goals affected migration decisions. Pastors encouraged migrants to remain in China even after years of economic failure. '[The migrant] should not return, because the money will come soon, and he will be able to fulfill the wish of his family', one pastor said. He presented returning to Africa with nothing to show for the stay abroad as an act of blasphemy. Whereas communal encouragement to retain faith in success in China inspired migrants to keep going, it also narrowed the range of morally acceptable choices.

The moral value assigned to hope may explain the negative reactions when Abel chose to leave China without having attained his objective. I had found his choice wise: he assessed the situation and confronted its implications head-on by returning home. However, I learned from the responses of Abel's peers that his decision could also be interpreted as a sign of weak faith in God's ability to turn desperate situations around. Abel was criticized for giving up, and I was reproached for accommodating his weakness rather than encouraging him to keep trying. Expecting these reactions, Abel left China without saying goodbye to the church members.

The ways in which Pentecostal pastors instill migrants with hope was not universally condoned by Nigerians in China. Some avoided the Pentecostal churches and blamed pastors for giving their compatriots unrealistic expectations that inspired bad behavior and damaged the reputation of all Africans. Nigerian migrants who had exhausted their funds regarded drug-dealing as a real and dangerous temptation. A number of Africans have been convicted and imprisoned for drug offenses in Guangzhou (Guangzhou People's Court Reports 2012). Drug crimes were a source of community mistrust. 'If I stay with people, I cannot know who is who. This place is China. It is not good to stay with people here', Chidike, an undocumented migrant, said with reference to the danger of being associated with narcotics trafficking. Three years after Chidike made this statement, in 2012, the police raided Liuhua Hotel, a center for the Nigerian-controlled drug-trade in Guangzhou (Li 2012). Several Nigerians jumped out of the windows to escape—rumor had it that a young man who was active in one of the African churches died in the fall. Chidike was among those who blamed the pastor of the deceased. 'If you tell people they will have a lot of money, some will do bad things to make it. The blood of this young boy is on the hands of the pastor', he asserted angrily. He had attended a non-African international church to avoid contact with other Nigerians and escape from the focus on the prosperity gospel. However, after the police checked passports at a church meal in 2010, the American pastors said they would no longer protect Chidike. He felt unwelcome and left the congregation.

## Hope without Restraint

In the moral universe promulgated by The Tower, unconstrained hopes and desires for astonishing success were valued more highly than realistic aspirations for incremental improvements. The congregants understood bold prayer requests as signs of strong belief in God's power, and church leaders condoned and encouraged this attitude. 'Just because you have some few thousand [dollars] does not mean that you have arrived', Pastor Paul said. 'You cannot get what you cannot see. You must see it to get it'. He often cited Ezekiel 37, a Bible passage where God gives life to piles of skeletons in the valley of dry bones. Churches across Africa interpret this tale as an attestation of God's ability to turn the most desperate situations around (Asamoah-Gyadu 2005). To believers in The Tower, the valley of dry bones symbolized China—a place of great hardship where sweeping improvements were imminent.

Pentecostal Christianity requires individuals to break with the past in order to access the boundless possibilities that come with being Born-Again. '[To be Born-Again] means you are free from the burden your family has brought upon you. [. . .] You have a new DNA. Nobody will ask who your parents are and judge you by it', Pastor Paul explained. Deliverance from the past is a long-term process rather than a one-off event. Believers must *continuously* create distance between themselves and their backgrounds, searching their souls for remnants of the past and evil intrusions. The dialectic practice of forgetting and remembering invokes the possibility of failure, together with the potential for improvement. Pastor Paul's sermons and his congregants' prayers and testimonies defined success as the appropriation of control over global flows, including one's own mobility across borders. Examples of achievements mentioned in the church were phone calls from wealthy people ordering goods, friends in high office, business branches in new countries, container-loads of goods shipped to Africa, residence permits for China, and visas for Europe and Australia.

In Guangzhou's trading malls, African migrants passed the time by relaying stories about people who resolved tough problems in spectacular ways. Their accounts described implausible and audacious escapes from difficult situations that involved the police, customs officers, or immigration officials. Such narratives were also incorporated into the church services. For example, Pastor Paul told the story of a migrant in China whose visa application was rejected by the British Embassy. The applicant had wept and said that he had no more hope left. The pastor then prayed for him and declared that the visa would be granted. The man went back to the embassy. Accompanied by cheers from the congregants, Pastor Paul described how the visa application eventually was successful:

> The visa officer said 'Why are you here?' The man then replied 'God said you must give me [a] visa'. The woman looked at him. 'God has said I must give you [a] visa?' she asked. He replied 'Yes'. And then the woman told him 'Come and collect your visa tomorrow!' And he went and got the visa.

Similarly, migrants provided testimonies about being saved from deportation through supernatural intervention: One man became invisible when the police did passport checks in a trading mall; a woman was captured by the police, showed signs of violent illness, was released by scared police officers, and immediately recovered her health.

The generic promises of wealth and success made in plenary in The Tower took on more concrete expressions as they were interpreted by the congregants. For example, a Kenyan woman, who lived from hand to mouth as a guide for visiting traders, planned to tap into global capital flows by buying vast amounts of land outside Nairobi and growing fresh strawberries to be airlifted to Europe. A Nigerian church member envisaged building schools that would serve as models for a better education system in his home country. These dreams were kept alive long after it became clear that life in China offered few opportunities to realize them.

The predictions of upcoming achievements presented in The Tower were, to some extent, real in their consequences. Promises of business success inspired people who had been unsuccessful for years to continue devising new plans and calling prospective customers at home to solicit orders. Prophesies about visas coming through encouraged congregants to put up with the hardship they experienced in China for a little longer. Hope was deferred, spatially and temporally—it was placed in new migration destinations, for which China was expected to serve as a springboard, and postponed, as migrants expected heavenly promises to be shortly fulfilled.

In Nigeria, Pentecostal churches give the not-yet geographical referents through the construction of self-contained towns. In these towns, the ministries express their visions for the future by providing the public infrastructure which most Nigerians lack: roads free of potholes, safe transport, clean water, electricity without power cuts, and premium health and education facilities. The website of the world's largest Pentecostal city, which was founded outside Lagos by the Redeemed Christian Church of God, presents the place as a spatial manifestation of the future:

> A billboard outside the gate shows a mother smiling down at her baby. It is a picture of complete satisfaction from both. [. . .] The prayers of the residents may have already been answered. [. . .] Unlike many Nigerian towns and cities where existence is dreary, nasty and often extremely disorganised, the Redeemed Camp is a town that works.
> (Redeemed Christian Church of God 2015)

In fact, these 'towns that work' house very few people except during special events. More than vehicles for concrete improvement in people's living conditions, the towns are effective as utopian visions. They project images of supreme fulfillment that are unfettered by the limitations of the present, representing, in Miyazaki's (2006) terms, 'prospective moments'.

African ministries have created spaces through which hope can be produced in Europe and the United States as well, albeit at a smaller scale than in Africa. The physical structures erected by Christian migrants allow them to put their economic resources and organizational capabilities on display, thus challenging the stereotypes of Africans in their host societies (Garbin 2010, 2013; Knibbe 2009). In China, by contrast, the strict regulation of religious activities denies foreign churches the opportunity to spatially manifest their presence. The African churches are shut down unless they show discretion. The churches' restrained mode of operation thus contrasts starkly with the uninhibited expectations and uncompromising attitudes which the pastors promulgate.

## Hope as an Embodied Practice

'Only God can save Nigeria'. 'If the immigration police come, I am covered by Jesus'. 'I trust nobody, not even myself. I only trust God'. As indicated above, Nigerians in Guangzhou understand such statements not as figures of speech but as examples of concrete ways in which divine forces intervene in their lives. The claims do not represent a fatalistic attitude; they call for action. Upon placing things in the hands of God, one must exert vigorous effort to combat the devil and promote the work of the Holy Spirit. Maintaining a sense of possibility—an expectation that God will ensure that the objectives that prompted migration to China are realized—requires both speech and movement.

In the Pentecostal tradition, the physical is valued higher than the cerebral. Conjuring belief in radical improvements requires the suspension of rational thinking. 'The voice of reason is the enemy of the Holy Spirit', Pastor Paul preached. At one of The Tower's 'miracle services', a visiting pastor singled me out to eject rational belief and to insert, in its place, true experientially based faith. He put his palm on my forehead and threw it backwards, as if physically pushing rationality out. To share the prospective momentum produced through Pentecostal services, reason must be suspended and a physical approach adopted in its place. The guest pastor guided me to use my body to summon what has not-yet-become rather than rationally assess the future based on past experiences (cf. Bloch 1986). The synchronic performances that invoke the future in The Tower represent a way of employing hope as method (Miyazaki 2006).

The African-run churches in Guangzhou demand energetic participation from their members. This form of worship is contrasted with the subdued and ritualized services of mainstream Catholicism. The congregants of Pentecostal churches confirm the pastors' words as they are spoken by repeating key messages and spontaneously utter 'Amen!' and 'Hallelujah!' Pastors invite believers to articulate what they want to achieve and, in narrative terms, these statements are completed the moment they are uttered (Coleman 2006). Pastor Paul asked that church members address each other as 'son of a rich man' and 'daughter of a king', thus declaring that the wealth and success to which congregants aspire have already arrived. The atmosphere became increasingly charged as the services progressed, and people variously fell down on the floor, walked around, and manifested the Holy Spirit by breaking into glossolalia. When the services ended, many congregants were soaked in sweat from the verbal and physical expressions of their spiritual agency.

The agency exercised in the Pentecostal services contrasts with the migrants' experiences outside their ministries. The churches provide congregants with the means to take charge of their own lives, thus with a sense of control over situations the outcome of which would otherwise depend on forces beyond their reach. Furthermore, congregants encourage each other to be loud and use their bodies expressively whereas, outside the church, migrants try to behave inconspicuously to detract attention from themselves.

A range of bodily techniques to be employed individually complement the collective exercises in the church. The core of these efforts is prayer, where migrants spell out their envisioned futures and name the forces holding them back. Fasting of various lengths of time can be added to improve the effectiveness of the prayers. The witches and demons that have the incentive and power to block the migrants' progress are located in the congregants' home countries, often among close relatives. Relations with Chinese people are not seen as arenas for spiritual combat, although evil forces can *use* the Chinese as a means to harm their victims.

Individual congregants may request help from their pastor to increase the potency of their prayers. Pastors pray and fast on behalf of others. If they have prophetic gifts, pastors can foresee in dreams whether the specific aspirations will be achieved. 'I have seen most of your faces in my dreams and visions', Pastor Paul assured his congregants. Because the actions of pastors are important mediums for advancement, worshipping with 'false men of God'—that is, leaders who lack divine connections—is dangerously obstructive. African pastors in Guangzhou cautioned against believing in the false promises of their rival churches. 'They will manipulate, tell you they will fast for you a lot of days', Pastor Paul warned people. 'They say the same to many others. It's not humanly possible to fast that much! [. . .] You must guard your heart! Deliver yourself from the hands of manipulative spirits!' The Tower frequently lost members to other churches. In Guangzhou's fiercely competitive religious landscape, Born-Agains easily find new places of worship when promises of success no longer feel effective. The pastors of the abandoned churches go from being trusted as agents for cleansing society of immorality to becoming targets of accusations of corruption themselves. The ability to induce hope is therefore a *sine qua non* for the success of the African churches in Guangzhou.

## Conclusion: The Paradox of Hope

Pentecostalism is an intensely future-oriented ideology. The ability to incite hope for material and social advancement has been central to its rapid global expansion. The concept of being Born-Again carries the promise of starting afresh without the afflictions of the past. Pentecostal theology provides migrants with certitude and ways of making sense of the world while facing circumstances beyond their control. However, the hopes mediated through a Pentecostal theology represent constraints as well as opportunities. The moral value assigned to hope shapes the migrants' relationship with the host society and the ways in which migration choices are assessed, making some options more accessible while constraining others. For those who eventually opt to return to their home country empty-handed, the choice represents a final failure in their migration endeavor: the failure to retain hope.

Despite the setback experienced by most Nigerian migrants in China, migration continues to be regarded as a path to improvement. The migrants maintain their faith in a better future by suspending it, projecting their expectations onto future points in time or new destination countries. The African Pentecostal churches provide spaces for generating hope through active participation and the exertion of great physical effort. Thus, the production of hope is an embodied as well as a collective process; to maintain aspirations requires both the hard work of the individual and the institutional support of the churches.

Participant observation is a particularly apt approach for studying hope produced through corporal and communal practices. However, there is also a need for an epistemological device that can capture the forward-looking orientation and ideology of discontinuity in Pentecostalism. As I have described in this chapter, Pentecostal practitioners often take a fiercely anti-intellectual stance and value fantastic expectations. The 'method of hope' proposed by Miyazaki (2006) provides a way for the researcher to reorient knowledge production so as to better understand hopeful practices. It represents a means to take religious belief seriously without explaining away its unknowable features.

African churches, as well as the migrants attending them, face a unique set of challenges in China. The migrants' religious practices have thus far been readily accommodated to the situation, and Pentecostalism has again proved extremely adaptable to local circumstances. Pentecostal institutions provide material optimism and promises of instant blessings in times of disruption, and seem to thrive off the contradictions they create rather than being undermined by them. There is no reason to believe that the hardship borne by Nigerian migrants in China will lead them to abandon Pentecostal faith and practices. Rather, the setbacks they experience in their migration projects sustain the need for methods of performing hoped-for achievements as facts of the present.

## Note

1. The names of persons and churches have been changed to protect the anonymity of the research participants.

## References

Adogame, A. 2003. Betwixt identity and security: African new religious movements and the politics of religious networking in Europe. *Nova Religio* 7 (2): 24–41.

Alpes, M. J. 2011. *Bushfalling: How young Cameroonians dare to migrate*. PhD, Faculteit der Maatschappij- en Gedragswetenschappen, University of Amsterdam.

Asamoah-Gyadu, J. K. 2005. Listening with African ears. *International Review of Mission* 94 (374): 343–353.

Bloch, E. 1986. *The principle of hope*. Oxford: Blackwell.

Bredeloup, S. 2008. L'aventurier, une figure de la migration africaine. *Cahiers Internationaux de Sociologie* 125 (2): 281–206.

Casanova, J. 2001. Religion, the new millennium, and globalization. *Sociology of Religion* 62 (4): 415–441.

Chinese People's Political Consultative Conference. 2008. *Cong chuzuwu guanli rushou jiaqiang dui zai sui juliu waiguoren de guanli* (Strengthening the management of foreigners living in rented houses in Guangzhou). Online at: http://

www.gzzx.gov.cn/lunzheng/content.aspx?id=633391252806005078442, accessed 01 February 2010.

Coleman, S. 2006. When silence isn't golden: Charismatic speech and the limits of literalism. In *The limits of meaning: Case studies in the anthropology of Christianity*, eds. M. Engelke and M. Tomlinson, 39–62. New York: Berghahn.

Ferdblack. 2009. Let our heart be strong. In *Obi si Anyi Ike by Chidubem Ferdinand Black*. Guangzhou: Self-published.

Garbin, D. 2010. Symbolic geographies of the sacred: Diasporic territorialization and charismatic power in a transnational Congolese Prophetic Church. In *Travelling spirits: Migrants, markets and mobilities*, eds. G. Hüwelmeier and K. Krause, 145–164. New York: Routledge.

Garbin, D. 2013. The visibility and invisibility of migrant faith in the city: Diaspora religion and the politics of emplacement of Afro-Christian churches. *Journal of Ethnic and Migration Studies* 39 (5): 677–696.

Guangzhou People's Court Reports. 2012. 2008–2011 年广州市外籍人员走私毒品案件情况调研报告 (2008–2011 Guangzhou expatriates' drug-smuggling cases: Investigation report). Online at: http://www.dsb.gov.cn/News/zazhi/lilun/201207/20120711153121_16592.html, accessed 02 July 2014.

Guyer, J. I. 2007. Prophecy and the near future: Thoughts on macroeconomic, evangelical, and punctuated time. *American Ethnologist* 34 (3): 409–421.

Hagan, J., and H. R. Ebaugh. 2003. Calling upon the sacred: Migrants' use of religion in the migration process. *International Migration Review* 37 (4): 1145–1162.

Haugen, H. Ø. 2012. Nigerians in China: A second state of immobility. *International Migration*, 50 (2): 65–80.

Haugen, H. Ø. 2013. African Pentecostal migrants in China: Marginalization and the alternative geography of a mission theology. *African Studies Review* 56 (1): 81–102.

Haugen, H. Ø. 2015. Destination China: The country adjusts to its new migration reality. *Migration Information Source*, 4 March. Online at: http://www.migrationpolicy.org/article/destination-china-country-adjusts-its-new-migration-reality, accessed 15 June 2015.

Hunt, S., and N. Lightly. 2001. The British black Pentecostal 'revival': Identity and belief in the 'new' Nigerian churches. *Ethnic and Racial Studies* 24 (1): 104–124.

Knibbe, K. 2009. 'We did not come here as tenants, but as landlords': Nigerian Pentecostals and the power of maps. *African Diaspora* 2: 133–158.

Lefkowitz, M. 2014. Strike hard against immigration: China's new exit–entry law. *China Brief* 13 (23): 13–15.

Li, Z. 2012. 在穗外国人称清查"三非"不影响城市开放包容 (Foreigners in Guangzhou say that the investigation of illegals does not affect the city's openness and inclusiveness). CRI Online at: http://gb.cri.cn/27824/2012/05/25/2625s3700335.htm, accessed 02 July 2014.

Marshall, R. 2009. *Political spiritualities: The Pentecostal revolution in Nigeria*. Chicago: University of Chicago Press.

Mbembe, A. 2004. Essai sur le politique en tant que forme de la dépense. *Cahiers d'Etudes Africaines* 44 (1–2): 151–192.

Meagher, K. 2010. *Identity economics: Social networks and the informal economy in Nigeria*. Suffolk: James Currey.

Meyer, B. 1998. 'Make a complete break with the past'. Memory and post-colonial modernity in Ghanaian Pentecostalist discourse. *Journal of Religion in Africa* 28 (3): 316–349.

Meyer, B. 2004. Christianity in Africa: From African independent to Pentecostal-charismatic churches. *Annual Review of Anthropology* 33: 447–474.

Miller, D. E. and T. Yamamori. 2007. *Global Pentecostalism: The new face of Christian social activism*. Berkeley: University of California Press.

Ministry of Public Security. 2012. *Exit and entry administration law of the People's Republic of China*. Adopted at the 27th meeting of the Standing Committee of the Eleventh National People's Congress of the People's Republic of China. Accessed 30 January 2015.

Miyazaki, H. 2006. *The method of hope: Anthropology, philosophy, and Fijian knowledge*. Redwood City: Stanford University Press.

Moltmann, J. 1967. *Theology of hope: On the ground and the implications of a Christian eschatology*. London: SCM Press.

Pieke, F. N. 2012. Immigrant China. *Modern China* 38 (1): 40–77.

Piot, C. 2010. *Nostalgia for the future: West Africa after the Cold War*. Chicago: University of Chicago Press.

Redeemed Christian Church of God. 2015. The largest city of God on earth. Online at: https://trccg.org/rccg/redemption-camp-largest-city-of-god-on-earth/, accessed 20 February 2015.

Robbins, J. 2004. The globalization of Pentecostal and charismatic Christianity. *Annual Review of Anthropology* 33: 117–143.

RVC. 2015. Royal Victory Church International. Online at: http://www.royalvictory.org/, accessed 22 February 2015.

Smith, D. J. 2001. 'The arrow of God': Pentecostalism, inequality, and the supernatural in South-Eastern Nigeria. *Africa* 71 (4): 587–613.

van der Meulen, M. 2009. The continuing importance of the local. African churches and the search for worship space in Amsterdam. *African Diaspora* 2: 159–181.

van Dijk, R. A. 1997. From camp to encompassment: Discourses of transsubjectivity in the Ghanaian Pentecostal diaspora. *Journal of Religion in Africa* 27 (2): 135–159.

Yan, S. 2012. Nigerian's death sparks demo. *The Global Times*. Accessed 31 August 2012.

# 7 Hope and Uncertainty in Senegalese Migration to Spain
## Taking Chances on Emigration but not Upon Return

*María Hernández-Carretero*

During fieldwork in Spain in 2010–12, I asked Senegalese migrants to recount their initial decision to migrate to Europe and their thoughts about returning to Senegal. Their accounts revealed a striking contrast in attitudes to uncertainty and taking chances with regard to emigration and return. Most had felt optimistic that, by emigrating, they could improve their lives and assist their families, and seemingly accepting of, or with limited concern for, the uncertainties that migration might entail in terms of unknowns or unforeseeable eventualities (see Williams and Baláž 2012, 169). When they discussed return, by contrast, they generally did so with a more cautious, even hesitant, attitude. Although virtually all wished to settle back home eventually, they stressed the need to first achieve certain financial objectives—reaching a particular level of savings, building a house in Senegal, or investing there—to ensure their own and their families' prosperity after leaving Europe. They were wary of going back unprepared, lest they return to a situation of livelihood uncertainty, shattering their families' hopes for a better life, and losing face for not succeeding through migration. In recounting their initial decision to migrate, my interlocutors communicated a sense of positive anticipation and confidence, largely expressed with a language of opportunity, hope, chance, and fate. By contrast, when discussing return they stressed concerns about preparedness and the possibility of failure and shame.

In this chapter I argue that the contrast in migrants' attitudes to uncertainty upon emigration and return lies in hope's power to mediate uncertainty: uncertainty related to migratory transitions may be approached with positive anticipation and a proactive disposition or elicit apprehension, depending on whether the transition inspires hope. Uncertainty and hope are both inherently temporal, connecting an individual or group's present with the future (Anderson 2006; Bloch 1986; von Benda-Beckmann and von Benda-Beckmann 1994). The interplay between hope and uncertainty affects migrants' willingness to take chances, by which I mean to engage with the uncertain with a sense of positive anticipation. An undertaking that entails uncertainty may inspire optimism when it implies opening one's future to new opportunities instead of remaining in a foreseeable situation

DOI: 10.4324/9781315659916-7

of stagnation (see Di Nunzio 2015; Horst and Grabska 2015). Yet in the absence of hope for positive change, uncertainty may only elicit a sense of insecurity. Overall confident that they could reach a better future through migration, my informants may consequently have been willing to take steps that involved confronting unknowns or unpredictability on the path towards this goal. By contrast they were more reluctant to return to Senegal—a setting poorer in opportunities and where others would be awaiting their successful homecoming—before having the necessary resources and plan to ensure a sustained, improved situation there.

My interlocutors shared their reflections about return at a time when precariousness in living and working conditions was no longer only an enduring characteristic of the Senegalese context but was gradually becoming, as a result of the sudden economic crisis, a new feature of life in Spain. Henrik Vigh (2008) distinguishes between crisis as context and crisis as temporary abnormality and argues that, in situations of uncertainty, hope 'does not necessarily die out but [. . .] becomes temporally or spatially transposed and related to other places or times' (Vigh 2009, 105). Following Vigh, I argue that persistent livelihood uncertainty may result in hope being placed elsewhere, prompting spatial solutions (migrating), whereas uncertainties considered temporary—such as lacking a job, residency permits or a sudden financial crisis in Europe—may be confronted and endured with temporal solutions (waiting) as hope for improvement is placed in future times.

Senegalese migration to Spain provides a rich case for examining ideas of hope and uncertainty at different points of migration trajectories and under changing contextual circumstances. Many people in Senegal dream of emigrating (Carling *et al*. 2013) but, as was the case among most of my informants, Senegalese labor migrants in Europe generally channel home much of their foreign earnings and intend to eventually return to Senegal permanently (Riccio 2002; Sinatti 2011). Spain, as a destination country, has undergone important transformations in recent years. In the early 2000s its booming economy attracted many immigrants, including Senegalese, who quickly became the largest sub-Saharan African group (Bernardi *et al*. 2011; INE 2014). With the financial crisis and consequent soaring unemployment from 2008, many migrants faced dilemmas over whether or not to stay, return, or migrate onwards.

## Methodology

My chapter is based on empirical data collected during eight months of ethnographic fieldwork in Spain and Senegal between April 2010 and October 2012. I conducted interviews and semi-participant observation with Senegalese migrants in Spain and with returnees, visiting migrants and non-migrants in Senegal, but here focus on migrants' perspective. My informants were a heterogeneous group, with different backgrounds and ages, who had emigrated from the 1980s to the 2000s through different channels, entailing a range of journey-related uncertainties. Most of them were men, although I interacted with both male and female migrants during fieldwork in Spain. Men have historically taken the lead in emigrating and represent the majority of the Senegalese population in Spain (INE 2014). The number of women is increasing steadily, but they were less accessible and more reluctant than men to be interviewed.

I used Spanish, French, and Wolof to communicate with my informants, and write in English. This entails several layers of translation and adaptation of vernacular terms. Informants used terms signifying luck, chance, progress, patience, suffering, endurance, success or hope, which sometimes bear different meanings across languages. *Chance* in French refers to both 'luck' and 'chance'. In addition to adopting these terms in their vernacular sense, I also use some of them in a broader, analytical sense, as with the expression 'taking chances', as I explain below. The contextualization provided by semi-structured, qualitative interviews and ethnographic fieldwork is essential to this process of analytical interpretation.

I use 'uncertainty' as a purely analytical term denoting unforeseeability, in relation both to general livelihood conditions and to the migration process. My understanding of the term is closely aligned with Marco Di Nunzio's definition (2015, 152–153):

> Uncertainty expresses the unpredictability and indeterminacy of what is going to be next, both immediately and in the long term. Living through uncertainty thus implies living in a state of contingency, that is, being dependent on courses of actions and events we cannot predict or know.

I write about uncertainty, on the one hand, referring to conditions of livelihood instability, precariousness, or stagnation that migrants had either experienced before emigration (contributing to their desire to emigrate) or feared encountering upon an unprepared return. The unpredictability and instability caused by such conditions affects individuals' ability to foresee how their life might develop—including whether or not they will be able to establish and adequately provide for a family—and to respond to contingencies.

I also refer to uncertainty in relation to the unknowns and unpredictable elements which my informants faced in relation to emigration. Williams and Baláž (2012, 168) write that, in the migration context, uncertainty arises from 'imperfect knowledge' and 'the unpredictability of the future' (see also Horst and Grabska 2015). Yet the fact that migrants had limited information or could not know exactly what they would encounter does not mean that they emigrated with a sense of uncertainty about migration *overall*. In fact they expressed a sense of determinacy, or *certainty*, about what they expected from Senegal and Europe, and were convinced that (or willing to find out whether) migrating to Europe would bring them greater prosperity than staying. I argue that it is from this positive confidence in—or hope on—the expected end result of migration that they garnered the determination to confront any intervening uncertainties: unknowns and unforeseeable elements along the path to their envisioned goal. Uncertainty thus exists at two different but related temporal horizons or scales: emigrating may entail engaging with uncertainty in the short term, with the expectation that this will eventually allow one to reach a more stable state of socioeconomic certainty.

I use the expression 'taking chances' to conceptualize what I interpret as migrants' proactive engagement with uncertainty, or their willingness to confront situations entailing unknowns and unpredictability out of a positive anticipation that a favorable outcome will probably result. The phrase 'taking chances' resonates with and encompasses the range of vernacular expressions which migrants used (such as intentar or *probar* in Spanish and *tenter* or *tenter sa chance* in French, or leaving *à l'aventure*) that all translate into trying something and venturing into the unknown. I interpret migrants' willingness to take chances (or not) as depending on their having a hopeful disposition in the face of uncertainty. Hope, which was also a vernacular term, here analytically conveys a positive, anticipatory disposition towards a better future condition (cf. Bloch 1986) with which my informants approached emigration.

## The Spatial Distribution of Hope and Uncertainty

Migration aspirations reflect how individuals unevenly allocate hope across settings: hopelessness regarding imagined futures at home is often expressed in contrast to the hope that migration will broaden one's range of possible futures (Mains 2012). 'I decided to come [to Spain] because over there, in Senegal, I no longer had any . . . hope, I had no more hope, so I told myself I had to leave, to go looking for a better life'. Like Babacar,[1] other informants expressed their original desire to migrate to Europe in terms of a differential assignation of hope for the future in Senegal and abroad. Pape more generally communicated a sense of stagnation at home that he expected to overcome by migrating:

> There was no work [in Senegal]. The good jobs, in the country, it's like an inheritance: I'm a minister, I hire my relatives. I run a company, I hire my relatives [. . .] or acquaintances, or someone who's recommended. But they don't hire qualified people . . . that's Africa. [. . .] There was no transparency. That's the problem! And me, who doesn't have a relative who is a minister, or who runs a company, I cannot access [those jobs]! And I don't want to stay . . . like that, living in poverty till I die! No. I had to do everything, everything, everything to go find another place.

Pape's frustration illustrates that of many others who highlighted the limitations imposed by structural circumstances in Senegal: scarce and badly remunerated employment, nepotism, high living costs, and extensive financial responsibilities towards family and friends. These combined factors generate a condition of socioeconomic uncertainty in which young people, especially men, are unable to transition to socially respected adulthood by gaining financial independence, establishing and providing for their own families, and assisting others (Buggenhagen 2012; Hernández-Carretero and Carling 2012; Melly 2011; Ralph 2008). This is common to youth elsewhere in Africa (e.g., Christiansen *et al*. 2006; Cole 2008; Hansen 2005; Honwana 2012; Masquelier 2013).

In contrast to the sense of stagnation many felt at home, migration offered a way to reach a more *enabling* environment, offering greater opportunities for progress and the possibility to reclaim control of one's future rather than resigning oneself to socioeconomic stagnation at home. Other young people around the world similarly yearn for a more promising future elsewhere (Bal 2014; Horváth 2008; Jeffrey 2010; Masquelier 2013). Imagining a better future attainable through migration is a way to reorient hope spatially instead of giving it up entirely (Vigh 2009). Migration may be seen as a solution to feelings of existential immobility: 'It is when people feel that they are existentially "going too slowly" or "going nowhere"', Ghassan Hage (2005, 471) argues, 'that they begin contemplating the necessity of physically "going somewhere"'. Migration is thus 'an inability or an unwillingness to endure and "wait out" a crisis of existential mobility' (Hage 2009a, 98). Where waiting does not resolve existential immobility, migration—by widening the range of possibilities for progress—offers a spatial fix to a temporal problem (Mains 2012, 135).

My informants' expectations that migration could accelerate socioeconomic progress largely developed from witnessing previous migrants' accomplishments (see also Fouquet 2007). Seeing others who, as several noted, were no more qualified than themselves improve their living standard in Senegal—building houses, buying cars, running businesses—and their ability to care for their families by working abroad convinced them that they could achieve the same. 'I thought that, if I myself managed to come to Europe, I could be like them', Modou said, recalling how he used to think of migrants as wealthy before he himself emigrated. 'I'd been working for years, and still hadn't managed to have my own house—I lived in my family's house, my father's house'. Relatives also sometimes encourage young men to migrate. Alpha recounted how, concerned about the possibility of an unsuccessful migration, he had initially hesitated to agree to his brother's idea to finance his emigration with family funds but eventually accepted, wary of being seen as not wanting to 'progress' if he turned down an offer intended to help improve his prospects.

## Confronting Uncertainty through Hope and Chance

Seeking a prosperous future, many Senegalese migrants left knowing little about how they would make a living abroad, what administrative hurdles they might encounter, or how they would ensure a sustainable return, even though virtually all intended to settle back in Senegal eventually. Confronting a degree of uncertainty need not be discouraging, however, if one is hopeful that the path chosen will bring positive results. 'Hopefulness', Hage (2003, 24) writes, 'is above all a disposition to be confident in the face of the future, to be open to it and welcoming to what it will bring, even if one does not know for sure what it will bring'. My informants did not indicate that they had been overly concerned or frustrated by imperfect information and unpredictability prior to emigration. This may have been due to the hopefulness with which they approached migration, encouraged by the prospect of emulating previous migrants' achievements and leaving stagnation behind.

Hope for positive change may be a motivating force with which to confront uncertainty by taking risks to overcome a condition of vulnerability (Hayenhjelm 2006), or by persevering in situations of uncertainty where imagined futures seem elusive (Pedersen 2012). '[Reimagining] the present from the perspective of the end', Hirokazu Miyazaki (2006, 157) suggests, allows hope for the future to shape actions in the present. Drawing on Miyazaki, Morten Pedersen (2012, 146, 148) argues that perseverance in the face of apparently unrealistic prospects can result from 'the work of hope', which prevents an individual from becoming 'imprisoned by the present' and succumbing to fatalism or 'passive resignation.' Similarly, Senegalese migrants may have confronted migration-related uncertainties driven by hope, 'leaping', like Pedersen's (2012, 144) informants, into futures they could not picture in detail—for they remained unknown—but which they did not for that reason consider any less promising. This resonates with Di Nunzio's (2015, 153) argument that individuals may regard uncertainty or 'the unforeseeability of existence' in a positive light when they see it as offering the possibility for change with respect to the present, and therefore bearing the potential to inspire action and hope.

In understanding migrants' willingness to confront intervening uncertainties in order to prosper through migration, we should also take into account that, before emigrating, most were mainly concerned with leaving stagnation behind and succeeding in entering Europe. Limited avenues for legal migration and tighter migration controls since the early 1990s have increased the difficulty and cost of entering Europe (Suárez-Navaz 2005), so for most Africans, the main perceived hurdle to succeeding through migration is leaving in the first place. Those who cannot afford safer means sometimes expose themselves to the risks of unauthorized border crossings (Hernández-Carretero and Carling 2012; Spijkerboer 2007).

Once abroad, my informants were confident that they could easily make a living, both because they believed that they were headed to a place with plentiful job opportunities and because they counted on being helped by fellow-migrants. Alpha explained that, although he left Senegal without specific ideas of what he would find abroad or the kind of work other Senegalese did, knowing that he would meet someone he knew was what reassured him the most: 'I wasn't leaving just like that . . . into the unknown'. Migrants' expectation of receiving solidarity and guidance from friends, relatives, fellow Senegalese, and religious brotherhoods abroad thus mitigates concerns about beginning anew in Europe (cf. Babou 2002; Castles and Miller 2009, 29; Diouf 2000; Massey *et al.* 1998, 43).

## Cultivating Fortune by Taking Chances

Through a language of chance, luck, or fortune, migrants expressed a positive engagement with uncertainty before and during migration. Some had barely contemplated the possibility of not succeeding through migration; others had been tentatively hopeful, regarding migration as an opportunity worth pursuing but counting on being able to resume their lives in Senegal if disappointed. Some, like Alassane, had left a job to which they expected that they could return. He recalls saying to himself: 'If, in a year from now, I have not found something certain, I'll have to go back, take up my job again'. Expectations of an unproblematic return might have made these migrants feel that they had nothing to lose by exploring opportunities abroad, encouraging acceptance of migration-related uncertainties. This 'try and see' attitude suggests an engagement with uncertainty through chance. 'In life, if you don't take chances, you will have nothing', Babacar explained:

> You have to try your luck. It's like a poker game: you win or you lose. If you lose, at least you know you played. It's like a football match. You can play well and lose. But at least, you'll feel proud that you tried. At least you tried something in your life.

Through these sentences Babacar expressed the idea, not unique to him, that trying one's luck or taking chances was intrinsic to any entrepreneurial undertaking and necessary for progress. This attitude reflects a positive, proactive orientation towards engaging with outcomes that cannot be entirely predicted and connects uncertainty with the possibility of success (cf. Hernández-Carretero and Carling 2012).

It has been suggested that the connection between migration, taking chances, and seeking progress relates to a broader trend towards individualization in Senegal. There, Caroline Melly (2011, 368) claims that 'migration is increasingly imagined as an individualized activity, as a matter of chance or luck, and as involving a personal engagement with risk'. This framing of migration in terms of individual entrepreneurship and investment has evolved, she argues, with the rise of a national neoliberal orientation. Relatedly, Havard (2001) argues that today's Senegalese youth express their desire for emancipation through the individualizing ethos of the '*bul faale*',[2] which places personal effort and work at the center of personal success. Individual aspirations for socioeconomic success are not, however, divorced from social expectations and encouragement which, as I discuss below, reflect the collective dimension of migration hopes. Migrants' desire to prosper is, moreover, intrinsically connected to their wish to fulfil interpersonal obligations and gain a socially respected position (Blanchard 2011; Hernández-Carretero 2015).

Informants' references to luck and opportunity shared a sense that luck had to be chased and mobilized. Biram explained that luck cannot be allowed to pass by—it must be seized. Referring to 'chance' as opportunity, Fadel indicated that opportunities must be sought, insisting that one had to be willing to be geographically mobile to find them: 'You can't stay arms crossed, thinking "It will work out, it will work out"—until when? You have to move! If you move, you'll find chances!' These assertions suggest a view that luck and opportunity need to be actively cultivated, not waited for. Fortune is to be attained through the 'bold deployment' of luck, requiring an 'active will, a display of bravery, an act of subjective determination' (da Col and Humphrey 2012, 4).

Relying on luck allows an optimistic interpretation of uncertainty as offering the possibility of positive outcomes. This might explain migrants' readiness to confront uncertainty in order to prosper through migration. Asked about his constant references to luck, Biram said 'I trust luck *a lot*. If I didn't trust it, I wouldn't have come here'. Others, too, insisted on their positive outlook before emigrating, suggesting that they would not have left if they had been overly concerned with the possibility of failure.

While insisting on the need to cultivate fortune by making moves that entailed confronting uncertainty, migrants also expected that their fate would ultimately be determined by a greater agency (cf. Hamayon 2012). Through locutions like 'Everyone has their luck', or 'If it is your luck that . . .' they suggested that the outcome of their attempts to progress depended on the fate assigned to them by God. Asked what would happen if, after investing in migration, he failed to reap the desired returns, Abdou matter-of-factly said:

> If it doesn't go well, it doesn't go well. It's a question of trying. [. . .] Whether it ends well or badly depends on . . . it depends on God. My things . . . a lot of my things, I put in the hands of God. I do what I have to do, but I can't know how it will turn out. What will happen, I leave in the hands of God. If God helps you be lucky and recover your money, good. If not, tough luck. [. . .] No problem, you go back to work [in Senegal] again!

Attributing one's ultimate fate to the work of a greater agency need not result in passivity: migrants tried their luck while accepting that the outcome was ultimately determined by divine will. Subjugation to the fate allotted by God provides an explanation of causality and may help in coping with unfavorable outcomes (see Hamayon 2012; Horst 2006; von Benda-Beckmann and von Benda-Beckmann 1994).

## Uncertainty and the Unexpected Difficulty of Return

The boldness with which informants appeared to have approached emigration gave way to a more cautious attitude when they spoke about returning. Most expressed concern over facing uncertainty upon return, including those who had originally thought that they would simply go back if disappointed abroad. Having migrated to improve their livelihoods, migrants were now wary of returning precipitately, without a job or the resources and strategy to subsist and invest. Alpha emphasized the importance of readiness:

> If I had the means, I would return to Senegal tomorrow. *Forever*. [But] I don't have . . . enough money to return to Senegal and invest there in order to stay definitely. [. . .] I could go back, and with the connections I have in my family, start working there. [. . .] I want to return, but . . . I don't want to *rush* it. I don't want to *rush* my return. I will go back, but, maybe in . . . I don't know.
>
> *What do you mean by 'rushing the return'?*
>
> Going back home . . . just like that. From one day to the next, taking my luggage and going back to Senegal without . . . without thinking about it, without preparing, without . . . without anything.

Alpha's quandary illustrates the distinction between *willingness* and *readiness* in migrant preparedness to return (Cassarino 2004). Among Senegalese migrants, expectations of returning successfully are very often tied to the motivations behind seeking one's fortune abroad (Sinatti 2011). The return that migrants work towards and that their relations expect is thus a return *ahead*, to an improved socioeconomic position, so the stakes are high for migrants to return displaying—and partly redistributing—the fruits of a successful time abroad. Despite the generalized wish to return eventually, hardly any informants felt that they had accumulated enough resources to live off or to run a business in Senegal. Rather than expressing a willingness to take chances *vis-à-vis* the uncertainties which a precipitate return would entail, most therefore spoke of the need to plan ahead and avoid a failed return ending in shame and ostracism.

The Spanish financial crisis has affected many migrants' employment, financial and administrative situation, and considerations of return. Unemployment, reduced salaries, higher costs of living, and assistance to fellow-migrants in a worse situation slows down migrants' capacity for accumulation and investment, which also delays their plans to return. Any uncertainty surrounding premature return is compounded if it implies relinquishing access to employment in Europe, as with those who do not yet have residence and work permits abroad and who would be unable to re-enter Europe if they traveled back to Senegal, or who could not meet the requirements for renewing a temporary permit if they left for an extended period. Greater unemployment as a result of the crisis has also increased migrants' vulnerability to remaining in or lapsing back into irregularity, since renewing temporary work permits or accessing regularization requires, respectively, staying employed or having an employment offer (Bruquetas-Callejo et al. 2011).

Nevertheless, some migrants accelerated their return plans as a consequence of the crisis, especially if they had enough financial security or a permanent permit abroad, both of which reduce the uncertainty associated with an early return. Savings, investments, a house or a source of income such as a family business in Senegal ensure the family's subsistence after the migrant's return. With a long-term permit or Spanish nationality, migrants can more easily make a tentative return to assess the viability of settling back in Senegal, permanently or temporarily, as they are still able to re-enter Europe. Indeed Sinatti (2011, 161) describes how Senegalese migrants in Italy, wary of others' failed return attempts, 'play it safe', returning only after obtaining permanent residency abroad and maintaining overseas connections that facilitate commercial activities after returning.

## The Affordability of Taking Chances

Seeing emigration and return as stages in the same project of socioeconomic prosperity rather than distinct processes helps to understand migrants' contrasting attitudes to uncertainty. Confronting uncertainty and the possibility of failure entails different consequences at each stage. Taking chances may seem necessary and justifiable when emigrating, but make less sense upon return which—even if not permanent—closes the cycle initiated by emigration. At that point, migrants are expected to show the success reaped through the migratory project and ensure their family's continued subsistence. It is thus not despite, but precisely *because of*, the chances taken on emigrating that return is not considered the right time to confront further uncertainty. 'I don't think many will risk going back of their own choice', said Lat, and explained:

> [We] have taken risks in coming here, because we didn't come with a job offer in hand. We went into the unknown,[3] so that's taking risks. We didn't know what we would find here. And when you return to Senegal, too, you don't know what you will find there. Because, if it's the same situation as you left behind . . . it could be worse than here.

An unsuccessful return could result from going back empty-handed or mismanaging one's assets and losing the gains made through migration. This could entail regressing to one's pre-migration situation, going 'back to zero', which could mean livelihood uncertainty—with the added shame of not having achieved something better through migration. Asked whether he might give up and return to Senegal after struggling in Spain for several years, largely without work and unable to accumulate any money, Pape strongly rejected that scenario:

> Noooo . . . I know that, it would be a failure for me! It's a failure! I have nothing! I have nothing, four years . . . outside of Senegal! Four years outside of Senegal, and you go back, to *zero*!? No, not that! [. . .] And when I return, if the people I meet there do not guide me . . . I won't know where to go. Because, after four years, I'm disconnected from Senegal! I don't know what's going on there! [. . .] But coming there with some money . . . I'll have the confidence that, even if disconnected, I can . . . get by with the little I have. But, arriving there, disconnected, and with zero euros? No way.

Earning a living as an immigrant abroad can be easier than as a returnee at home, because migrants are generally flexible in accepting jobs abroad but face limited opportunities back in Senegal. Most intend to become self-employed after return, so insisted on the extensive capital needed for investment. Comparing migration to a well, Abdou claimed: 'If you have no money to invest in your country, then what? You don't get out of the well'. He assured me that it is virtually impossible to uphold the standard of living attained through migration by other means than developing one's own business, as returning migrants from rural areas would no longer be physically capable of working in agriculture, and salaried jobs in industry or construction are scarce. Older returning migrants would, besides, probably have difficulty competing with the numerous unemployed youths in the Senegalese labor market.

Those who were living in a precarious situation in Spain felt strongly that they could *not* afford to take chances in relation to return. Babacar, without money to establish a business in Senegal or any certainty of finding a job there, explained:

> Even though you didn't find what you were looking for here, you can't go back just like that! [If you do], what are you going to do with your life, then? [. . .] Going back now without certainty [*wóorul*]. And you're at an age when you no longer have the right to make mistakes. You shouldn't make mistakes. Do you understand? Since you made a mistake by coming here, don't make a mistake in your return!

Babacar, who had been willing to take chances on emigrating, highlights both the notion that taking chances on emigration and return are connected, and that doing so is justifiable at certain life stages—e.g., youth—but less so when one is expected to show results. His words also illustrate how migrants who had achieved little abroad would generally avoid returning empty-handed, with nothing to show for their time abroad or to sustain themselves.

## Interpersonal Aspects of Hope and Uncertainty

In Senegal, hope in the power of migration to bring about socioeconomic progress is borne collectively: young men are often encouraged to migrate by others who already have or by relatives who expect to benefit from their successful migration. The weight of interpersonal responsibilities to and expectations from non-migrants in Senegal also influences migrants' experience of hope and uncertainty in relation to return which, if unsuccessful, would affect not only migrants' wealth, status, and reputation but also their dependents' livelihoods and hopes.

Migrants may therefore experience the return decision as not being theirs alone. Relatives may voice reservations about what the migrant's return may mean for them, as Lat illustrated: 'I was talking with my wife [. . .] and I said "This country [Spain] is not looking good. I think it's time to go back home". You know what she said? "Yes . . . that's OK. But as far as we're concerned, we don't envy the wives of those who return"'. Lat explained that his wife's wariness stemmed from having seen that others gradually lost their wealth after returning. Concern about maintaining the living standard achieved through migration can create pressure to not break the migration cycle. Adama explained that it is difficult to go back 'because when you have [migrated], you place the standard very high. So, if you return to your country, you have to bring the standard back down. [. . .] in order to maintain the standard, you need to stay abroad'. Sinatti (2011, 163) has similarly observed Senegalese in Italy who feel 'trapped in migration' because of their interpersonal responsibilities.

A migrant's unsuccessful return affects not only others' livelihoods but also their hopes: migrants become repositories of hope for relatives and friends who count on them to improve their situation or assist them when they become wealthy. Hope for the future helps relatives to cope with hardship in the present, for instance, when a migrant is abroad but not yet able to adequately provide for them. As Pape explained, families support migrants and sometimes rely on solidarity networks, encouraged by the conviction that their hardship is temporary:

> What I was looking for, right now . . . there is none of it: work. There is no work. But . . . Africa is always difficult. Here, it's difficult, I know. But Africa is always difficult. Because over there, your family is there, you're seen, you're surrounded by ten people . . . and they see you, and you have nothing to give them. [*He pauses, then chuckles*] But when you're here, *they* don't see you. But you can talk to them and relieve them. Give them hope. For . . . yes, give them hope to wait . . . that one day things will be good. And *they* can feed on that hope.

Pape's suggestion that his family can 'feed on the hope' for a better tomorrow highlights the relationship between hope and coping, and the significance of the interpersonal dimensions of hope and uncertainty to migrants' decisions.

Shattering others' hopes and generally failing to succeed through migration carries implications for the migrant's social status and authority (see also Cole 2014). Hope embedded in social networks connects individuals who expect to extract favors or profits one day (Pedersen 2012). Failing to live up to others' expectations results in them ceasing to believe in the individual's capacity as a provider and benefactor. For young men who had migrated to Europe to escape the shame of being unable to fulfil gender- and age-specific roles and to rectify this situation, failing through migration represents an additional discredit. 'The fact alone of leaving is already in itself a solution to worry, shame, distress and disarray', writes Mamadou Mbodji (2008, 310). Migration provides not only a path to restoring one's dignity, but also a way to preserve it by shielding one's shortcomings. Abroad, migrants are alone with their financial troubles whereas, in Senegal, they are exposed to the critical gaze of others.

The social repercussions of failing to meet expectations of a successful time abroad create a strong motivation for avoiding an unsuccessful return. Migrants fear being confronted with the discredit and shame of being unable to provide for their families and regarded as having failed to succeed through migration. Returning empty-handed therefore requires exceptional emotional strength and courage, as Alpha explained:

> Since it's going into the unknown [*à l'aventure*], it means . . . you go exploring. You don't have to stay. If you go, and you find something that can keep you there, you stay, otherwise . . . if you're brave, you make the decision to return to Senegal. Because it's very difficult to *leave* Senegal, and then return. That, that's a very touchy question in Senegal. From the moment you leave Senegal to come to Europe, those who are in Senegal say 'Ah! Alpha is gone'. Well, they start counting the years. 'He's been there two years, three years, four years. Ah! He must have money, eh? Certainly when he returns, he will . . .' With these hopes that people place in you, you don't dare return to Senegal without succeeding. It's embarrassing! To leave, emigrate, and return without succeeding. That's why . . . there are people here who've spent . . . more than ten years without returning to Senegal, because they have failed. And they're ashamed of returning home.

Shame results from moralizing judgments that hold the individual migrant personally responsible for not achieving success, allegedly as a result of having been undisciplined, lazy, or wasteful while in Europe. This stands in stark contrast to migrants' reliance on luck and fate upon migration, which implies a belief that causality is partly beyond individual control and, therefore, responsibility (see Giddens 1999). Research in other settings has also found migrants feeling shame and distress at failing to achieve the success expected from migration and consequently losing touch with their home communities or avoiding return (Dünnwald 2010; Kleist 2017; Mapril 2011). Several of my informants explained that they would rather stay in a difficult situation in Spain and suffer away from their relatives and acquaintances than endure hardship amongst them, unable to help them or themselves.

## Stuck in Europe

Most migrants indicated that it was only when they were abroad that they became fully aware of the hardships of migrant life and the obstacles to accumulating the wealth necessary for a successful return. Several even described migration as a kind of entrapment: a 'hole', a 'well', an 'addiction', a cycle easier to enter than to exit. Having emigrated to break out of socioeconomic stagnation in Senegal, they now felt trapped by a new set of factors. Entrapment metaphors often arose as migrants told how they tried to explain to others back home why they persevere abroad despite unfavorable conditions. 'Migration is so tempting', Lat explained,

> But once [someone] leaves, and sees, for example, that over there it isn't paradise either, that it isn't El Dorado, once he sees the difficulties that exist, *then* he begins to say 'Ah, if only I could go back'. But by that point you can't! And, why can't you? Because, it's very simple: there's a social sanction. [. . .] What's the social sanction? It's that so-and-so has left, and he has achieved this. [*He pauses*]. You tell yourself, '*I* too, am going to leave to achieve it'. So once here [in Spain], on the ground, you have to struggle to achieve this. [. . .] Then when you fail, when things don't work out . . . people over there [in Senegal], they're going to think, why, why haven't *you* put in all the courage necessary to achieve it? *That* is the social sanction.

Migrants' metaphors of entrapment encapsulated a sense of both socioeconomic and spatial immobility. Many felt unable to progress at their desired pace and blamed factors beyond their control: migration regulations, financial responsibilities to and expectations from others in Senegal, or macroeconomic conditions in Spain—all of which affected their capacity to earn and save for their return. Although they may not have envisaged a specific duration to their migration, many said it had already been longer than they had imagined: 'Before we know it, we're going to retire here!' Lat exclaimed, only half-jokingly. Those without residence permits experienced additional dimensions of entrapment: their financial and social mobility was constrained by their limited capacity to seek work in Spain or elsewhere in Europe, earn some money, and travel to Senegal to start or add to a family.

## Waiting and Patience

The unexpected onset of the financial crisis compounded many migrants' sense of entrapment. Some reacted by initiating or exploring the return process and others considered moving onward. Most, however, stayed in Spain, either believing in a future recovery or having scant hopes of better prospects elsewhere. The impossibility of re-entering Europe for those without residence permits or the financial and social implications of returning unsuccessfully complicate the decision to return, even if staying brings little apparent benefit. Those who stayed out of hope were waiting for positive change. Waiting 'may be considered both as a gap and as a link between the present and the future' (Gasparini 1995, 30). It is also 'a consciousness of time embodied, of time endured' (Schweizer 2005, 782).

Migrants' waiting reflects a specific, comparative articulation of the temporal, spatial, and interpersonal dimensions of hope in relation to different settings. It can be interpreted as passive or active (Brun 2015). As indicated by their metaphors of entrapment, migrants often spoke of waiting or plans delayed, expressing frustration at their immobility or inability to control their own progress. This is reminiscent of settings where individuals are described as burdened with an overabundance of time, resorting to 'timepass', 'killing time' or 'sitting' as they wait to be able to migrate or otherwise emerge from stagnation (Jeffrey 2010; Mains 2012; Melly 2011; Ralph 2008). In general, however, migrants did not present themselves as idly waiting for better times to come. Although they acknowledged the force of structural circumstances beyond their control, they strove to make the best of their situation, struggling daily to make a living while hoping for macroeconomic stability to be restored.

Those who were hopeful that circumstances would again improve found, in this, the motivation to endure difficult conditions in the present. When talking about waiting for the time when the crisis would end or their goals would be accomplished, they recurrently used the Spanish locution *aguantar* (to hold on, endure) and the Wolof *muñ* (to exercise patience, endure). One migrant explained that many told themselves that, even though things were difficult, they would eventually improve and, being already abroad, it was better to stay and see the better times return. 'They simply live on hope', he concluded. This sentence parallels the notion, introduced earlier, that a migrant's relatives back home could 'feed on the hope' that he would one day improve their situation. Together, they illustrate how hope may help to endure hardship in anticipation of better times to come.

In explaining that one could not and should not 'rush one's luck', some presented patience as a requirement of fortune, suggesting that, although luck may be cultivated, it will come in its own time. Patience can therefore be seen as a form of actively nurturing hope—rather than giving up—while simultaneously submitting to luck's own temporality. As Crapanzano (2003, 6) writes, hope depends not only on the individual's desires but also on 'some other agency—a god, fate, chance, an other—for its fulfilment', and therefore requires 'expectation, constraint, and resignation'. Using expressions like 'before the good times must come hard times', 'bad times are followed by good times', or referring to the cyclical nature of droughts and abundance described in holy scriptures, migrants regularly indicated that hardship and fortune were interrelated and neither was everlasting. Their determination to endure hardships was nourished by the expectation that conditions would change.

My informants furthermore described patience as a virtue related to the cultivation and display of faith, closely connected with faith in God's intervention in bringing about a better future (see Gasparini 1995, 37). Some spoke of enduring hardship as a test of faith, or part of their God-given destiny. 'God is with those who are patient. If you hold on, God will reward you', Babacar assured me. Reflecting on his difficult situation in Spain, he confidently explained: 'If God loves you, you will struggle. The way I see it, God loves me. That's why I'm having a hard time, because God loves me. But the hardship is only temporary'. Patience thus implies submitting one's fate to divine will, and carries the expectation of an eventual divine reward for faith and endurance. Fortune is cultivated through the patient endurance of everyday struggle.

Many also stressed the connection between endurance and masculinity, explaining that men were expected to endure hardships that would be unbearable for women. Several admitted that they feared they would be perceived as cowardly if they returned empty-handed, running away from hardship instead of confronting it stoically. Whereas returning in such conditions requires considerable psychological strength, staying on does, too: someone who is not mentally strong might just give up and leave the hardships brought on by the crisis behind, one veteran migrant affirmed.

Migrants' hopeful waiting may be viewed as active engagement with their circumstances, involving a state of anticipation *and* the exercise of patience (see Lakha 2009, 122). Refusing to give up, migrants' display of endurance in times of hardship conveys hope and agency in a challenging situation of uncertainty (see Hage 2009b). They were not merely waiting: they were *expecting* a particular event or transition. As Gasparini (1995, 31) argues, the difference between 'merely waiting' and expecting 'that an event will take place at a given time [. . .] is represented by the state of anticipation implied in the latter which, to a certain extent, gives an actor control over the situation'. Although migrants could not know exactly when things would change, they were confident that they eventually would. Whereas they regarded crisis in Senegal in the sense of livelihood insecurity as a permanent condition, they saw the crisis in Spain as a 'temporary abnormality', a rupture with the regular state of affairs that would end someday (Vigh 2008, 6, 7). It is this distinction in the perception of crisis that gave migrants hope for the future in Spain, and encouraged them to wait for that change. Theirs was a particular form of waiting, the kind of 'waiting out' that entails waiting not for something to happen but, rather, for something undesirable to end (Hage 2009a, 102). This kind of waiting, Hage argues, entails an ambivalent passivity that involves simultaneously subjecting oneself to, and braving, the conditions one is waiting out.

Patience is thus not only different from idle waiting, but the opposite of giving up—a demonstration of agency and tenacity under uncertainty. As Hage (2009a, 101) notes, the idea of endurance implies 'asserting some agency over the very fact that one has no agency by not succumbing and becoming a mere victim'. Discussing agency with respect to waiting, Peter Dwyer (2009, 23) makes an important distinction between the availability of 'options for choice' and the 'capacity to choose'. Under difficult conditions, migrants may have little room for choosing between giving up and enduring, and may even come to question the hope that motivates their patience:

> When I thought of coming to Spain, I thought I'd get a good job—I don't have one. I thought I'd obtain residency—I don't have it. Still. Three or four years pass. I always keep on hoping. I always keep on hoping. Well, why don't I go back now? I always think that, alright, by the end of this or that year, I might have my residency, and I can go back. [. . .] The worst part of being a foreigner is this: you always keep on hoping for a time in the future. *That's the worst part*. [He pauses] I am young, but every day I've lost a day, every week I've lost a week, every month I've lost a month. Every year . . . I've lost a year. And always, it's the fault of being hopeful.

Blaming hope for his investing time in waiting for a better future that may never come, Mbaye points to the motivating power of hope and to the fact that, as Gasparini (1995, 31) notes, waiting does not imply certainty: 'Waiting is at the crossroads not only of the present and future, but also of certainty and uncertainty. One can wait for an event, the occurrence of which is either certain (although not always determined in time) or completely uncertain'.

## Conclusion: Uncertainty, Hope and Taking Chances

Hope, I have shown, mediates uncertainty: individuals may be willing to confront uncertainty and take chances when hopeful that this will yield positive change, but may prefer to minimize uncertainty in the absence of hope. This can explain migrants' contrasting attitudes to uncertainty and taking chances with respect to emigration and return—with many willing to accept some uncertainty when seeking fortune through migration, but preferring to delay return until they feel ready to undertake it successfully. The interaction between hope and uncertainty in relation to migration produces different temporal and spatial responses: moving, when hope is placed elsewhere; staying or waiting, when it is placed in a future time. Patience, in the face of crisis and hardship, emerges as a response to uncertainty when taking chances seems unaffordable: it represents an active, brave engagement with uncertainty and hope based on the expectation that better times will arrive.

Personal circumstances, contextual factors, and interpersonal dynamics shape the interplay between hope and uncertainty in migration trajectories. Macroeconomic, political, and social conditions in different geographic locations may inspire hope for the possibility of socioeconomic progress—or instill a sense of unavoidable stagnation. Hope and the availability of perceived alternatives affect one's sense of affordability with respect to taking chances. Individuals may feel they cannot afford to stay put in a situation of livelihood stagnation without taking action to alter their circumstances, or feel comfortable taking chances because they have alternative options in case of failure. Financial and social resources, access to international mobility, and one's stage in the migration and life cycles—with differing responsibilities and expectations from others—affect possibilities for reversing one's actions, the expected costs of failure, the ability to handle contingencies, and consequently whether individuals feel they can afford to take chances—or to not take them (cf. Hernández-Carretero and Carling 2012).

Individuals might feel more hopeful about trying their luck in settings that they perceive as enabling—relative to others where they feel constrained in their possibilities to progress. In migrating to Europe, migrants felt confident in the likelihood of succeeding and left the final outcome in the hands of fate. When considering return to Senegal, associated with limited opportunities and livelihood uncertainty, they were less willing to take chances, stressing the importance of a well-prepared return. The context of financial crisis in Spain highlighted the salience of the sense of affordability with respect to engaging with uncertainty: migrants with a relatively secure financial and administrative situation were better positioned to take chances in making a tentative return.

Taking chances in relation to emigration and return are thus related: if emigration fails to bring success, migrants may be more reluctant to make an uncertain return, perhaps opting to wait for circumstances to improve. The consequences of an unsuccessful return, in terms of unfulfilled responsibilities to others, loss of status, and shame, combined with greater hope in Europe than in Senegal, may help to explain why many postpone return even in times of crisis in Europe.

## Acknowledgements

I am indebted to the men and women who made this research possible by kindly sharing their time and stories with me in Spain and Senegal. I am also very grateful to Nauja Kleist and Dorte Thorsen for inviting me to take part in this book project and, together with Mattia Fumanti and two anonymous reviewers, for giving thorough and insightful comments which have been very helpful in developing my chapter. The research was funded by the Research Council of Norway under grant number 191369.

## Notes

1. All names are pseudonyms.
2. Translated by Havard as '*T'occupe pas*' or 'Don't meddle'.
3. '*À l'aventure*' in the French original which, as he explains, implies not knowing what lies ahead.

## References

Anderson, B. 2006. Becoming and being hopeful: Towards a theory of affect. *Environment and Planning D: Society and Space* 24 (5): 733–752.
Babou, C. A. 2002. Brotherhood solidarity, education and migration: The role of the Dahiras among the Murid Muslim community of New York. *African Affairs* 101 (403): 151–170.
Bal, E. 2014. Yearning for faraway places: The construction of migration desires among young and educated Bangladeshis in Dhaka. *Identities* 21 (3): 275–289.
Bernardi, F., L. Garrido and M. Miyar. 2011. The recent fast upsurge of immigrants in Spain and their employment patterns and occupational attainment. *International Migration* 49 (1): 148–187.
Blanchard, M. 2011. Note de recherche: Entre logiques de redistribution et volonté d'entreprendre: Les relations complexes des migrantes sénégalaises avec leurs familles d'origine. *Revue Européenne de Migrations Internationales* 27 (2): 139–159.
Bloch, E. 1986. *The principle of hope*. Cambridge, MA: MIT Press.
Brun, C. 2015. Active waiting and changing hopes: Towards a time perspective on protracted displacement. *Social Analysis* 59 (1): 19–37.
Bruquetas-Callejo, M., B. Garcés-Mascareñas, R. Morén-Alegret, R. Penninx and E. Ruiz-Vieytez. 2011. The case of Spain. In *Migration policymaking in Europe: The dynamics of actors and contexts in past and present*, eds. G. Zincone, R. Penninx and M. Borkert, 291–323. Amsterdam: IMISCOE/Amsterdam University Press.
Buggenhagen, B. A. 2012. *Muslim families in global Senegal: Money takes care of shame*. Bloomington: Indiana University Press.
Carling, J., P. D. Fall, M. Hernández-Carretero, M. Y. Sarr and J. Wu. 2013. *Migration aspirations in Senegal: Who wants to leave and why does it matter?* Brussels: European Commission, European Policy Brief.
Cassarino, J.-P. 2004. Theorising return migration: The conceptual approach to return migrants revisited. *IJMS: International Journal on Multicultural Societies* 6 (2): 253–279.
Castles, S., and M. J. Miller. 2009. *The age of migration: International population movements in the modern world*. Houndmills: Palgrave Macmillan (4th ed.).
Christiansen, C., M. Utas and H. Vigh, eds. 2006. *Navigating youth, generating adulthood: Social becoming in an African context*. Uppsala: Nordiska Afrikainstitutet.
Cole, J. 2008. Fashioning distinction: Youth and consumerism in urban Madagascar. In *Figuring the future: Globalization and the temporalities of children and youth*, eds. J. Cole and D. Durham, 99–124. Santa Fe, NM: School for Advanced Research Press.
Cole, J. 2014. The *téléphone malgache*: Transnational gossip and social transformation among Malagasy marriage migrants in France. *American Ethnologist* 41 (2): 276–289.

Crapanzano, V. 2003. Reflections on hope as a category of social and psychological analysis. *Cultural Anthropology* 18 (1): 3–32.

da Col, G., and Humphrey, C. 2012. Introduction: Subjects of luck-contingency, morality, and the anticipation of everyday life. *Social Analysis* 56 (2): 1–18.

Di Nunzio, M. 2015. Embracing uncertainty: Young people on the move in Addis Ababa's inner city. In *Ethnographies of uncertainty in Africa*, eds. E. Cooper and D. Pratten, 149–172. Houndmills: Palgrave Macmillan.

Diouf, M. 2000. The Senegalese Murid trade diaspora and the making of a vernacular cosmopolitanism. *Public Culture* 12 (3): 679–702.

Dünnwald, S. 2010. *Failed migrants in Bamako: The mental pressure of return.* Lisbon: Paper presented at the 7° Congresso Ibérico de Estudos Africanos, 9–11 September.

Dwyer, P. D. 2009. Worlds of waiting. In *Waiting*, ed. G. Hage, 15–26. Victoria: Melbourne University Press.

Fouquet, T. 2007. Imaginaires migratoires et expériences multiples de l'alterité: Une dialectique actuelle du proche et du lointain. *Autrepart* 41 (1): 83–97.

Gasparini, G. 1995. On waiting. *Time and Society* 4 (1): 29–45.

Giddens, A. 1999. Risk and responsibility. *The Modern Law Review* 62 (1): 1–10.

Hage, G. 2003. *Against paranoid nationalism: Searching for hope in a shrinking society.* Sydney: Pluto Press Australia.

Hage, G. 2005. A not so multi-sited ethnography of a not so imagined community. *Anthropological Theory* 5 (4): 463–475.

Hage, G. 2009a. Waiting out the crisis: On stuckedness and governmentality. In *Waiting*, ed. G. Hage, 97–106. Victoria: Melbourne University Press.

Hage, G. 2009b. Introduction. In *Waiting*, ed. G. Hage, 1–12. Victoria: Melbourne University Press.

Hamayon, R. N. 2012. The three duties of good fortune: 'Luck' as a relational process among hunting peoples of the Siberian forest in pre-Soviet times. *Social Analysis* 56 (1): 99–116.

Hansen, K. T. 2005. Getting stuck in the compound: Some odds against social adulthood in Lusaka, Zambia. *Africa Today* 51 (4): 3–16.

Havard, J.-F. 2001. Ethos 'bul faale' et nouvelles figures de la réussite au Sénégal. *Politique Africaine* 82 (2): 63–77.

Hayenhjelm, M. 2006. Out of the ashes: Hope and vulnerability as explanatory factors in individual risk taking. *Journal of Risk Research* 9 (3): 189–204.

Hernández-Carretero, M. 2015. Renegotiating obligations through migration: Senegalese transnationalism and the quest for the *right* distance. *Journal of Ethnic and Migration Studies* 41 (12): 2021–2040.

Hernández-Carretero, M., and J. Carling. 2012. Beyond 'kamikaze migrants': Risk taking in West African boat migration to Europe. *Human Organization* 71 (4): 407–416.

Honwana, A. 2012. *The time of youth: Work, social change, and politics in Africa.* Boulder: Kumarian Press.

Horst, C. 2006. *Buufis* amongst Somalis in Dadaab: The transnational and historical logics behind resettlement dreams. *Journal of Refugee Studies* 19 (2): 143–157.

Horst, C., and K. Grabska. 2015. Flight and exile: Uncertainty in the context of conflict-induced displacement. *Social Analysis* 59 (1): 1–18.

Horváth, I. 2008. The culture of migration of rural Romanian youth. *Journal of Ethnic and Migration Studies* 34 (5): 771–786.

INE. 2014. *Estadística del padrón continuo*. Madrid: Instituto Nacional de Estadística.
Jeffrey, C. 2010. Timepass: Youth, class, and time among unemployed young men in India. *American Ethnologist* 37 (3): 465–481.
Kleist, N. 2017. Disrupted migration projects: The moral economy of involuntary return to Ghana from Libya. Forthcoming in *Africa*.
Lakha, S. 2009. Waiting to return home: Modes of immigrant waiting. In *Waiting*, ed. G. Hage, 121–134. Victoria: Melbourne University Press.
Mains, D. 2012. *Hope is cut: Youth, unemployment, and the future in urban Ethiopia*. Philadelphia: Temple University Press.
Mapril, J. M. F. 2011. The patron and the madman: Migration, success and the (in)visibility of failure among Bangladeshis in Portugal. *Social Anthropology* 19 (3): 288–296.
Masquelier, A. 2013. Teatime: Boredom and the temporalities of young men in Niger. *Africa: The Journal of the International African Institute* 83 (3): 385–402.
Massey, D. S., J. Arango, G. Hugo, A. Kouaouchi, A. Pellegrino and Taylor, S. E. 1998. *Worlds in motion: Understanding international migration at the end of the millennium*. Oxford: Oxford University Press.
Mbodji, M. 2008. Imaginaires et migrations. Le cas du Sénégal. In *Le Sénégal des migrations: Mobilités, identités et sociétés*, ed. M.-C. Diop, 305–319. Paris: Karthala.
Melly, C. M. 2011. Titanic tales of missing men: Reconfigurations of national identity and gendered presence in Dakar, Senegal. *American Ethnologist* 38 (2): 361–376.
Miyazaki, H. 2006. Economy of dreams: Hope in global capitalism and its critiques. *Cultural Anthropology* 21 (2): 147–172.
Pedersen, M. A. 2012. A day in the Cadillac: The work of hope in urban Mongolia. *Social Analysis* 56 (2): 136–151.
Ralph, M. 2008. Killing time. *Social Text* 26 (497): 1–29.
Riccio, B. 2002. Senegal is our home: The anchored nature of Senegalese transnational networks. In *New approaches to migration? Transnational communities and the transformation of home*, eds. N. Al-Ali and K. Koser, 68–84. London: Routledge.
Schweizer, H. 2005. On waiting. *University of Toronto Quarterly* 74 (3): 777–792.
Sinatti, G. 2011. 'Mobile transmigrants' or 'unsettled returnees'? Myth of return and permanent resettlement among Senegalese migrants. *Population, Space and Place* 17 (2): 153–166.
Spijkerboer, T. 2007. The human costs of border control. *European Journal of Migration and Law* 9 (1): 127–139.
Suárez-Navaz, L. 2005. *Rebordering the Mediterranean: Boundaries and citizenship in Southern Europe*. New York: Berghahn.
Vigh, H. 2008. Crisis and chronicity: Anthropological perspectives on continuous conflict and decline. *Ethnos* 73 (1): 5–24.
Vigh, H. 2009. Wayward migration: On imagined futures and technological voids. *Ethnos* 74 (1): 91–109.
von Benda-Beckmann, F., and K. von Benda-Beckmann. 1994. Coping with insecurity. *Focaal—European Journal of Anthropology* 22/23: 7–31.
Williams, A. M., and V. Baláž. 2012. Migration, risk, and uncertainty: Theoretical perspectives. *Population, Space and Place* 18 (2): 167–180.

# 8 The Migratory Adventure as a Moral Experience

*Sylvie Bredeloup*

## Introduction

The term 'adventurer' is sometimes used as an analytical category with which to classify migrants who have overcome risks and dangers to traverse the various barriers and borders introduced to curb migratory movements. Yet it also resonates with *emic* descriptions common among sub-Saharan people of various origins, living in different places. Migrants from the Sahel in West Africa, for example, who settled in Brazzaville in the 2000s, describe their travels and migratory choices as adventure and characterize themselves as adventurers (Whitehouse 2012). Likewise, migrants from Guinea Bissau living in Lisbon speak of adventure (*aventura*) to describe their experiences of migration and migrant life (Sarro 2009). This *emic* usage is not new; the desire for adventure has a history. Thus, it is important not to essentialize what we understand by adventure. It is, above all, a social construction offering insights into societies and their imagined utopias. By tracing the history of the category, we discover that it has been used for a long time by migrants from the Senegal River Valley engaged in diamond smuggling between the two Congos, Angola, and Belgium. Through studying their trajectories we begin to appreciate that the term adventurer covers not only a particular form of migration but, more importantly, a particular lifestyle that allows migrants to escape their predictable, and possibly gloomy, everyday lives and pursue their dreams (Bredeloup 1994; 2007).

Elsewhere I argue that the emic notion of adventure expresses a deeply felt desire to live in another way, one which is not possible where the migrants come from or where they currently are (Bredeloup 2008; 2013; 2014). Thus, migration is not just determined by misery and danger. Individual ambitions and motivations are important catalysts for people who are planning to set off on the migration journey in order to radically change their everyday lives. This may, or may not, result in what would be deemed rational behavior from a micro-economic perspective. In other words, migratory choices are not entirely economic—migrants also travel to explore far-away places, real or imaginary, and to invent new ways of life. It is thus important to explore in more depth the different elements that constitute migration as adventure. Is it a generic expression of migrants' aspirations for the future? Is the desire for elsewhere also the desire for otherness? Through this lens, migration is similar to a moral experience.

Through an exploration of desires, dreams, and subjectivities among West African migrants at different historical times, this chapter examines the symbolic dimensions of migratory adventures. In particular, I explore the dialectic between hope and faith and between dignity and shame. First, I highlight some of the recurring patterns of adventure in African migrations and show that adventure is not only a shared *emic* label across West African cultures but also a social construction shared and reiterated by migrants, the regimes governing migratory movements, and media representations alike. Second, I examine how faith and religion impact on the construction of hope among adventurers, especially in circumstances where the hope for a better life might compel migrants to take the initiative and make decisions instead of awaiting their destiny. Finally, I investigate the trajectories of adventurers deemed successful and of those deemed failures to examine the effects of such views on their status in the community of origin.

## A Longitudinal Study

My analysis is based on longitudinal field research conducted with West African migrants in Senegal, Mali, Burkina Faso, Côte d'Ivoire, and Libya who migrated in search of employment in Europe and North Africa, or who went to look for diamonds in Central and Southern Africa.[1] Many of the latter became involved in diamond smuggling and it is the reconstruction of their trajectories that has allowed me to demonstrate how the multiple twists and turns on their migratory paths foster their insertion into an international circuit of diamond trade and facilitates their management of the permanent insecurities integral to fraudulent activities such as smuggling. Additionally, this research has helped to foreground the individual dimension of the migration project more objectively, without losing sight of the ways in which individual and collective strategies intertwine at the family and village levels. Thus, I have shown that individuals' search for economic independence does not necessarily imply existential autonomy. It can, when failing, lock an individual into perpetual dependence and collective heteronomy. Across several field sites I have drawn attention to the heterogeneity among African migrants and the fluid identities forced upon them structurally—e.g., through drawing links to the hardening of immigration politics in a study carried out in Marseille, France (Bertoncello and Bredeloup 2004) and through exploring the effect of increasing migration from sub-Saharan Africa to North Africa in a study carried out in Sebha, Libya (Bredeloup and Pliez 2005). By taking a longitudinal and multi-sited perspective, these studies document the different forms of migratory adventure and the logic underpinning them which, in turn, allows us to see how they differ from migration organized within collective frameworks involving families, village communities, and the 'communities of circumstance' built along the migratory path.

My methodological approach involves a combination of interviews, narratives, and observations. Moreover, I also turn to literary accounts of migratory adventures because they examine many of the same questions as those posed by social scientists. Novels focusing on African migrants, even if the main characters are invented, offer critical insights into representations of migrants and the expectations their societies have of them at a given moment in time. This approach is not aimed at validating existing social theories; rather, it is a methodological step to tease out new elements in migratory strategies, and even new fields surrounding migration, that would otherwise escape the sociological gaze. Thus, it is interesting to compare and interrogate further the divergences and similarities between the singular discourses presented in fiction and those presented by migrants in interviews. Migration becomes adventure as soon as the migrants' practices are re-enchanted and highlighted through the accounts; in these conditions, writers and *griots* (praise singers, musicians, poets, and story-tellers who maintain oral history traditions in West Africa) as well as migrants can be considered as potential 'adventure makers'.

## African Adventure or Adventure in Africa?

In the West,[2] literary accounts have traditionally given life and consistency to images of exceptional fictional persons, turning them into adventurers. The term adventure has different connotations in Africa than in the West; it follows a different set of rules and mechanisms. In the West, today, the term is primarily used to invoke a particular set of images of African migrants. Adventure used to be shrouded in mystique, enhanced by the fact that early adventures were the privilege of colonial explorers. Since the nineteenth century, the African continent has become a favorite location for Westerners seeking adventure containing exotic elements and a measure of authenticity. Thus, in the Western perception, the idea of the adventurer has changed from 'the man who came from somewhere else' to 'the man who went somewhere else' (Venayre 2002).

This contrasts with the way in which contemporary adventurers from Africa think about elsewhere. In Africa, today, going (to the Western) elsewhere is not necessarily linked with the ideas of strangeness and exoticism but with ideas of opportunity and membership of a globalized world. Europe occupies a central place in migratory imaginaries among most Africans and the 'European elsewhere' is far from being a *terra incognita*. Televised images diffused across the globe flow into the very villages that are often deemed the most backward by the media and, through television series and sitcoms, African villagers discover intimate details about everyday life in Europe and America. Even if these places are distant physically, they are not necessarily so culturally. Migration may thus allow Africans to participate even more in the processes of globalization that create new connections while simultaneously exacerbating marginalization (Ferguson 1999; 2006; Salazar 2010). For instance, for young Guinea-Bissauans from the Bijago Islands, migration to Europe appears to supplant all other possibilities and be elevated as the only viable means to escape isolation and become reconnected with the rest of the world (Bordonaro 2009). Similar motivations are found among Ghanaian fishermen, who have a strong sense of being disconnected. As they can no longer earn a living from fishing, they take tremendous risks in order to migrate to Italy and escape the shadow of globalization (Lucht 2011).

Finally, Europe constitutes a place of reference that is associated with colonial legacy and the collective historical memory shared by African people. Without necessarily being experienced directly by all individuals, this collective memory is, nevertheless, passed on from generation to generation. This is what Abdourahman A. Waberi[3] reminds us of in his novel *Transit*:

> I have an old debt of memory to settle with France: people think migrants arrive naked in a new land at the end of their odyssey; yet migrants are loaded with their own personal stories and heavier still with what is called collective history.
> (Waberi 2003, 6)

*Adventure: The Spice of Life*

Philosophers and sociologists have shown less interest in adventure as an event than as a process. Georg Simmel was the first scholar to consider adventure as an object of study. According to him, the intensity with which an event is lived determines whether or not it can become an adventure. The adventure allows people to feel the *spice of life* (Simmel 1912). It is not necessarily an unexpected or extraordinary event, mixing danger with the pleasure of discovery, but part of the collective life experience. For writers such as Jean-Paul Sartre (1972) or Pierre Mac Orlan (1998), the adventure exists first and foremost in the mind of the subject who lives it or talks about it. The risks taken, the trials endured, and the achievements are transcended by the importance of recounting them.

> Adventures are found in books [. . .]: to transform even the most banal event into an adventure, it is necessary—and it is enough—to recount it. This is what dupes people: a man is always a story-teller.
> (Sartre 1972, 61–62)

Thus, an adventure ensuing in silence or in solitude remains an episode without future. It is not enough to leave or to take risks; it is necessary to make known how the adventure unfolds. Essentially, an adventure only stands out because of the way in which it is narrated and how particular twists and turns are highlighted—'Adventure is the essence of fiction' (Tadié 1982, 5).

Among African migrants interviewed in Senegal, Burkina Faso, Libya, and France, 'adventure' thus signifies migrants' aspirations to try different ways of living that involve fewer constraints and are more intense and more dignified. The young men I interviewed explained that their lives as migrants were more turbulent and fast-moving than those they led at home. Instead of meeting up with their friends at home every day to discuss what had happened during the day while being bored and dreaming of a better life, they find themselves in the midst of action as migrants. They constantly have to be on the alert in order to negotiate border crossings, avoid having their papers checked, and, as explained by Alioune, who was deported back to Senegal:

> All my life, I've felt the pressure daily, even in France. I didn't have papers. Pressure when you leave, pressure when you come home! Even at the borders, you think about that, about control. Everything can fall apart one day—no, that is just too difficult. Ah, this is the reason why I feel so tired!

Alioune returned home because he felt he was growing old, not because he felt he had earned enough money. Whereas he had been excited about taking risks in the early days of his adventure, he had now begun to feel that risks made him tired.

Among Francophone migrants, '*chercher la route*' and '*chercher la vie*' (to look for a better path, to look for a better life) are expressions commonly used to describe their own practices and reasons to depart. These metaphors have been used by several generations of African migrants, despite them being a heterogeneous group and originating from different places and social classes. Before their departure for Europe, Ivorian migrants want to 'look for their life', to sublimate their life—that is to say, to break the monotony of daily life and become authors of their own destiny (De Latour 2001). The adventure is undoubtedly the opposite of both boredom and seriousness (Jankelevitch 1963). To leave equates with mobilizing 'a philosophy of action' that gives priority to the intensity of each moment in time. Thus, the departure connotes abandoning everything in order to find oneself and to open up new and more stimulating horizons.

### The Time of Youth?

An interesting question to explore is how youth are defined and represented when the focus is on the figure of the adventurer. Are the definitions grounded in notions of chronological or social age? Invariably, both researchers and migrants alike present the taste for adventure as a desire of youth that disappears with the onset of maturity. For Georg Simmel, as well, 'Adventure does not square with the lifestyle of old age . . . it is *par excellence* the lifestyle most suited to youth' (Simmel 2002, 82). What ties youth to adventure lies in the intensity of the tension with which it allows us to feel life, the 'spice of life'. A youthful disposition facilitates taking risks and is open to adventures. In return, the adventure has an element of locking people into an eternal youth. In several of the adventure novels for young people published in Europe in the middle of the nineteenth century, adventure was described as a youthful folly which ended as soon as the heroes married and thereby entered adulthood and gained social recognition. 'First and foremost the adventurer is a bachelor', André Malraux enthused in his *Antimémoires* (1967, 378). His idea was that, at some point in life, a young frivolous man would leave behind his adventures and undergo a complete transformation to become an orderly man for the sake of the good fortunes of marriage!

Another interesting issue relates to the question of whether migratory adventures are also associated with youth. The media systematically represents migratory adventures as the behavior of youth in the Global South who dream of living better lives in the Global North. Such representations are quite hard to verify, considering the difficulties of collecting statistical data of pathways marked by their fluidity and, to a large extent, by happening clandestinely. Even based on the empirical material collected in the course of my research, it is difficult to assess whether the migrants considered all or only some of their migratory pathway as adventure. However, migrant diamond miners born in the 1930s to 1940s, whose journeys I have followed over several years, were very clear. They unmistakably associated adventure with youth. Whereas they spoke in nostalgic terms about the golden age of diamond mining, which corresponded with their own entry into the world of risk-taking at the time of decolonization, they no longer spoke about themselves as adventurers. Those whom villagers in the Senegal River Valley label as adventurers today are a new wave of young people who engage in the smuggling of precious stones in Angola, but who do not maintain strategic relationships with their ageing countrymen. From the point of moving into new careers, the earlier generation of adventurers has been relabeled from 'diamond smugglers' to 'big men' (Bredeloup 2007). 'Nothing says that an adventurer remains one throughout his life, we live out our youth' recounts Jean-Daniel Gandoulou, who studied Congolese migration in Paris in the 1970s and depicted their *arts of getting by* between 'Paris and Bacongo' (Gandoulou 1984; 1989).

## Links between Adventure, Hope, and Faith

Adventurers look for something better. Central to the migratory adventure is the fact that it is appreciated as a lifestyle allowing one to escape a gloomy and predictable everyday life and to find fulfillment. It is premised on the hope of going elsewhere, the hope of returning with the Western modernity attributes of accumulating wealth and exhibiting the achievement of success. The time of adventurous projects must be followed by a time of building one's career. But if hope is related to desire, 'it is its passive counterpart . . . Desire is effective. It presupposes human agency', argues Vincent Crapanzano with reference to the work of Walter Pater, a Victorian novelist (Pater 1911). In contrast, hope depends on a god, fate, or chance for its fulfillment; 'Although desire presumes a psychology, hope presupposes a metaphysics' (Crapanzano 2003, 6).

In potential migrants' deliberations, the migratory adventure is elevated to an antidote to boredom and seriousness (Jankelevitch 1963). This is rooted in migrants' biased portrayal of their journeys, in which they underline the most extraordinary elements. They prefer to talk about how they have crossed deserts or lived rough in forests and how they have managed difficult relationships with the police and the military in different places rather than to talk about their everyday lives, the repetitiveness and the boredom while waiting to move on. In other words, they prefer to talk about the journey rather than about the temporary settlement in between the different legs of the journey—amongst other reasons in order to keep their audience dreaming. Thus, everything becomes possible when focusing on hope. Expulsion, theft, imprisonment, and assassination were considered as occupational hazards by the diamond smugglers I met. During a longitudinal survey conducted between 1994 and 2004, twelve of the 376 diggers and traders from the Senegal River Valley died a violent death before the end of our study, a much higher mortality rate than I have come across in the other sites under study (Bredeloup 2007). All the life stories gathered make mention of danger. Some speak of danger shamefully, others evoke it in a romantic manner, intending thereby to defuse their uneasiness about the inherent dangers or hoping that their adventures might be immortalized by the researcher who, in this context, is perceived as a modern-day poet who glorifies the daily life of the Senegalese diggers. Such ideas are linked to the history of diamond smugglers. In the past, *griots* followed the richest diamond smugglers and sang their praises in the countries they traversed, as well as at home. In their performances they compared the migratory and professional trajectories of diamond smugglers to those of the traditional Tukulor[4] heroes, thereby reinserting the hope of glory in those who had already begun their migratory adventure and motivating those who had not yet set off from home.

## *Mystic Journey*

Phillip Mar has shown that the concept of hope is strongly embedded in Muslim and Christian religions, due to its long association with faith, hope, and love, and thus with discourses of salvation and redemption (Mar 2005). To the majority of the migrants I interviewed, the migratory experience appears to take on the meaning of a mystic journey. Their actions are grounded in an interminable hope of being able to change their fate, by themselves and by the grace of God. This sentiment of hope gives them the strength to face the high expectations others have of them and to meet the dangers with determination. The majority of the migrants I met referred to God when explaining their luck in avoiding prison or death but also when rationalizing their capability to support the agony of separation or the pain and anguish endured physically. On the one hand, they wanted to describe the ways in which they were fortunate: 'I never fell into the hands of the police. It's a work of God! I cannot say that it's because I know the road well. No, that is God's work! Because nobody has his luck'. On the other hand, they wanted to emphasize their ability to tolerate suffering:

> When you leave here [Burkina Faso] to arrive in Niger, the trip after Niger, it's not a small pain. As soon as you're on this part of the journey, you ask God that he leads you and that you arrive in Libya in good health... It's thanks to God, otherwise the journey isn't easy. The walking in the desert is a story which we can't tell to anybody.

In the course of their migration, both Christian and Muslim migrants from sub-Saharan Africa draw on religious ideologies in their most general sense as well as on much narrower discourses embedded in particular denominations to better endure the waiting, instill meaning in their suffering, invigorate their migration project, and, where required, obtain material or symbolic assistance (Bava and Capone 2010). When the migrants feel discouraged, the appeal of collective prayer in churches or mosques is that it helps to give meaning to their migratory quest. Thanks to the transformation of dangers into ordeals, the migratory route can then be converted into a spiritual route.

Muslim migrants tend to construct exile as an experience similar to that of the Prophet Mohammed, who was in exile in Medina for ten years. For the devotees of the Murid Brotherhood, the imprisonment in Gabon for more than a decade of their spiritual leader, Sheikh Amadou Bamba, has a similar value. Every year they commemorate the *magal de Touba*,[5] the idea that going into exile is connected with unavoidable ordeals. To travel far away from Senegal, confront the unknown to increase one's resources, progress, and demonstrate one's faith is an integral part of the Murid spiritual trajectory (Bava 2005). To migrate, then, symbolizes the devotees' pursuit of the same path as their spiritual leader, and they contribute to the reproduction of the myth about exile as a path to personal enhancement. Such religious discourses also work to reinforce the devotees' faith, their confidence, and their capacity to act and to endure the ordeals along the migratory routes and temporary stops.

Similarly, Pentecostal churches offer their adherents encouragement to tolerate the separation from home and maintain the hope for a better life in the near future (Bava and Picard 2010). When seeking to make the migratory experience of the adherents easier to endure, the Pentecostal discourses refer in particular to the Exodus and to the reassurance of having chosen a good path when turning to the preaching of the gospel (Maskens 2008). Pentecostal devotees believe that their migratory paths are strewn with pitfalls and ordeals that they will endure and pass by means of their unshakeable faith in God and in the manner in which their pastors encourage them in collective prayer.

In other words, religion helps migrants who begin to deviate to bolster their faith, regain hope, and envisage new possibilities. As a contrast, we find that those who have sunk into despair have lost their faith and no longer believe in the power of God. Writing about clandestine Moroccan migrants in Europe, Stefania Pandolfo presents examples of such migrants:

> The risk of madness in despair is paralleled by a risk of doubting the foundation of faith or even challenging God, therefore entering heresy . . . The person in despair has thoughts of being abandoned by God.
> (Pandolfo 2007, 349)

## Epic Journey

In addition to religion, the epic story is an important cultural element in rousing hope in migrants across West Africa. The history of diamond smugglers reveals that the epic story incited the hope for change harbored by peasant sons who left to enrich themselves in Central Africa, far away from their region of origin (Bredeloup 2007). In Fulbe societies, the epic story or *fergo* is defined as emigration and, at the same time, rebellion or dissidence. The Fulbe princes who went into exile opposed the hierarchical heritage system or the political system in their region. Ousmane Kane describes vividly how a prince called Sammba Booyi began an open rebellion against one of his relatives, Siree Sawa Laamu, who reigned over the Fuuta Tooro[6] in the eighteenth century, to contest his conciliatory politics with the Moors. When falling in disgrace, Sammba Booyi followed the example of Samba Gueladio, who had gone into exile in Gadiaga[7] and lingered in anticipation of making a glorious return to his country (Kane 2004, 408).

The first generation of diamond smugglers from the Senegal River Valley reinterpreted their trajectories across Africa in the light of these famous *fergos*. Throughout their migration, they drew on oral heritage to legitimate their search for moral independence, to justify their elation, and to maintain hope for a better future. According to El Hadj Omar Tall, the famous Fulbe leader and military commander who founded a short-lived empire, exile was the condition for success of all Fuuta Tooro migrants. Rejecting colonial domination, the young descendant of a large and very religious family left the Senegal River Valley. Owing to his journeys to contemporary Sudan, Niger, and Egypt, he perfected his knowledge of Islam before being imprisoned by the King of Ségou. He was obliged to go into exile in the Fouta-Djalon (a region of what, today, is Guinea), where he began to preach the doctrine of the *Tidjaniya*[8] and plan the *Jihad*[9] (Robinson 1988). His well-known conquests later permitted numerous marginalized groups within the *fuutanke* society to seek revenge in order to gain entry into the kingdom of God. In the same way, Samba Guéladio, a young Fulbe prince, left Fuuta accompanied only by his *griot* after his uncle barred him from his legitimate role as leader of the country upon his father's death. With the aim of regaining the throne, he gathered an army in Mauretania. Samba Guéladio returned to his country to fight his uncle and take his rightful place. The epic story emphasizes the individuality of the person who seeks to take charge of his destiny and, at a more general level, seeks to liberate himself from the confinement of Fulbe society.

The two epic stories presented elate the liberty of African heroes to take initiatives, insist on the heroes' courage, and justify exile as the only means of recapturing one's place in society. Through associating migratory adventurers with the conduct of heroes, migrants indicate that they are not just puppets controlled by fate but, in fact, actors shaping their lives. In this sense they feel that they have the right to break off family relations temporarily in order to construct or consolidate their lives. Numerous migrants from the Senegal River Valley identify themselves with these heroes, who knew how to overcome the dangers and prohibitions on returning home triumphantly. Thus, the epic stories work to legitimize adventures (Lahire 1998), but they also imply certain outcomes. The trials along the route must be overcome convincingly if the migrants are to return triumphantly to their country. Contrary to the heroes who were led by awe-inspiring ideals, the adventurer is partially released from the world of the gods and is left to decide on his own what he ought to do and what he can refuse. In this situation his deepest desire is to know his destiny and to be able to direct it. In short, even if the commencement of the journey and its many trials is common for both adventurers and heroes, their relations to death differ. The adventurer plays with death but seeks life, whereas the hero must die to become famous and the object of particular cults.

Similarly, the literature on Mandinke cultures shows that some social markers are antagonistic. For example, contrasting markers such as the *badenya* and the *fadenya* are part of the social construction of life as a migrant as much as they structure everyday life for Malian villagers (Jónsson 2007). The *fadenya*, which generates an opposition among children of the same father but of different mothers, drives young men to engage in heroic acts to stand out among their brothers. Jealousy thus becomes a powerful motor in the drive to rise out of anonymity. The *badenya*, on the other hand, which is a metaphor for harmony, is more likely to stimulate people to accept their situation and the constraints imposed by the authorities. The notion of *fadenya* reflects, in the same way as adventure, an act of rebelliousness. Youth are incited to lift themselves out of their disadvantaged situation, to migrate to find their own path in life. '*Fadenya* spins the head-strong youth into the world of adventure' (Bird and Kendall 1980, 22). So, once again, the hope of a better life and a superior position in their society drives young people to see a journey to other places as the only means to achieve this. It is this deeply internal conviction that helps them to endure the ordeals and suffering in exile. Thus, instead of paralyzing them, it is this invincible hope for a better life and a different social position that stimulates migrants to stand out from the crowd, to distinguish themselves and to seek material wealth. However, this quest for difference does not mean that migrants necessarily impact on existing social norms upon their return. In my study of diamond smugglers, I demonstrated how those who had left their community at a very young age in a challenge to the gerontocratic hierarchy, accepted and used this hierarchy upon their return some years later. They put aside upon their return whatever provoked their challenge to the hierarchy and subsequently their migration, in order to reintegrate themselves socially. The material wealth gained through migration could not emancipate them from being subjugated by the social hierarchy in the village. In fact, existing social hierarchies were strengthened in that return migrants ensured their reproduction, because rejecting them would be at the returnees' expense.

## Dialectics of Dignity and Shame

### Dignity in Foreign Places?

In the introduction to his book about Malian migrants from Togotola living in Brazzaville, Bruce Whitehouse points to the everlasting actuality in Soninke society of the Bamanan proverb *tunga te danbe don*—exile knows no dignity (Whitehouse 2012, 21). In a study focusing on Malian migrants from another Soninke village—Kounda—who have left for France, Gunvor Jónsson comes to the same conclusion: 'A foreigner has no value in foreign places' (Jónsson 2008, 45). Those who go abroad lose their *danbe* or dignity, and they can only recover it once they return home. Migration, then, is perceived as an alternative route via which an individual can find his or her social place at home. While abroad, migrants do not need to worry about shame, they have no social obligations and no expenses. This allows them to engage in physically degrading jobs and endure social humiliation without this having any durable negative consequences for their social status at home. This dynamic is the reason why the Dogon, who are of a noble caste, can allow themselves to work in the metallurgy industry once they have migrated to Cameroon, despite the fact that, in Mali, such work is reserved for the caste of blacksmiths (Cisse 2009). Likewise, Malian and Senegalese migrants of noble Haalpulaar and Soninke descent sweep the streets of Paris without repercussions for their gentry.

### Glorious Return or Shameful Return?

Migrants' return to the country of origin must either stand out gloriously or not happen at all. Whether migrants return voluntarily or as a result of expulsion, their family and community cannot conceive that they might return empty-handed. 'The adventure is not without charge; it is surrounded by an obligation to succeed in accordance with the collective imagination'

(De Latour 2003, 187). In other words, migrants need to manage the end of their adventure carefully. The return home must be triumphant: what is at stake is the achievement of social fulfillment after having 'repaid the debt of life' (2003, 186) to all the people who contributed to the migrant's upbringing and education and helped to finance the adventure. Thus, it is equally important for the returning migrant to support his relatives upon his return and to expect favorable consequences of this support.

In the Senegal River Valley, we were told regularly about adventurers who had left for Zaïre or Nigeria in the 1960s and were never heard of again. Just as often, the story went on to describe how the brothers attempted to follow in the adventurer's footsteps to draw them back into the family circle. Whitehouse also shows that some of the Malian adventurers in Brazzaville find themselves in a dire economic situation but nevertheless deem an empty-handed return to be out of the question (Whitehouse 2012, 89). In the film *Le cri de la tourterelle* [*The Dove's Call*] a female *griot* invites Nigerien migrants, who for years have been lost in Côte d'Ivoire, to return home. 'The dove has called out that it wants to go home'. This *griot* was the one to incite them to take migratory paths and seek adventure through her songs in the 1960s; now she once again seeks to influence their paths by calling them home, using exactly the same discursive means but this time focusing on the shame of leaving: 'Fleeing is cowardice'.[10]

Contrary to the received wisdom, migrants' desperate actions cannot only be interpreted as a consequence of a lack of knowledge or of criminality. From their perspective, social death is far worse than physical death. Rather than losing face, many migrants prefer losing their mind or losing their life. In the transit countries, and in particular in Libya, I met migrants who had completely lost contact with their family and friends, who were homeless or who had sunk into madness. They no longer counted on their family, and they no longer seemed to be counted on by their family. They had lost all awareness of time.

This kind of sentiment is reflected in the novel *Paradis du Nord* [*Northern Paradise*]: 'Shame! I feel too ashamed', exclaims a Cameroonian migrant:

> I can already hear them whisper behind my back: 'See Anselme, he went to France but came back poorer than when he left'. You know very well that, in the popular belief in my country, those who don't get rich while in this country [France] where you only need to bend down to pick up money, are good-for-nothings.
>
> (Essomba 1996, 120)

Thus shame is an extremely effective emotion in driving migrants to take enormous risks, to cross deserts and the sea, to push their boundaries beyond previous limits in order to avoid social death. As Essomba suggests in his novel, it is impossible to return if the return does not enhance the reputation of the family.

## 'Failure on the Journey is Worse than Immobility at Home'

Deportation often leads to the denigration of the deportee, who may be deemed a disgrace to the family. Relatives never see deportation as an injustice orchestrated by a repressive political apparatus but rather as an individual failure. The culpability of the migrants is foregrounded and their morality is challenged. In one interview, a Senegalese migrant who had been deported from Italy ten years earlier and who had still not found stable employment, described his experience of returning involuntarily.

> Some people say you're a loser, that you had all the opportunities in the world but didn't know how to exploit them. If you go to Europe, you *must* succeed. It's mandatory . . . But you, you keep your calm, you manage to control yourself, you let them talk, but in the evening you are alone . . . Maybe one day they will understand. But you can't begin to discuss these matters, you can't convince them that their ideas of Europe are wrong. I just can't, but one day, I'll be proven right! The first thing I would like to set right is why people like myself get into their heads that going to Europe is the only option.

Relatives think that the migrants have done something wrong, that they have strayed off the right track—read: that they have committed a crime—although often they are deported after a random control of identity papers. Migrants are thus blamed for not knowing how to benefit properly from the abundance of opportunities they are believed to have from the moment they arrive in the destination country. Moral judgments are measured out quickly and migrants find themselves ostracized by their relatives and labeled as good-for-nothings, lazy, vagrants, delinquents, and, even worse, murderers, without having the means to challenge such devastating prejudice.

'Failure on the journey is worse than immobility at home: poor at the outset, the warrior becomes a loser' (De Latour 2001, 174). Some deportees prefer to disappear as soon as they have been expulsed rather than to make contact with their family and face the disgrace of returning empty-handed. Some who could not escape the empty-handed return have become the laughing-stock of their community and have subsequently sunk into silence, alcoholism, or madness, or have tried to take their own life. I remember a young man lost in the suburbs of Dakar and dressed in rags, who drew circles on the pavement in ink. Unlikely to respond in an intelligible way, he nevertheless described how he had lost his footing in the trade in emeralds in Zambia. He had not been able to endure repeated detention in the prisons of Kitwe. Contrary to what Suzanne Roth (1980) has argued, even if adventurers recoil from misfortunes, they are nevertheless harmed by them. In the streets of Dakar and Saint-Louis in Senegal, one regularly meets men who, according to rumors, have lost their senses and have gone mad after a failed migration because they could not cope with others' prejudice.

Not everybody has the psychological and physical resistance necessary to retain their composure in the face of the extraordinarily high frequency of humiliations, imprisonment, and abuse they experience along their way, the renouncement by their family and the rejection by their community of origin. Mamoutou Tounkara describes how a Malian migrant deported from France, after having worked there for more than ten years, was brutally pushed away by his mother when he wanted to embrace her. 'Whether a child has succeeded, has gone mad or something else, the child usually is loved and respected by his mother. My mother, however, quickly made me understand that I lived in another world' (Tounkara 2013, 288). Behind the anguish of returning empty-handed is the anxiety of facing others and their views, and of humiliating one's relatives because of one's failure. How a person is judged reflects on his mother and, as soon as he fails, the reliability of his mother is challenged. In some of the communities in which I have conducted my research, returning empty-handed can result in the migrant being considered irresponsible and, in some cases, being rejected by his or her community, like the migrant described by Tounkara. Such rejection also excludes the migrant from participating in community meetings and from speaking up in public.

*Words Describing Failure*

The words used by migrants and their relatives to describe the different categories of failed migrants are informative for understanding the symbolic violence in relation to this ostracism, to this social killing. If migrants express their shame at not being able to fulfil their part of the migratory 'contract'—this implicit and moral contract according to which family members back home benefit from migratory adventures whether the family was implicated in the decision or not—the open acknowledgement of failure may even reiterate the shame (Vermot 2015). According to Mamoutou Tounkara, all deported migrants in Mali are treated as vagrants by their relatives; this is a radical way of expressing the perception that deported migrants have messed up their lives. Despite having had the family's blessing on their migratory project, the migrants fail to fulfil their obligations towards the family when deported and they therefore become *danga-den* (Tounkara 2013, 286). On the other side of the Senegal River Valley, the Halpulaaren use a similar extensive vocabulary to describe the situation for failed migrants. Generally, they distinguish between those who return successfully after accumulating material wealth (*jajaade*) and those who have lost their way and do not return (*luttude*). Failure can be further nuanced in distinctions between those cursed because they no longer remit money to the family but do not return (*kudaado*), those deemed irresponsible because they did not foresee their deportation (*ala haaju*) and those returning empty-handed, described in terms of nudity (*bolo*) to humiliate them the most (Dia 2010, 382).

During one interview, a migrant who had been deported from France described how he and his friends always had a suitcase ready in case of deportation. It was packed with new clothes which could be distributed to the members of their family to circumvent shame in case of an untimely return.

> One day I was deported. Before being sent back to Senegal I was accompanied by the police to my room, where I quickly packed my things. I was prepared. I'd got this idea because I knew that, as an undocumented migrant, I could be deported any day, especially since the control of papers is frequent. Thus, as soon as I earned a bit of money, I bought jeans to pack away in my suitcase. I didn't want to return to Africa without nice clothes because, at home, they say that you returned empty-handed and that you are a loafer if you don't have nice clothes to wear. But as soon as you are well dressed and use a nice after-shave, they will say that you've succeeded and that you've become someone, even if you were deported.

By preparing for an unplanned return, migrants are better equipped to cope with the reality of deportation by making them look like they returned voluntarily. The permanent insecurity with which migrants are faced incites them to engage in all kinds of illegal activity, to experiment with new strategies to make their everyday lives more endurable, and to preserve their dignity amongst their own people.

The notions of *sutura* (dignity, tact) and *koyera* (shame) are not only mobilized by migrants from the Senegal River Valley who have traveled to Europe or to the diamond mines across the African continent, they are also part of the vocabulary used by Burkinabé migrants interviewed during their migration or upon their return, after having been expulsed from Libya or Côte d'Ivoire (Bredeloup 2014). The importance for them of returning with dignity has burgeoned with the many obstacles they have had to overcome. Failure can be interpreted differently depending on whether the unlucky candidate is viewed as a strong or a weak person in his community of origin. Accordingly, the person who is considered weak is often judged to be responsible for his own failure whereas the person who is perceived as resourceful is perceived to be the victim of bad luck. Scrutiny of the prevalent vocabulary used to describe migrants who are unable to materially honor the expectations of their relatives should be more systematic if we are to understand how norms of solidarity within the family and among peers function in contemporary societies.

### Fiction Describing Shame

Shame rarely surfaces in verbal communication. Often researchers need to interpret articulations of shame *a posteriori* through analyzing a larger empirical material surrounding migration. This is because talking about shame to a foreign researcher, and especially one coming from the country from which the migrant was deported, is not easily done. This difficulty often creates silences during the interview, leads to the omission of the parts of their story that are just too painful to describe or to adaptations of the truth so that they do not lose face but can preserve a less-devalued self-image. This is why it is interesting to turn to the literature and analyze how writers address these difficult emotions. The novel *L'Impasse* [*The Dead End*] published in 1996 by the Congolese author Daniel Biyaoula recounts the everyday battle of an African split between nostalgia and the desire for elsewhere. The author stresses the shame felt intensely by his main character during a vacation in his home country. The Congolese community ostracizes him because he refuses to adhere to the canonical representations of success in the West and thus to comply with the demands of his family.

> All that rested on me were disapproving and inquisitive eyes. I didn't hear anything but silences and overwhelming words. My father's voice and that of uncle Titémo relegated me to the bottom of the abyss where one is blind. They restrained me, criticized me. I'm a disgrace to the family, I'm told. [. . .] Foregone dead that I am.
> 
> (Biyaoula 1996, 141)

Several other African authors evoke the symbolic violence associated with an untimely return; migration then becomes a metaphor for existential social and cultural anxiety among Africans. In the novel *Le Ventre de l'Atlantique* [*The Belly of the Atlantic*] by Fatou Diome, a young Senegalese author, one of the leitmotivs is 'Every scrap of life must serve to win dignity' (Diome 2006, 63). The main character, Moussa, is young football hopeful who, after failing his trial in a French club, is deported. His dignity is undermined when his father sends him a letter ending 'Spare us this shame among our people. You must work, save money and come home' (2006, 69). Moussa disappears in the waves of the Atlantic, close to his village, when trying to escape the intolerable guilt that torments him and the humiliation at the hands of his peers. To preserve one's dignity through thick and thin when experiencing one humiliation after the other requires an extraordinarily strong character and distinctive strategies to preserve one's identity. Not to be stripped of their social dignity spurs migratory destinies.

Finally Vincent de Gaulejac's 1996 study of the sources of shame and 'social suffering' demonstrates the pertinent links between concrete living conditions and their consequences for individuals. His work merits being highlighted for its insights into the ways in which being (shame) and doing (culpability) differ and can be mobilized differently by migrants. If the culpability can be lessened by confession, compensation, or punishment, shame on the other hand 'requires a transformation of oneself. It is the being in its most profound sense that is at stake, as if something irreversible had happened' (de Gaulejac 1996, 142).

## Conclusion

In this paper I have tried to clarify the underlying moralities and beliefs of a new category of migrant, the adventurer. I have shown that, among African migrants, the word 'adventure' is not just a generic expression of their aspirations for the future nor is 'the adventurer' an analytical category invented by researchers to group migrants who overcome various risks and dangers to transgress the barriers and borders which have been put in place to stem the flow of migrants. The notion of adventure, of being an adventurer, is an emic label that expresses a deeply felt desire to live in another way than is possible where the migrants come from or where they are. 'Adventure' thus signifies migrants' aspirations to try different ways of living that involve fewer constraints and are more intense and more dignified. The migratory adventure is indeed envisioned as a stage in the life of a man, as is his settling down. The adventure would be a passage, a transition.

As soon as the symbolic dimensions of adventure are considered, it is necessary also to take into consideration the desires, dreams, and subjectivities. Migration adventures are, first and foremost, a moral experience, a way of existence. Religion, as well as the epic stories of the past, is invoked in migrants' legitimation of their trajectories and choices to reconfirm their faith in a better future far from their home. Besides this dialectical relationship between desire and hope, I have endeavored to better understand the subtleties in the enunciations of dignity and shame which are at the heart of migration adventures. The migrants are prepared to risk their lives for a precarious future, in order to know the present-day misery of emigrants, to put up with shame in the hope of being recognized at home once they return to their country, and recover their dignity. But their migration adventures do not always turn out the way they had anticipated, nor do they necessarily end at their own initiative. Despite the hope which emigrants nourish, the new ways of living and being that they experience as migrants are very different to those which they had imagined before they left home. Notwithstanding that migrants' desires change throughout their uncertain and turbulent journeys, the outcome of migration is appraised upon their return and comes at a high price. The ideal exit from migration adventures is experienced by the few who have succeeded in accumulating sufficient money or skills to reclaim a space—more or less prestigious—in the community of origin. At the other end of the scale are the numerous migrants who have exhausted the possibilities of a dignified return to their country or who, after having been deported, experience general humiliation. These migrants pay the heavy price of social relegation for having failed in the task which they had been assigned by their family or which they themselves had instigated.

## Notes

1. This study began in 1992 and is still ongoing. Whereas the key questions have remained the same, additional themes have been introduced over the years, reflecting changes in migration flows and regimes.

2. Novels describing adventure have always existed but they have had different functions in the popular imagination over the course of time. Only in the nineteenth century did they develop into a literary genre in Europe.
3. Waberi is a Francophone writer from Djibouti. His 2003 novel *Transit* is a succession of monologues addressing the agony of exile related to the civil war in Djibouti (Djibouti was the last French colony to gain independence in 1977). The theme of separation is the *fil rouge* connecting the characters presented in the novel.
4. Tukulors belong to a sedentary group related to the Fula of West Africa. However, contrary to the pastoralist Fulbe, the Tukulors have farming and fishing as their main activities.
5. Sheikh Amadou Bamba was born in Touba, Senegal.
6. Fuuta Tooro was the generic name which Fulbe people used to describe the area between present-day northern Senegal and southern Mauretania, where they lived.
7. Gadiaga was a medieval kingdom founded by the Soninke (Galam).
8. The Tidjaniya is a Sufi brotherhood within Sunni Islam that prioritizes culture and education. Originating from North Africa, it has become the largest Sufi order in West Africa. Ahmad Tijani Ali Cisse was the spiritual leader of this brotherhood, founded in 1781 in reaction to the Qadiriya order, which was judged as too conservative.
9. Umar Tall conquered several non-Muslim regions in present-day West Africa, then constructed fortifications near Kayes (Mali), before declaring war on a number of smaller Islamic states nearby.
10. For an analysis of the semiology of this film, see Marina Lafay and Carola Minck (2014).

# References

Bava, S. 2005. Variations autour de trois sites mourides dans la migration. *Autrepart* 36 (4): 105–122.
Bava, S., and S. Capone. 2010. Religions transnationales et migrations: Regards croisés sur un champ en mouvement. *Autrepart*, 56 (4): 3–16.
Bava, S., and J. Picard. 2010. Les nouvelles figures religieuses de la migration africaine au Caire. *Autrepart* 56 (4): 153–170.
Bertoncello, B., and S. Bredeloup. 2004. *Colporteurs africains à Marseille: Un siècle d'aventures*. Paris: Autrement.
Bird, C., and M. Kendall. 1980. The Mande hero: Text and context. In *Exploration in African systems of thought*, eds. I. Karp and C. Bird, 13–26. Bloomington: Indiana University Press.
Biyaoula, D. 1996. *L'Impasse*. Paris: Présence Africaine.
Bordonaro, L. 2009. *Sai fora*: Youth, disconnectedness and aspiration to mobility in the Bijago islands, Guinea-Bissau. *Ethnogràfica* 13 (1): 125–144.
Bredeloup, S. 1994. L'aventure contemporaine des diamantaires sénégalais. *Politique Africaine* 56: 77–93.
Bredeloup, S. 2007. *La Diams'pora du fleuve Sénégal: Sociologie des migrations africaines*. Toulouse: IRD/PUM.
Bredeloup, S. 2008. L'aventurier, une figure de la migration africaine. *Cahiers internationaux de Sociologie* 125 (2): 281–306.
Bredeloup, S. 2013. The figure of the adventurer as an African migrant. *Journal of African Cultural Studies* 25 (2): 170–182.
Bredeloup, S. 2014. *Migrations d'aventures: Terrains africains*. Paris: CTHS.

Bredeloup, S., and O. Pliez, eds. 2005. Migrations entre les deux rives du Sahara. *Autrepart* 36 (4): 3–20.

Cisse, P. 2009. Migration malienne au Cameroun à la conquête du secteur informel. *Hommes et Migrations* 1279: 38–51.

Crapanzano, V. 2003. Reflections on hope as a category of social and psychological analysis. *Cultural Anthropology* 18 (1): 3–32.

De Gaulejac, V. 1996. *Les sources de la honte*. Paris: Desclée de Brouwer.

De Latour, É. 2001. Du ghetto au voyage clandestin: La métaphore héroïque. *Autrepart* 19 (3): 55–176.

De Latour, É. 2003. Héros de retour. *Critique Internationale* 19 (2): 171–189.

Dia, H. 2010. *Espaces domestiques, espaces villageois, espaces urbains multisitués. Cinquante ans de migrations à partir de la moyenne vallée du fleuve Sénégal 1960–2010*. PhD thesis, Ecole des Hautes Etudes en Sciences Sociales.

Diome, F. [2003]2006. *The belly of the Atlantic*. London: Serpent's Tail.

Essomba, J.-R. 1996. *Le paradis du Nord*. Paris: Présence Africaine.

Ferguson, J. 1999. *Expectations of modernity: Myths and meanings of urban life on the Zambian copperbelt*. Perspectives on Southern Africa 57, University of California Press.

Ferguson, J. 2006. *Global shadows: Africa in the neo-liberal world order*. Durham, NC: Duke University Press.

Gandoulou, J.-D. 1984. *Entre Paris et Bacongo*. Paris: Editions du Centre Pompidou.

Gandoulou, J.-D. 1989. *Dandies à Bacongo: Le culte de l'élégance dans la société congolaise contemporaine*. Paris: L'Harmattan.

Jankelevitch, V. 1963. *L'aventure, l'ennui, le sérieux*. Paris: Aubier Ed Montaigne.

Jónsson, G. 2007. *The mirage of migration: Migration aspirations and immobility in a Malian Soninke village*. Master's thesis in Anthropology, University of Copenhagen.

Jónsson, G. 2008. *Migration aspirations and involuntary immobility in a Malian Sonink village*. University of Oxford: International Migration Institute Working Paper No. 10. Online at: http://www.imi.ox.ac.uk/pdfs/imi-working-papers/working-paper-10-migration-aspirations-and-immobility

Kane, O. 2004. *La première hégémonie peule: Le Fuuta Tooro de Koli Tenella à Almaami Abdul*. Paris: Karthala.

Lafay, M., and C. Minck. 2014. A l'écoute du 'Cri de la tourterelle'. La performativité du chant et du cinéma sur la migration au Niger. *Cahiers d'Etudes Africaines* 213–214 (1): 499–527.

Lahire, B. 1998. *L'homme pluriel: Les ressorts de l'action*. Paris: Nathan.

Lucht, H. 2011. *Darkness before daybreak: African migrants living on the margins in Southern Italy today*. Berkeley: University of California Press.

Mac Orlan, P. 1998. *Le petit manuel du parfait aventurier*. Paris: Mercure de France.

Malraux, A. 1967. *Antimémoires*. Paris: La Pléiade.

Mar, P. 2005. Unsettling potentialities: Topographies of hope in transnational migration. *Journal of Intercultural Studies* 26 (4): 361–378.

Maskens, M. 2008. Migration et pentecôtisme à Bruxelles. Expériences croisées. *Archives des Sciences Sociales des Religions* 143: 49–68.

Pandolfo, S. 2007. 'The burning'. Finitude and the politico-theological imagination of illegal migration. *Anthropological Theory* 7 (3): 329–363.

Pater, W. 1911. *Marius the Epicurean: His sensations and ideas*. London: Macmillan.

Robinson, D. 1988. *La guerre sainte d'al-Hajj Umar: Le Soudan occidental au milieu du XIXème siècle*. Paris: Karthala.

Roth, S. 1980. *Les aventuriers au XVIIIème siècle*. Paris: Galilée.
Salazar, N. B. 2010. *Tanzanian migration imaginaries*. Oxford: Oxford University, International Migration Institute Working Paper Series.
Sarro, R. 2009. La aventura como categoria: Reflexiones simmelianas sobre imigracion subsahariana. *Revista de Ciências Humanas* 43 (2): 501–521.
Sartre, J.-P. 1972. *La Nausée*. Paris: Gallimard.
Simmel, G. 1912. *Mélanges de philosophie relativiste: Contribution à la culture philosophique*. Paris: Alcan.
Simmel, G. 2002. *La philosophie de l'aventure*. Paris: L'Arche.
Tadié, J.-Y. 1982. *Le roman d'aventures*. Paris: Presses Universitaires de France.
Tounkara, M. 2013. *Les dimensions socioculturelles de l'échec de la migration: Cas des expulsés maliens en France*. PhD thesis in Sociology, Université Paris-Est Créteil Val de Marne.
Venayre, S. 2002. *La gloire de l'aventure: Genèse d'une mystique moderne, 1850–1940*. Paris: Aubier.
Vermot, C. 2015. Capturer une émotion qui ne s'énonce pas: Trois interprétations de la honte. *Terrains/Théories* 2. Online at: http://teth.revues.org/224; DOI: 10.4000/teth.224.
Waberi, A. A. 2003. *Transit: Continents noirs*. Paris: Gallimard.
Whitehouse, B. 2012. *Migrants and strangers in an African city: Exile, dignity, belonging*. Bloomington and Indianapolis: Indiana University Press.

# 9  Death of a Gin Salesman

## Hope and Despair among Ghanaian Migrants and Deportees Stranded in Niger

*Hans Lucht*

## Introduction

Based on three months of fieldwork in 2010 among Ghanaian migrants stranded in Niamey, Niger, the principal transit country for African overland migration to Libya, this chapter discusses the notion of hope and its connectedness to migrant sacrifice and death on the desert migration routes. Each year, tens of thousands of young people travel from West Africa through the desert towns of Niger towards Libya and some further to Europe. Although little is known about the trans-Saharan route from Niger into Libya—and even less is known about the routes connecting the Horn of Africa with Libya via Sudan—it is clear that it represents a massive risk for undocumented migrants and refugees (Simon 2006, 54) and results in a substantial number of deaths each year, deaths that are most probably unaccounted for due to the lack of monitoring and absence of security in this vast and largely ungoverned area. Often migrants run into problems on the route. Perhaps the old trucks taking them across the desert break down, or they are cheated or robbed by the smugglers or they simply run out of money (see Lucht 2011, 160–176). In many instances, they will relocate to Agadez or Niamey or other transit points, and wait for another opportunity to go to North Africa. For many, however, the waiting becomes permanent and they end up doing menial work, sometimes cutting off connections with their families out of shame.

Focusing on the unexpected death of a Ghanaian migrant stranded in Niamey, this chapter explores how hope is understood and maintained under such stressful and dangerous circumstances. Hope, I argue, is a belief in a sense of continuity between an individual's efforts and the responses they generate in both the here-and-now and in death, whereas a sense of despair represents a breakdown of this moral economy of human lifeworlds, i.e., the experiential sense that a person's actions matter and are responded to, even if the response is delayed or transferred to other times and places—even if the individual will not prosper her/himself. Hope is underpinned by a notion of existential reciprocity (Lucht 2011; 2015), a fundamental belief that, in the future, one's efforts will be rewarded in a form that justifies the many sacrifices made.

DOI: 10.4324/9781315659916-9

## Hope and Existential Mobility

Migration is an expression of the hope that one's needs and desires will be accommodated elsewhere, Ghassan Hage argues; migrants, like all human beings, need to feel that 'they are going places in life' and, if they cannot obtain that sense of existential mobility at home, they will travel to obtain it (Hage 2005, 470, see also the Introduction in this volume). Seeking the fleeting warmth in promise, and in a near future or in a different location altogether, where 'losses are made good, injustices redressed, patience rewarded, and knowledge achieved' (Jackson 2011, 197) is a fundamental trait of the human imagination. It speaks of the eternal existential unrest of human life that, according to Schopenhauer, resembles

> the course of a man running down a mountain who would fall over if he tried to stop and can stay on his feet only by running on; or a pole balanced on the tip of the finger; or a planet which would fall into its sun if it ever ceased to plunge irresistibly forward.
>
> (1851/2004, 52)

In fact, running downhill without stumbling appears to be a relevant analogy for the kind of human struggle that migration represents in the globalized world because how to keep moving, both physically and existentially, in spite of the many obstacles on the road, appears to be a recurrent theme of migrant life. During fieldwork in Naples in 2005, for instance, I noticed that my Ghanaian assistant carried a golden key around his neck, a gift from his sister. He explained that it was the key which would unlock the doors of opportunity (Lucht 2011, 92). In spite of the many challenges and setbacks in Naples or, perhaps, because of them, he was constantly concerned with clearing the channels for his continuous migration trajectory.

The immediate barriers and suffering that so many migrants experience *en route*, or after their arrival in Europe, seldom extinguish hope that they can find another place in which to express themselves, however unlikely it sometimes appears from the outside. Henrik Vigh, for instance, records how Bissauan migrants who find themselves down-and-out in Lisbon, exchanging one kind of stasis with another, say that Portugal is just a 'trampoline' for their next move; hope opportunistically migrates ahead of the migrants to new destinations. It becomes 'temporally or spatially transposed and related to other places or times' (Vigh 2009, 105). Hope, Jarret Zigon argues, is both the motivation to endure times of hardship or 'breakdowns' where a person's life and existence is called into question as well as a continuous motivation 'for persevering through the life into which one has been thrown. In this way, hope is not necessarily aimed at the future good, but primarily at the perseverance of a sane life' (2009, 258). Michael Jackson, drawing on Gabriel Marcel, describes hope as the belief that there is still time left to change one's circumstances (Jackson 2011, xii) or, one might add, that there is still time left to preserve the things that 'really matter' (Kleinman 2006).

This, to me, is an approach that appears close to the experiential truth of hope—namely that hope is a vernacular term for the sense of existential continuity between a person's efforts and the responses they generate; a sense that one's desires will somehow be accommodated in due time and in a shape appropriate to the intensity and extent of the struggles. Hope, and the continuous desire for existence, is constantly formed, and transformed, and fixed to new objects, ideas and routes, and challenged by social and political reality. Yet, sometimes hope becomes impossible to believe in or disappears or can lead to stasis or even 'paralysis', as Vincent Crapanzano has argued, 'One can be so caught up in hope that one does nothing to prepare for its fulfilment' (2003, 18). Hope can also be substituted by another form of future management, a kind of *defeatist agency*—that is, a form of proactive fatalism or despair that consists in playing down hope and aspirations and elaborating endlessly on the many pitfalls that wait around the corner, to the extent that nothing unfortunate the world has in store for you comes as a surprise. Again, this is a way of predicting or even collaborating with one's continued negative trajectory and is, therefore, in principle, empowering, even if psychologically demanding, in the sense that one stage of life substitutes another in predictable ways (Lucht 2011, 82). Despair, in this sense, is not necessarily a passive attitude but a negative grasp of the social world, ensuring that one moves nowhere fast. The complexity of the situation is that, among African migrants in Niger, hope and despair are interchanging modes of managing the future that both belong to the human repertoire of struggling for whatever makes life worth living, and seem to substitute each other constantly.

## Hope in the Globalized World

Perhaps Pierre Bourdieu is right to argue that the dispossessed are a lot more resigned than we usually imagine—resigned to the impossibility of radical social and economic change—and that, 'Having adapted to the demands of the world which has made them what they are, they take for granted the greater part of their existence' (2000, 231). To Bourdieu, the hope that still lingers—in its more fantastic and unrealistic forms—is an effect of a person's marginal position in the world system. In other words, below a certain threshold of power, where social and economic mobility are unobtainable, fantasies such as lotteries and other almost occult promises of instant wealth and social prominence—that have little or no 'objective chance' of realization—flourish because, if nothing is possible, everything is possible (2000, 226). Yet there is still a margin of freedom. Individual hope and the desire for existence are, of course, informed by socioeconomic and political forces but they are not mere expressions of these constraints. Even negative, fantastic, or unrealistic forms of hope are important and should not be ignored or pathologized in that, even if they do not change a person's objective situation—whatever that means—it is an experiential reality that may make a real difference to individuals. To grasp this perpetual intersubjective tension between structural constraints and human subjectivity, Robert Desjarlais has coined the term 'critical phenomenology' (1997, 24), with a view to linking the political and the phenomenal. In migrant studies, Sarah Willen, working with undocumented migrant workers in Israel, has elaborated on the notion of critical phenomenology to address 'the conditions of structural inequality and structural violence that shape migrants' positions' and, at the same time, 'the impact of these contextual factors on migrants' individual and collective experiences' (Willen 2007, 13). Indeed, even in the most difficult circumstances, people have the sometimes emancipating force of hope.

One example of this is anthropologist Morten Axel Pedersen's perspective on hope among marginalized hustlers in Ulaanbaatar, Mongolia. Drawing especially on Miyazaki (2006), hope to Pedersen is not conceived as a flight into fantasy but a 'multi-temporal attitude' of 'pre-experiencing' the 'tiny but innumerable cracks through which the promise of another world shines'. Hope, in this context, creates a kind of sought-after irregular life on the margins that is not unwanted but represents a 'systematic unwillingness to plan' (2012, 10, 13). In the same vein, Joel Robbins (2013) has recently argued for an 'anthropology of the good', a strand of anthropology that challenges, according to Robbins, the dominating focus on the 'suffering subject' and seeks to reinstate human agency and play in the face of seemingly insurmountable difficulties—i.e., to explore ways in which 'people come to believe that they can successfully create a good beyond what is presently given in their lives' (2013, 458). In this connection, a focus on hope could be one avenue to understanding—especially but not only—poor and disenfranchised people's resistance to their circumstances or, at least, their experiential lack of acceptance of the undesirable *status quo*. Yet, to Pedersen and others, the insistence on the 'surprisingly hopeful' dimension of life among the marginalized and the continued hope that 'tomorrow will be a better day' are not only forms of future management or a recasting or playing with a difficult situation which has no desirable alternatives but 'a continual colonization and expansion of the present' (2012, 2, 6). It offers an alternative reality or ontology that is chosen and lived by the marginalized to the extent that they abstain from making long-term plans.

Although I sympathize with the effort to reclaim and rehabilitate hope, I want to take this chapter in another direction. Perhaps informed by fieldwork among 'the floating population' of the EU–African border zones (Bayart 2007, 272), it appears to me that any perspective on hope needs to be grounded in but not determined by socio-economic and political reality, to a greater extent than Bourdieu's many critics appear willing to admit. A critical phenomenological position does not entail that people are some kind of robot, passively enacting their fate but in a constant struggle for a life worth living. The death-defying journeys in the desert and the Mediterranean, for instance, are ways of transgressing the borders imposed on them in more than one way. Although not political acts *per se*, migrant suffering and sometimes death are forms of iconoclasm that question the moral legitimacy of the system (even though, to a growing extent, likely to be received as unfortunate but inevitable in Europe). More than seeking to create another or a better world, West Africa migrants experientially seek to drag the globalized world that is so unresponsive to their lives and longings into their sphere of influence via disproportionate sacrifices with great risks. It is an attempt to pollinate the global political economy that has doomed some people and places to oblivion. Hope, in this connection, speaks of the existence and continuity of a morality that is based on exchange—a world where a person's actions matter and the brutality of life on the margins is understood to be a prelude to better times. Sometimes, however, the stressful running downhill comes to an abrupt and painful end when a migrant dies and the futility of subaltern life is brought out.

## Life and Death in Niamey

During fieldwork among Ghanaian migrants and deportees in Niamey, Niger, I had the possibility of attending the funeral of an acquaintance, Dominic, who unfortunately passed away before I could sit down and talk with him about his migrant trajectory. It was a critical event (Das 1995, 6) in the lifeworld of stranded Ghanaian migrants in the sense that, here, the individual struggle for life, the fragile and vulnerable struggle of undocumented migrants *en route*, was overwhelmed by ungovernable circumstances and the ultimate loss conceded. As such, his death became both a focal point of practical attention, concern, and collective action, and a sinister promise of dark things to come. It was the enactment of a probable future that was the antipode to the hopes and dreams of his stranded colleagues: to die without having achieved anything, in a strange country, far from friends and family.

The death of Dominic, and how he ended up in Niamey as another stranded Ghanaian migrant, hustling through life, became a social event that brought together the perhaps most unfortunate section of the Ghanaian community in Niger. Methodologically, talking about his life with his fellow migrant hustlers became a way of paying tribute to a deceased colleague and an interesting insight into the lives of migrants who shared in Dominic's fate. They, too, were struggling with the haphazard distribution of life and death that characterizes life among the stranded. To this group of strangers, his death did not appear to come as a great shock but constituted a term of life under these circumstances, on the bottom of society, far away from home; everybody understood the risk of ultimately yielding to such a term of life unless they kept moving forward one way or the other. The hope that existed, that they would make it out somehow, was just about enough to keep them persevering although, in some cases, the constant breakdowns led to great psychological strain. This was, for instance, the case with Mr. James, the plastics repairman, whom my two informants, Bobby and Kantinka, took me to visit one day.

Bobby and Kantinka worked as migration brokers and hustled at a bus station in Niamey. Their position as observers and facilitators of migrant life on the road, combined with their own failed adventures, became in themselves an interesting story that I have written about elsewhere (see Lucht 2013). But on that day they took me to see Mr. James. He lived with a dog in a wooden shed surrounded by what looked like a plastic junk heap, with small stinking fires burning all around him. In those fires he kept glowing iron rods that he used to burn and melt plastic and reconstruct and fix broken chairs or even whole car fronts. He was an expert on various types of plastic and demonstrated their qualities to us in both hard and liquid form, reminding us that plastic may be considered a low-quality product to people in more affluent societies but has real value in other places. To manage the smell of and the headaches from the ever-burning plastic, Mr. James drank hot spirits, he explained with a laugh; a filthy bottle filled with moonshine was permanently placed underneath his chair.

Bobby and Kantinka warned me that, on bad days, he would suddenly shout at imagined intruders, although this never happened when we met with him. Although he was fearful of strangers and unwilling to fix a time for an interview—because he was always busy, he explained—we managed to exchange a few words. From our brief conversation I understood that, 'due to financial difficulties', he somehow lost his way in the desert, ended up in Niamey and had lived here for so many years that his children were, by then, grown up. I asked him if he wanted to go home, then immediately regretted asking such an insensitive question. He shook his head as if almost disgusted. Of course he wanted to go home, he said, but not before he had managed to save up a little money to take back to the family in Ghana. And when might that be, I asked him. Shaking his head in frustration, he put his hands into his empty shirt pocket and turned it inside out, and said peevishly 'Only my pocket knows'. He excused himself because a big man was coming to pick up an important job, a Toyota bumper, and he wanted to get back to work.

### They Love to Travel too Much

To better understand the situation of the stranded we met with Mr. Frimpong, one of the leading figures in the Ghanaian diaspora, and former president of the Ghana Association in Niamey. Mr. Frimpong found nothing extraordinary in Dominic's narrative except the unfortunate story of so many young Ghanaians who set out to search for greener pastures but lose their way. We met Mr. Frimpong one night at the outside bar of *La Tombée*, close to the Ténéré bus station where travelers depart for the desert. A former professional footballer in Burkina Faso and currently employed as an electrician at the U.S. embassy, Mr. Frimpong initially welcomed the appointment to head the association after meeting with the Ghanaian ambassador to Burkina Faso in the Grand Hotel, but he retired six months ago because 'the stranded boys became too much'. The Niger police would call him in the middle of the night to come and pick up deportees, and arrange for them to travel back to Burkina Faso, where the embassy would handle the rest. One time he had to charter a whole bus. Although the Ghanaian Embassy would refund the money for the transportation, he still had to put up the money first, and had to pay for the deportees' food and drink out of his own pocket. He asked the embassy for an office or a house where the stranded migrants could sleep until transportation was ready, so that he did not have to take them to his own house but, when that, too, was turned down, he decided to step down as president. Although he had left the position six months earlier, he still received calls from the Nigerian police in the middle of the night—'President, your people are here!'—when stranded or deported migrants came back from the desert. Mr. Frimpong was fiddling with his two mobile phones on the table—one phone was his own and was constantly ringing with the Ghanaian national anthem, and the other was a work phone paid for by the American Embassy. He also had a walkie-talkie where he apparently answered to the codename Elmina. 'Ghanaians' he said, shaking his head and smiling, 'They love to travel too much'.

## Taking Care of the Dead

Basically, the group that came together to arrange Dominic's funeral were all lost migrants—most were chronically lacking any financial means and living from hand to mouth, whereas some, like Bobby and Kantinka, had turned their exile into a livelihood. Arranging a funeral for someone in their own unfortunate situation was an unwelcome and expensive obstacle—yet, morally and religiously, it was unthinkable not to conduct the proper rites and secure the passage of Dominic's soul to the spirit world of the ancestors. Broadly, this responsibility—taking care of people with even less money than oneself—however unwanted, was a common theme of life on the margins in Niger. To Bobby and Kantinka, assisting would-be migrants in transit and guiding them along the desert routes, the handling of such matters was a current topic of conversation and worry. They would, for instance, receive back migrants who had had accidents in the desert because, since they 'pushed' them, they felt that it was their responsibility. Moreover, unnecessary attention from the local police was not desirable to the brokers. If a migrant, for instance, wandered about, mad or injured, and told his story to the authorities, it could be a problem not only for the brokers but also for the drivers and the station owners. Once they had a young boy who was sitting on the wrong side of the four-wheel drive in the desert when the car hit a landmine and both his legs were badly injured from the knees down. On the way back, his colleagues had to spray him with perfume to cover the smell of gangrene. Bobby and Kantinka took him to the hospital and covered the expenses themselves. They also had to dip into their own pockets when, another time, a jeep somersaulted in the desert and caught fire and a young Ghanaian who they had 'pushed' to Libya was badly burned on his back. He came back almost naked, Kantinka explained, and covered in iodine to keep him from 'rotting'; his friends were covering him with a piece of cloth that they made sure did not touch his skin. They also had a couple of mad people, 'shouting and misbehaving', who lost their minds in the desert because of 'the pressure'; normally they would tie them to the seats, Kantinka explained, and send them back to Ghana. For this reason they were skeptical about helping would-be migrants who looked sure to fail the journey, and were always weighing up the expected profits against the possibility that a migrant could represent a future loss. But other concerns than business played into it, also. They were not monsters but failed migrants themselves, trying to make ends meet, and they appeared to have real pity for compatriots going through the same events that had so severely dented their own future plans.

## Migrant Brinkmanship

One such case was Muhammad, a young Ghanaian migrant on his way to Libya, whom Bobby and Kantinka had advised to turn back to Ghana instead because the amount of money he had was 'too small' to see the journey through. When we sat down and talked about his now shattered hopes and dreams, Muhammad's disappointment and sense of injustice were considerable. He explained how he had to leave school because the family struggled and it hurt him deeply, because he loved schoolwork and was even good at it. Before, he was working on odd jobs in Accra while his former colleagues were 'moving ahead', even though he was a better and more serious student than they were, as he bitterly remarked. His dream was simple. He would travel to Libya and make money, go back, set up a small shop, and then finish school. He had all the details worked out.

> I will study in the morning then, in the afternoon, after school and after taking my bath, I will go to the shop and go over the accounts with my friend. He will get the key and run the shop when I am in school. This way I will finish my education. That's my dream.

But his father, who sold sugar, could not help him with money, his mother was 'weak' and in the house, and his uncle had left for the Ivory Coast long ago and was never heard of again. So it was up to him, and him alone, to change his life around. But now, clutching his ticket from the station, he had to give up those plans. The next day, Muhammad announced that he had decided to travel into the desert anyway, which came as no surprise to the brokers. He explained that he believed that, when he reached Agadez, God would help him and his friends in Libya would come through somehow and send him more money. 'He will suffer', Bobby said later, 'he thinks when he reaches Agadez he's almost there, but that's only the beginning of the journey'. The next morning, Muhammad left on the bus for Agadez, and Bobby and Kantinka had another client hanging on to life by a thread in the desert.

Yet Muhammad's decision was understood and sympathized with, even if it did not represent the recommended course of action. It denoted a necessary form of *migrant brinkmanship* and perhaps a deep-seated understanding that advances are not distributed in any predictable order and that disaster travels along anyway, however well one prepares. It also spoke of the power of hope in a future where wrongs would be corrected and where Muhammad would be able to continue his disconnected education and lead the kind of life that he felt morally belonged to him, to the extent that risking his life in the desert to obtain it was a risk worth taking. Bobby, himself, caused 'fire damage' at home before leaving—he sold something that did not belong to him—whereas Kantinka suffered greatly on the road and almost lost his bearings. So the brokers understood well that difficult and dangerous choices are a feature of undocumented migrant life in transit, and sometimes hope is all there is, in the sense that, even with all the evidence stacked against you, there is still a sense that one's unfortunate circumstances can be changed for the better. Moreover, they were resigned to the fact that, whatever they said, people went anyway, and only when they came back did they really understand what was asked of them in the desert or on the sea. It was like joining a secret society of members who had experienced shameful and undignified events that could only be discussed with those who had already been there. But most often the details were suffered in silence.

This conspiracy of silence, and its positive counterpart—the confidential sharing of important information about the mesmerizing life in the big cities of Europe—has an important effect, John Berger posits. His argument is based on labor migration to Europe in the 1970s, an effect that has a parallel in today's current African labor migration. The migrant 'visualizes himself entering their conspiracy. Then he will learn their secrets. And he will come back having achieved even more than they, for he is capable of working harder, of being shrewder and of saving more quickly than any of them' (Berger and Mohr 2010, 33). To understand Muhammad's choice, one has to take into account the fragile hope that somewhere else one's talents and efforts will be given the attention and respect they deserve; that somewhere else will be a 'launching pad' for one's existential self (Hage 2005, 470). And, if not, so be it. This is the gamble of migrant brinkmanship in the desert; it literally boils down to life or death. The reality in Europe is therefore often a big disappointment, too, because surviving the journey is not a voucher that can be cashed in. Instead, another kind of stoppage awaits.

## Selling Gin

The only time I met Dominic was one evening when we were heading for a Ghanaian street kitchen across from an empty bus station, where the street kids—as Bobby informed us while we were walking through the labyrinth of then-deserted stalls that surround the station—allegedly 'like to stab people too much'. Bobby said he had something special in store for us as we passed a roadside motorcycle repair shop—where a group of mechanics were sitting under a thatched roof, smoking cigarettes in the darkness—and then turned down an unlit corridor that cut between the mud walls of the neighborhood houses. The corridor led to a kind of small square where others corridors met, with a couple of large trees and five or six cars parked outside the gates of the houses; a boy with a table top, selling cigarettes and bonbons, appeared out of nowhere. Bobby knocked quietly on a large green iron gate before pushing it open with two hands. We stepped into a compound of three terraced houses. Bobby knocked on the door of the first house, and there was a mumbled response from inside as Dominic slowly got to his feet, having apparently been lying on a mattress on the floor, watching television, and wearing only shorts. He was a big man, probably in his late thirties. We exchanged greetings, and Bobby explained that we were on our way to eat at Bobby's wife's food stand, and that we would like something to whet our appetite beforehand. Dominic nodded, disappeared into the backroom and came back with a string of gin shots wrapped in plastic, like lollipops. They were contraband goods that he imported from Ghana. Tommy, my assistant, and I took one each; it was really strong and warm and did not go down all that easily. Bobby knocked back two and also took two for the road, whereas Kantinka rarely touched alcohol. We sat for a while in Dominic's bare room and talked about Ghana, and about the photo poster on his wall—as in any decent Ghanaian migrant home at the time—celebrating the Ghanaian national football team winning the 2009 World Cup for players under 20, beating Brazil in the finals and becoming the first African team to win the competition. We agreed to go back and see him soon and take down his long migration story. Dominic smiled and warned us that we would need a lot of notepads but said we were always welcome and walked us to the gate.

Unfortunately, the interview failed to materialize, as Dominic lost his life only ten days later. The official story that was given at the funeral, and that nobody believed, was that his leg suddenly swelled up and he went to the hospital for treatment. They apparently managed to solve the problem but, after having been discharged from hospital, Dominic suffered a massive heart attack, collapsed in his home, and somehow almost severed his right middle finger as he grabbed at the window bars for support. Mr. Frimpong, for instance, had a different version. He said that one would have to consider the fact that Dominic was a ladies' man, and that he was taking a big risk by chasing a certain married lady. Mr. Frimpong pointed to the strangely severed finger as proof that he been attacked by a jealous husband with a knife or a cutlass: 'He was trying to protect himself but they got him'. Whichever story happened to be true, in this hostile environment it appeared that all the Ghanaian migrants had a small amount of fear to pour into Dominic's death.

## The Wrong Medicine

Seeking to know what really happened to Dominic, we sat down with a number of the Ghanaian dignitaries who came together to arrange the details of the funeral, and they all gave a small part of his story. We never came close to fully understanding what led to his death except that he, like most of his compatriots, had plans to go to Europe but had met 'difficulties' on the way and for one reason or another had ended up in Niger, where he was waiting for a new chance when fate caught up with him. One of the senior figures in the community, Mr. Francis, an accountant who nurtured a dream of returning to Ghana and playing a part in the political life of the country, explained to us that Dominic was from the Volta Region; his father was dead but his mother and sisters were still living there. 'They should have been here [for the funeral] but, because of financial problems, they could not come. Now, the sister says she's coming next Friday . . .'. Prior to Niger, Dominic spent time in Liberia and Cape Verde and later in Guinea and Nigeria, traveling for 'many, many years'. But he wanted to see Europe, too, and was trying to reach Libya when something 'unfortunate' happened on the road and he ended up in Niamey, working as a part-time painter. Last year he was planning to go to Spain, Mr. Francis explained, but a brother 'deceived' him. Later, an uncle in Lesotho told him to come down, and Dominic was making plans to leave that very Christmas, when disaster struck. He had had a problem with the leg which had swollen up, and he went to the lorry station and bought some drugs from a local pharmacist, Mr. Francis said. However, when he took the medicine he instantly felt ill, and his heart was paining him. He easily felt tired, and could not move around or work. 'So that killed him; he was moving somewhere when he fell down. The medicine was not correct; you know, the Chinese, and the Nigerians too, they put anything inside a paper and sell us so maybe it was a wrong medicine he bought. It wasn't a good medicine'.

## 'Nobody Knows I'm Here'

It quickly became evident that, instead of obtaining meaningful information about what really happened to Dominic, his unfortunate death became a vantage point for other migrants in similar circumstances to open up. To Mr. Francis, the dream of making a name for himself in Europe, and his ultimate failure to do so, also underscored the story of his own life. An accountant from the Kwame Nkrumah University of Science and Technology, he traveled to Germany in 1978 and found work as a machine operator in a food-processing company on the river Rhine. 'The people were so good, and so warm and generous, people who have not been there think the Germans are wicked but it's not true, they are helpful and polite and, of all the countries I have been to, Germany is the place I loved the most'. He managed to make the most of his time there and traveled back to Ghana six years later with money to invest, which is when things started to turn sour. While working for the government, he bought shares in a fishing company that operated out of Jamestown. 'But those fishermen are not serious; you can't rely on them. They'll go somewhere and sell the fish and tell you there was no catch; they'll really bring you down'. The fishermen cheated him and spent most of his money before he quit the industry and invested the remaining savings in an electronics shop, selling televisions and cassette decks. To concentrate on business, Mr. Francis quit his low-paying government job. Yet his investment was not yielding sufficient profits, and, when the opportunity presented itself for him to travel to America and stay with a younger brother, he cashed in everything and made the fateful decision to buy gold. 'I am an Ashanti, I know gold', he said. Yet, at the time of Jerry John Rawlings, it was illegal to smuggle gold out of Ghana and, before he even reached the checkpoint at Aflau on the Togo border, Mr. James was arrested and brought up before a military tribunal in the city of Ho in the Volta Region. His plan had been to reach Nigeria and buy a ticket for the United States but, instead, he was sent to James Camp Prison in Accra. 'It was terrible time; a very rough time. They took everything from me. There was no access to a phone, and I had no communication with my parents; even my wife didn't know my whereabouts'.

Upon his release, two years later, he managed to raise enough money to go to Libya, with a view to somehow reaching Germany again. His stay in Libya was short-lived, however, since he could not accept the racism. 'Things were so rough there; they don't have any respect for human beings. Your heart cannot be at rest; always, you're filled with fear'. He then relocated to Algeria and worked as a money exchanger at international hotels there, making good use of his language skills. Once again, he managed to save enough money to make a new investment. This time he bought aluminum and powdered milk in Tamanrasset and chartered a truck for Niger where, according to his calculations, he could sell the load and make a great profit. However, a Tuareg gang who threatened to kill him if he looked back stole the milk powder. When Mr. Francis finally reached Niger with the aluminum, he was shocked to find that the price for the transportation from the mountains had suddenly risen, and was now greater than the value of the goods. Thus, cheated and penniless, Mr. Francis ended up in Niamey, where he has now been for 12 years, surviving on small business deals. 'My parents, my wife, my children—nobody knows I am here. They think I am dead or somewhere in Europe.'

## 'I Cannot Go Back Empty-Handed'

Although he had now retired from traveling, having suffered such great misfortunes on the road, Mr. Francis sympathized with Dominic's dreams and with the hopes of the young Ghanaian 'boys' coming through Niamey on a daily basis to look for opportunities in Libya or Europe. They come from poor families, he explained, and there was no money to buy an airline ticket so they take to the dangerous road. 'They know there's an element of risk, but if they want to be rich, they have to do it. Unlike in Europe, for us here, in black Africa, just to feed yourself is a problem'. He put it down to the economy and the hunger for consumption:

> When people come back from Europe they bring so many things, so people in Ghana think it's an economic paradise, a consumer wonderland, where everything you want, you can get, so they, too, want to go. They know if they can make it to Europe or America they can become someone.

Although Mr. Francis' own dreams of becoming someone—in the eyes of his family and the country that he loved and repeatedly talked about 'serving'— had taken such a wrong turn, he had not given up. 'My plan now is to open a bar and restaurant, gather money and go back to Ghana. I have a wife, she's working as a civil servant but for a very long time there has been no contact'. He thought of them often, and sometimes imagined what had happened to them during his long exile:

> If I go back empty-handed, I will be a burden to her. A civil servant in Ghana is not too rich—unless the person is corrupt—and looking after three children is not easy. I suppose she has been struggling but I don't know.

He completely refused the idea of going back and explaining the truth to the family—that he had struggled but things just had not worked out.

> I cannot go back empty-handed, that's impossible. That's the last thing I will ever do. I have three children whom I left so many years ago; imagine if I go back and greet them with nothing. It would be so shameful; I will never do it. But I have to go; I have to find money and go and serve my country. Here, I can't do anything.

Amazingly, having such bad luck and being in a tight spot for years had not erased Mr. Francis' hope that, in the future, his ship would come in. 'I am very hopeful that things will change for the better and that I can open a bar and get a little money', he said.

## The Prophecy

The hope that still made Mr. Francis persevere in life was connected to a prophecy that had been given to him from an unexpected source. Indeed, just as the negative forces in his life appeared to be so unevenly and unpredictably distributed, so too did the positive influences appear to happen at random. Yet these little enigmatic openings seemed to keep him from stumbling in his tracks despite the setbacks. During his time in Germany, Mr. Francis worked closely with an Indian migrant from the Punjab; they became close friends and did everything together like 'brothers'. If there was a social event at the workplace, they would always go together. The Indian was a Theosophist—a member of a religious society which celebrated esoteric knowledge of the world's spiritual secrets—and one day he read Mr. Francis' palm and foresaw many of the things that had later come about and that would happen in the future. Through him, Mr. Francis joined the international Theosophical Society in Madras and, he explained, he knew today what the spiritual nature of his problem was, but he also knew that whatever happened to a man occurred for his own good:

> Any problem you face, there are certain things you can learn that will help your development. The important thing is to not lose hope but to strive and do good things and shy away from anything evil. Strive for anything you want and you can achieve it.

The Indian told him that what he had planned—to eventually go home to Ghana, build a house, and start a company—would one day materialize but that he would struggle initially and all his plans would come to nothing. 'Later, I will become rich. That is what he told me, and that is what I believe'.

## The Wretched of the Earth

In Mr. Francis' example we see that, even though 'The lack of a future, previously reserved for the "wretched of the earth", is an increasingly widespread, even modal, experience' (Bourdieu 2000, 234), hope still lingers among the lost migrants and plays an important part in the maintenance of a moral universe—that is, a universe where one has the attention and responsiveness of the powers one is sustained by. This universe is also where there is a belief that one's fate is not entirely out of one's hands, or ridden with arbitrariness, but where there exists some deep grammar of reciprocity in the world that will, ultimately, receive a person's sacrifices and, in due course, redress the losses he or she has suffered (Lucht 2011, 246). Despair, on the other hand, appears to be a breakdown of this notion of existential reciprocity.

Among the Ghanaian migrants in Niger the risk of despair was ever-present, as in the image of Mr. James, the plastic repairman, sitting in the black smoke of his open fires, talking to himself (although I had the impression that, to himself, however bleak his situation looked, there was still time for another throw of the dice). Even Kantinka, the most clear-headed of the brokers, suffered a breakdown prior to going into the broker business after losing his family's money in the desert, and was literally and mentally lost on the streets of Niamey until Bobby found him and took him in (see Lucht 2013 for Kantinka's story)—lost as in a lack of existential direction and at the complete mercy of circumstances. Hope in its most basic form, as Jackson, inspired by Alain Badiou, argues, does not necessarily include the idea that justice will be done or a person's wishes granted but only that it is not the end, that the individual is not lost and that his or her subjectivity will persevere (Jackson 2011, 79). Like Mr. Francis, one must suffer and be patient and agree to yield to powers greater than oneself, or to resign from having control in order, paradoxically but according to the existential give-and-take of life, to regain that control by a leap of faith. The obligation to give (or be forced to give up, which reciprocally demands a response, too) in order to receive what is vital to sustain life, often demands a sacrifice of the social world in order to reaffirm it (Lucht 2011, 246). Just like Mr. Francis, who sacrificed the very life he longed for—to be with his wife and children in his own country—in order to secure his family's sustained well-being, even to the extent that dying in Niger, like Dominic, would be a better option than returning empty-handed. This is because coming home with nothing would not only be his social death, it would spell a return to the grip of stagnation that caused him to leave so many years ago. If Mr. Francis could give nothing else, he could at least not be a burden. But the desire for life is not easy to extinguish; it is 'amorphous and volatile', writes Michael Jackson, and the imagination always travels beyond the immediate social world and experiments with new beginnings and the limits of what a person can actually become (Jackson 2013, 212). Mr. Francis, for instance, still had hope, meaning that what the Indian friend saw in the lines of his palm caused him to believe that his suffering would eventually come to an end; in his exile he found in that hope the justification for continuing to sacrifice the present for a future which, from the outside, appeared hard to believe in.

## Death is not the End

On the day of the funeral, after Dominic had been lying in a freezer for a week, we all met up at the morgue to claim his body, Bobby and Kantinka appropriately dressed in black. There was quite an impressive group of people there, taking into consideration that his family from Ghana had failed to appear. 'That's how it is', my assistant Sammy said. 'When you're rich, they'll rush to the funeral, they will even sell their land to get there in time, but when you're poor nobody will show up'. Nevertheless, a large group of resident Ghanaians had come, among them the former president of the Ghanaian Association and Mr. Francis, the accountant. As we sat outside the white walls of the city morgue to await the arrival of the coffin, Dominic was, according to tradition, being washed down before his final journey. His wife borrowed a razor blade from Sammy, and Dominic's hair, nails, and pubic hair were cut; the hair would be returned to Ghana and buried there when the family arrived. 'Death is not the end', Mr. Francis leaned over and said to me as we sat waiting outside, the slender and eloquent man smiling enigmatically as if he were conveying a happy secret—'Do you understand?

Death is the beginning'. Then a beat-up truck arrived with a white coffin on the back accompanied by three young men in work attire, and began backing up into the yard of the morgue. The coffin was taken down and disappeared into the building, where suddenly the sorrowful screams of Dominic's wife and her fellow mourners rang out, as they were given one last glimpse of the dead body. But Dominic was heavy, a big man—although perhaps not 'obese' as Mr. Francis rather coolly noted—and they had to put him down halfway to catch their breath.

In the end they managed to lift his coffin onto the back of the truck; half of the funeral party joined him, standing up and singing as the truck moved down in the direction of the river Niger, past the flower garden on the river banks before arriving at the Christian burial ground. The caretakers had been weeding the place and burning a pile of yellow grass, causing the whole graveyard to be covered in a layer of smoke that—this being an unusually quiet day—still lingered in the downtrodden paths between the small mounds, with their tombstones and crosses. The pastor, who was a young energetic Nigerian man, stood bareheaded under the hot sun, regularly wiping his neck and forehead. He preached about the insignificance of human life in the grand scale of things, and how easily we are blown away, obliterated by circumstances, which led him to point out that, in such a world, where life can disappear in the blink of an eye and, to our confusion and frustration, continually does, there is only one solution. Turn to God in order to save your soul, and better today than tomorrow, for only the soul will have eternal life. This prompted the female mourners to begin singing a traditional Ghanaian funeral song, which touched on the same theme: '*Human being, you're pitiful, human being, you're pitiful, when you die it's finished, when you die it's finished*'. Bobby, who had a dislike of pastors—who, he claimed, were the most corrupt big men in terms of 'chopping people's money'—had withdrawn about five yards away from the funeral party, watching everything and smoking a cigarette. When Dominic was lowered into the ground, and the coffin covered with earth, Bobby shrugged his shoulders, flung away the cigarette and said 'Last, last', meaning 'That's the end of it'. We then took a taxi to Dominic's house. Four rows of plastic chairs had been arranged under a canopy in the yard, a very loud stereo had been rented, and soon the older ladies—some intoxicated to a greater or lesser degree from the liquor that was consumed around the corner—started dancing. We greeted the older people among them, and went to Dominic's semi-darkened room, where the widow, as is customary, was sitting alone on the floor. Mr. Frimpong informed us that he had advised the widow not to keep the hair and the nails from the corpse in the house but to bury the whole thing in the back yard until such time as his family could take it back to Ghana because, if there was foul play, as he expected, you would not want the angry soul of the dead person hovering about, seeking revenge over the living. The widow thanked us for coming and for the small donation to the funeral expenses, and then we went outside and sat in front of the gate, chatting for a while before we left.

## Conclusion

The solemn, yet spirited nature of the funeral seemed to speak of a sense of acceptance of and resignation to the unpredictability of migrant life in the borderlands, even if this event, to many, served as an unpleasant reminder or even a rehearsal of the fate that loomed over their own futures. Indeed, a year later, Bobby would suddenly fall sick with stomach pains and be admitted to hospital, where he died a few days later without his friends knowing or understanding what had happened to him. However, if Dominic's death was an example of the unsuccessful migrant brinkmanship that attempted to steer a course between the hope and need for growth and the dangers and death that awaited on the road and in the border zones, what did Mr. Francis mean when he said 'Death is not the end'? Apart from the obvious Christian understanding that Dominic's soul was now in the hands of God and his seat among his forefathers secured, as the priest said, there was perhaps also the deeper existential meaning. In this context a person's subjectivity goes on, and death—the final boundary in life—is there to be crossed, too; a person's struggles in the here-and-now may come to an end, but the soul, unlike on earth, will be set free to pursue what was not possible in life: a free and dignified life among one's peers. Indeed, the afterlife is characterized by liberation from the brutality, the insults, the waiting, and the nothingness that characterize life among the 'floating population'—that growing class of people scattered on the edges of richer regions, suspended in a life of 'expectancy' (Bayart 2007, 274).

This sense of continuity, even on the margins, may be what Schopenhauer, the otherwise gloomy and misanthropic thinker, is pointing to when he argues that the reason why we are not 'frantic' at the idea of our little 'unacceptable' lives 'ebbing away' is that we are 'secretly conscious in the profoundest depths of our being that we share in the inexhaustible well of eternity, out of which we can forever draw new life and renewed time' (1851/2004, 52). Beyond religious cosmology, I argue that hope draws strength from a notion of continuity or existential reciprocity which is not necessarily obliterated by loss but which inscribes loss in the logic of sacrifice as a giving up of that which cannot or should not be given up—one's life proper. This is done in the hope that, by making this movement or leap, life will be reinstated in some form in the due course of time, and something new may appear, even if the individual will not him/herself prosper. This hope, that life can be drawn into a relationship of exchange by way of sacrifice, is a way of instituting what is missing in the first place, namely a moral horizon one can have trust in and, to some extent, exercise control over. To many, this hope of responsiveness and mobility beyond immediate existence appears more desirable than returning empty-handed. At present, the death-defying journeys represent people taking action in the hope that the borders that confined them to a life of stasis can be transgressed—the very reason for traveling in the first place—and not just geographical borders but social and political borders, too, in the sense that, in this migrant brinkmanship of risking one's life in the desert and on the sea, the prize is a complete reversion of one's social status. In other words, becoming 'someone' at home by refusing to accept an order that otherwise appeared unchangeable, or as Bourdieu argues, 'The symbolic transgression of a social frontier has a liberatory effect in its own right because it enacts the unthinkable' (2000, 236). Clearly, these journeys had a symbolic meaning; it was possible to challenge the impossible. For all the might and power of European nation-states and private security companies operating in the borderlands, it was possible to breach the borders—the geographical, social, and political borders—that impose limits and subordination on people in the Global South.

The resulting suffering and death on the borders, although not political acts *per se*, are powerful acts of iconoclasm that challenge both the repressive geopolitical order and the sincerity of European commitment to humanitarian values. In fact, in order for this form of iconoclasm to appear legitimate at all, instead of being rejected as scandal (which, of course, is often the case in the alarmist discourse of media and politics), the structures that are contested must be in a state of uncertainty and crisis, argues Pierre Bourdieu (2000, 236). Perhaps the unease with which we witness people dying in the Mediterranean Sea speaks of such a potential insecurity in the system. However dangerous, and sometimes fatal, these journeys are, they represent to the migrants a margin of freedom to make more out of the lives into which they have been thrown (Zigon 2009, 258).

# References

Bayart, J.-F. 2007. *Global subjects: A political critique of globalization*. Cambridge: Polity Press.
Berger, J., and J. Mohr. [1975]2010. *A seventh man*. London: Verso.
Bourdieu, P. 2000. *Pascalian meditations*. Stanford: Stanford University Press.
Crapanzano, V. 2003. Reflections on hope as a category of social and psychological analysis. *Cultural Anthropology* 18 (1): 3–32.
Das, V. 1995. *Critical events: An anthropological perspective on contemporary India*. Oxford: Oxford University Press.
Desjarlais, R. 1997. *Shelter blues: Sanity and selfhood among the homeless*. Philadelphia: University of Pennsylvania Press.
Hage, G. 2005. A not so multi-sited ethnography of a not so imagined community. *Anthropological Theory* 5 (4): 463–475.
Jackson, M. 2011. *Life within limits: Well-being in a world of want*. Durham and London: Duke University Press.
Jackson, M. 2013. *The wherewithal of life: Ethics, migration, and the question of well-being*. Berkeley: University of California Press.
Kleinman, A. 2006. *What really matters*. Oxford: Oxford University Press.

Lucht, H. 2011. *Darkness before daybreak: African migrants living on the margins in Southern Italy today*. Berkeley: University of California Press.

Lucht, H. 2013. Pusher stories: Ghanaian connection men and the expansion of the EU's border regime into Africa. In *The migration industry and the commercialization of international migration*, eds. T. Gammeltoft-Hansen and N. N. Sørensen, 173–190. New York: Routledge.

Lucht, H. 2015. Kierkegaard in West Africa: Hope and sacrifice in a Ghanaian fishing village. In *Anthropology and philosophy: Dialogues on trust and hope*, eds. S. Liisberg, E. O. Pedersen and A. L. Dalsgård, 243–255. Oxford and New York: Berghan.

Miyazaki, H. 2006. Economy of dreams: Hope in global capitalism and its critiques. *Cultural Anthropology* 21 (2): 147–172.

Pedersen, M. 2012. A day in the Cadillac: The work of hope in urban Mongolia. *Social Analysis* 56 (2): 1–16.

Robbins, J. 2013. Beyond the suffering subject: Toward an anthropology of the good. *Journal of the Royal Anthropological Institute* 19 (3): 447–462.

Schopenhauer, A. 1851/2004. *Essays and aphorisms*. London: Penguin Classics.

Simon, J. 2006. Irregular transit migration in the Mediterranean: Facts, figures, and insights. In *Mediterranean transit migration*, ed. N. N. Sørensen, 25–66. Copenhagen: Danish Institute for International Studies.

Vigh, H. 2009. Wayward migration: On imagined futures and technological voids. *Ethnos* 74 (1): 91–109.

Willen, S. 2007. Toward a critical phenomenology of 'illegality': State, power, criminalization, and abjectivity among undocumented migrant workers in Tel Aviv, Israel. *International Migration* 45 (3): 8–36.

Zigon, J. 2009. Hope dies last: Two aspects of hope in contemporary Moscow. *Anthropological Theory* 9 (3): 253–271.

# 10 Returning with Nothing but an Empty Bag

## Topographies of Social Hope after Deportation to Ghana

*Nauja Kleist*

Kwaku[1] did not feel good, worried sick about how to provide for his family and secure their future. At night, he would pretend to be sleeping, closing his eyes to avoid his wife worrying about his insomnia. The days were not much better. A man in his thirties with little schooling, he could not find a job and spent most of his time in the rented room that he shared with his wife and their three children, ruminating about his life and avoiding contact with townspeople, who would laugh at him. This kind of life was not what Kwaku had hoped for when he left his Ghanaian home town, one fine December morning in 2012, and headed to Libya to earn money to support his family and, in due course, travel onwards to Europe. It was not that he had thought that the journey would be easy, knowing how many townspeople had struggled on the way to Libya. However, he also knew that some of them had made it and sent money back home to take care of their families, establish businesses, and build houses, and he could not face a life without a similar future. His journey did not go well: first he was first kidnapped by armed robbers, then he was detained by the Libyan authorities, and finally he was deported to Niger, from where he managed to find his way back to Ghana. Just two months after Kwaku had left, he was back with nothing but an empty bag in his hands. 'I did not feel happy', he bitterly explained, 'because there was nothing in my pocket, and there are no jobs here, so I am not feeling lucky. My family is not feeling good either, they were not feeling good. Even the little money that I had, I have lost it'. Nevertheless, Kwaku wanted to go to Libya again, perceiving it as one of the few options for progress in his life.

In this chapter I examine hope in the context of high-risk migration and restrictive mobility regimes, with a particular focus on life after deportation to Ghana. For many migrants and their families, deportation signifies the ultimate failure of migration projects, implying an enforced disruption of mobility and livelihoods abroad, the termination of (eventual) remittance flows, economic problems, and shame *vis-à-vis* one's family, peers, and wider community. As several other chapters in this volume show (e.g., Lucht, Bredeloup, Hernández-Carretero), returning empty-handed is considered a personal and collective catastrophe, to be avoided at almost all costs. Whereas some migrants prefer—or put up with—destitute and precarious living conditions rather than return empty-handed, deportees do not have this option. Based on fieldwork in Kwaku's hometown, my aim is to analyze, first, the ways in which deportation and high-risk migration are embedded in conflicting notions of the good life and how to achieve it and, second, how deportees perceive and cope with their situation. In this way, I endeavor to shed light on two seeming migration paradoxes: first that, despite widespread knowledge about the dangers of high-risk migration, including deportation, migration continues to constitute a perceived pathway to a better life in some contexts; second, that much migration is weaved around collective hopes for a good life abroad but, when migration fails, as in the case of deportation, the individual migrants are blamed as having brought it on themselves. I suggest that, inspired by Ghassan Hage's work on social and societal hope (2003) and Phillip Mar's notion of topographies of hope (2005), analyzing the different modalities of hope is a productive way of exploring these paradoxes.

## Methodological Considerations: Topographies of Social Hope

Employing hope as an analytical framework, I analyze the simultaneous uncertainty and potentiality of an imagined or anticipated future (Mar 2005; Webb 2007) and what this means for people affected by deportation. I am particularly interested in the conditions of possibility for different modes of hope, and how these are negotiated and generated at different scales and by diverse groups. Hope, in this sense, is relational and embedded in historical and structural contexts; it is neither pure fantasy nor completely individualized but refers to 'a temporalized sense of potential, of having a future' (Mar 2005, 365).

Ghassan Hage's work on social and societal hope (2003) is a useful way of approaching such a sense of having a future and of distinguishing between different modes of hope. *Social hope* refers to social imaginaries and collective visions of the good and meaningful life and future among particular groups, be they large or small—or, in Mar's words, to the '"public" evaluation of possibility' (2005, 365). *Societal hope* constitutes a more delimited form of social hope, focusing on how the state generates and distributes visions of the good life and possible achievement within society. Such visions may be related to upward social mobility, security, and prosperity. Whereas these visions may not be realized, they are based on—or are meant to convey—the confidence that this future is not beyond reach.

Societal hope may refer to the well-known tale of the newspaper boy (or the occasional small-business owner or computer-science student) rising to glory and riches or to the equally well-known promises of a better education and hence a better future for children and young people. It constitutes a mode of governing (Turner 2015) through the invocation of future scenarios and the belief—be it patient or avid—that these scenarios can be realized in accordance with the overall political project of the state. Hence, distributing hope is not an unequivocal process whereby a pre-determined result is produced by the state and uncritically consumed by citizens, but, rather, one which attempts to install a belief in the future and in the ways of realizing or accessing this future which, again, is perceived and negotiated in different ways by diverse groups.

A focus on the distribution of hope in relation to migration and deportation raises the issue of its spatial dimension and how different places and zones are associated with opportunities or stasis in a world of stratified globalization and inequality. I am here inspired by Phillip Mar's notion of 'topographies of hope' (2005). Mar has suggested the term to capture how migrants map opportunities and principles for engagement with the world—e.g., accumulation, security, or pleasure—onto different places or regions, including migrants' countries of origin and (possible) destinations. Such topographies may originate in an experience of living in a place devoid of opportunities, marked by loss, insecurity, poverty or, simply, a lack of imaginable progress for certain groups (cf. Vigh 2009). In such cases, hope may be placed elsewhere, perhaps to be reached through mobility.

The word 'topography' is evocative in terms of implying distances and the density of imagined or experienced opportunities and stagnation, constituting 'mental' maps of places. I propose that the concept can usefully be combined with Hage's thoughts on social hope and hence a focus on how not only migrants but also states and other actors create, sustain, and (attempt to) govern topographies of societal or other kinds of social hope. This makes it important to distinguish between the different topographies of hope in terms of who are hoping or distributing hope and, not least, who and what are included or excluded in these topographies. Not all parts of the citizenry or the national territory are necessarily included in the state topographies of hope and not all subjects share the same topography of hope. As Hage (2003) has pointed out, states do not distribute societal hope equally, which creates differentiated scenarios of possible futures for different subjects. Likewise, some subjects' topographies of social hope may not reflect or include the state's topography of societal hope.

Examining the tension between state and local topographies of hope among deportees allows me to explore how the different modalities of hope and the good life are related to high-risk migration and deportation. The argument I present is two-fold. First, I demonstrate that deportation implies social and financial problems, shame, and the (at least) temporary suspension of hope. Nevertheless, some deportees may be perceived as successful if they have managed to return with savings. This implies an individualization of migration success and failure which enables the continued social hope of migration as a means to a better life. Second, and in consequence, I demonstrate a discrepancy between the distributions of societal hope in Ghana and the local topographies of social hope in relation to high-risk migration.

Whereas the state emphasizes opportunities for the good life in Ghana through educational achievement and hard work and discourages irregular or 'aimless' migration, many aspiring and deported migrants and their families still perceive high-risk migration as a pathway to upward social mobility.

I base this argument on a total of seven months of fieldwork, carried out between February 2012 and April 2015, on involuntary return to Ghana, such as deportation and the emergency return of labor migrants from the civil war in Libya in 2011. Fieldwork took place in a rural town, here called Amanfo, characterized by much overland and high-risk migration to Libya and sometimes onwards to Europe or other destinations. I carried out observation, participant photography, informal conversations, and interviews with involuntary return migrants, their families, prospective migrants, local political and traditional authorities, municipal officers, representatives from institutions and NGOs working with migration, and government agencies. Fifteen men and one woman among the interlocutors had been deported from primarily Libya but also from other North African countries, Israel, Europe, and North America. Most of the deportees were in their twenties or early thirties and many were school drop-outs, although a few had finished senior secondary school. They all had relatively poor backgrounds although some had managed to earn good money during or after their migration. I also carried out interviews with national and international institutions and organizations in Accra and Tamale, such as the Ghana Immigration Service, the Ministry of Foreign Affairs and the International Organization for Migration (IOM). Finally, I draw upon data from a previous research project in Ghana on diaspora politics, a total of seven months of fieldwork in 2008 and 2010 among policy-makers, government officials, and transnationally engaged return migrants from Western countries.

## A Brief History of Societal Hope in Ghana

Since the advent of the Ghanaian nation-state in 1957, the country has gone through periods of progress and crisis. The first sub-Saharan African country to achieve independence from its European colonizer, economic and political optimism in Ghana was widespread in the late 1950s and early 1960s (McCaskie 2008). The situation changed in the middle of the 1960s with an economic and political crisis and a succession of *coups d'état* until the end of 1981, with the establishment of Rawlings' left-populist military regime. During the 1970s, many Ghanaians migrated to Nigeria to work in the booming economy. However, following the economic crisis there in the 1980s, all irregular migrants were expelled from the country, including more than one million Ghanaian labor migrants in 1983 and about 100,000 Ghanaians in 1985 (Van Hear 1998). The 1983 expulsion coincided with an unusually tough year in Ghana, with widespread bushfires, droughts, and bankruptcy as well as the adoption of IMF-induced structural adjustment programs and neoliberal policies (Osei-Assibey 2014). This situation spurred large waves of out-migration throughout the 1980s, with the opposition fleeing from political persecution and skilled and unskilled labor migrants looking for better economic opportunities and employment elsewhere.

Migration from Ghana has continued since then but within a changed political context. Constitutional rule and multiparty democracy were established with the Fourth Republic in 1992. Changing governments have continued neoliberal policies since the 1980s with a range of economic liberalization programs. Despite challenges, since the late 1990s Ghana has slowly but steadily climbed the human development index, with the most dramatic increase in 2008.[2] Oil was found in the Ghanaian territorial waters of the Gulf of Guinea the year before, spurring economic and political optimism (Darkwah 2013; McCaskie 2008). At a press conference in June 2007, then-President Kufuor (NPP) exclaimed: 'We're going to really zoom, accelerate and, if everything works, which I pray will happen positively, you come back in five years, and you'll see that Ghana truly is the African tiger, in economic terms for development'.[3]

As Kufuor's statement suggests, the finding of oil was evoked to generate societal hope. The president both targeted the Ghanaian nation in terms of general economic development—as his statement was widely quoted in Ghanaian newspapers—and emphasized Ghana's future competitive position *vis-à-vis* other states. At the more quotidian level, I witnessed an example of the local distribution of societal hope when I spent some time in 2008 with a Ghanaian politician in his rural home town. Visiting a school, he embarked on a long speech to encourage the pupils to be ambitious. 'You can become an ambassador, an astronaut or rich', he exclaimed, 'because we have found oil. You study hard and pray' (see also Kleist 2015). The focus on education as an avenue for a better and more prosperous future, funded by oil money, has continued since then.[4] The belief in a more promising future grew even greater when Ghana was ranked as a middle-income country in 2010, nearly ten years earlier than expected. By 2011 the growth rate was an impressive 14 per cent.[5] During the 2012 election campaign, education was the most salient theme, with the government focusing on quality education as the means to a better future, whereas the contesting party promised free Senior High School for all.

These statements send messages of societal hope about social upward mobility and wealth to the population. Whereas economic growth should not be equated with societal hope, it can be evoked in the narratives of a promising future, sustaining the idea that this promised future is likely to happen. The articulations of a promising future for Ghana as an African Tiger and of Ghanaian village children as ambassadors and astronauts are examples of how the Ghanaian state distributes societal hope, based on faith in economic and societal progress. Ghana is situated as the locus of hope for realizing an attractive future although, interestingly, the profession of ambassador involves traveling in a highly regularized and comfortable way, and astronauts travel in space. However, hope is also characterized by uncertainty and it is notable that both Kufuor and the politician's articulation of hope emphasized praying rather than absolute certainty.

However, in spite of poverty reduction and economic growth, Ghana is also characterized by rising inequality (Osei-Assibey 2014). Dissatisfaction and disillusion among disadvantaged parts of the population are rife. Whereas the number of new private cars seems to be ever-expanding in Accra and other major towns and there is a construction boom in all major cities in Ghana, with big houses being built by the growing middle class and/or international migrants (Smith and Mazzucato 2009), many people struggle to get by. The growing assortment of expensive consumer goods in Accra and elsewhere is out of reach for the large majority of the population, who can, in both a literal and an abstract sense, see the goods but not enjoy them.

The conspicuous consumption and highly visible wealth create frustrations among those who feel excluded from the economic growth in the country. Unemployment, especially among youth and people with little education, is high and is often linked to an alleged rise in armed robbery and other social problems. What is more, the economy has slowed down, with growth rates dropping to 7.6 per cent in 2013 and 4.2 per cent in 2014.[6] Nevertheless, the confident distribution of societal hope in the early and euphoric oil-finding days was wide in scope by the end of 2012 and the first part of 2013, when I did my main fieldwork. In combination with the visible but inaccessible presence of prosperity and progress, this may well have added to the sense of disappointment and disillusion and the urge to seek a better future elsewhere which was expressed by many people.

Today Ghanaian migration takes on a multiplicity of forms, ranging from high-skilled persons to students and labor migrants. The total number of Ghanaians living outside Ghana today is unknown but is estimated to be more than 1.5 million people (Quartey 2009). About 70 per cent of them are estimated to live in the Economic Community of West African States (ECOWAS) zone, with the United States, the UK, Italy, and Germany as other main destinations (Quartey 2009). As indicated above, political stability and economic growth have not halted Ghanaian migration, which continues to play an important role in terms of livelihood strategies, education, and what is often articulated as 'exposure' to other places in the world. However, different types of migration and destinations are seen as enabling different opportunities and prestige, which together constitute a variety of topographies of hope.

In the context of high-risk migration, it is particular interesting to take a closer look at the *Borga* figure. *Borgas* (sometimes spelled *Burgers*) is a Pidgin English word for Ghanaians living abroad. Etymologically, it is related to Ghanaian migration to Hamburg in the 1980s and early 1990s, when a large number of young, mainly male labor migrants managed to save money through doing blue-collar work and living austere lives. When visiting Ghana, they displayed their hard-earned wealth, distinguishing themselves from their peers as well as from educational return migrants and other elite strata of the population (Nieswand 2013). Today the term *Borga* is widely used to refer to successful migrants—or at least migrants who appear so through the sending of remittances, presents, cars, gadgets, and Western clothing from the country of residence or when visiting or returning. As Nieswand (2013) aptly notes, *Borgas* embody a transnational status paradox: being working-class in the country of settlement while performing and consuming a middle-class lifestyle in Ghana—much like the *Vadimbazakas* in Madagascar (Cole 2014a). This makes the *Borga* figure contested in some circles in Ghana in that *Borgas* typically lack the conventional legitimation of high social status, such as higher education or prestigious family background, and jump social and economic hierarchies through their speedy accumulation and display of wealth. However, *Borgas* are still held in high regard in Amanfo, to where I now turn.

## Connected to the World: Amanfo as a *Borga* Town

Amanfo is the capital of a district located in the Brong Ahafo Region in the western part of Ghana. The district has an estimated population of 95,000 persons, of whom about 30,000 are estimated to live in Amanfo. Being located in the Cocoa Belt, agriculture is the most important livelihood. Amanfo is distinctly rural, with tractors, farmers in rubber boots, and goats and chickens everywhere. There is a hospital, several schools, and many churches. Women sell dried fish and vegetables from wooden structures in the back alleys. Hairdressers, shoe shops, and convenience stores in containers or wooden kiosks abound at the roadside, and spots (as bars are called) play blazing highlife music or the latest *azonto* hits—a Ghanaian dance and music style which has become immensely popular in large parts of West Africa. A few years ago, a new market was established on the outskirts of town, as the old one had become too crowded. Each Tuesday, Amanfo is full of people from the nearby towns and villages, selling all kinds of goods at the New Market, as it is now called. Old *Tico* cars (small, and often extremely battered, cars produced in South Korea) serve as shared taxis up and down the few tarred roads, whereas bigger cars drive between Amanfo and the neighboring towns. The houses in town are a mix of old run-down structures and new big houses painted in bright colors. Likewise, there are several hotels, of which the smartest has an outdoor restaurant serving chicken or fish with *banku*—a favorite staple throughout Ghana, made of boiled fermented corn and cassava dough.

At first sight, Amanfo thus seems like a quiet rural town, mainly connected to the surrounding villages and towns in the district. It is a far cry from the hustle and bustle of Accra or other major cities in Ghana. However, even the occasional visitor, if he or she takes a closer look, will notice how many bars, stores, and schools have names that refer to places from *outside*—as places outside Ghana are usually called—such as Chicago Hardware Store, Benghazi Bar, Jamaica Spot or Cambridge Private School. Like the internationally named barbershops in Arusha, Tanzania (Weiss 2002), the references to *outside* demonstrate multiple connections to the world, as do the persistent 'Hello's from people who will tell you that they have been to Italy, Spain, or Libya or, at least, that they would like to go there.

International migration from Amanfo dates back to the 1960s. Townsmen started to migrate to Nigeria, inspired by the country's booming economy at the time, the presence of Nigerian traders in town, and the economic crisis in Ghana, and brought back money and built houses in Amanfo. This migration continued throughout the 1970s and early 1980s, until the migrant workers from Amanfo were expelled from Nigeria, like other Ghanaians. They returned to Amanfo with tape recorders and transistors, which they placed in front of their houses or carried on their backs, playing loud music for everyone to hear and see that this person had been to Nigeria. However, the political and economic crisis in Ghana during these years, aggravated by droughts and severe bushfires that resulted in the loss of agricultural land and an ensuing famine, made it difficult for returnees to provide for their families (Bob-Milliar and Bob-Milliar 2013; Nieswand 2013). One of the results was re-migration to other West African countries, especially neighboring Côte d'Ivoire. From the late 1980s and early 1990s, Libya[7] became a prominent destination for Amanfo migrants, who primarily found work as masons or construction workers. Likewise, a number of migrants continued—or aimed to continue—onwards to Italy and Spain as the most popular destinations and also to Germany, the Netherlands, the United States, Canada, and Israel, constituting a hierarchy of destinations in the local topographies of hope. It is estimated that, today, about 15 per cent of the population of Amanfo are international migrants.[8]

Walking around Amanfo with this in mind and in the company of a local friend, one quickly realizes that the town has its fair share of *Borgas*, and of their houses, businesses, and cars. The smartest hotel is owned by a returnee from the United States, who drives around in a big car, enjoying his retirement by running his business and drinking with his friends. Likewise, the other hotels and the big new houses are almost all built by international migrants, the wealthiest ones carefully repainting their houses every year so that they keep on looking new. Many of the bigger and more comfortable shared taxis driving between Amanfo and surrounding towns are owned by migrants in Europe or North America who have friends or family members to drive for them, whereas the cheaper and battered *Tico* cars running in town are mostly owned and driven by less-prosperous return migrants. The school fees for pupils at private schools with fancy names are paid by migrants (and a small but growing middle class of non-migrants) who do not trust the state schools and want their children, nephews, and nieces to attend good schools so that they can become 'big' men and women when they grow up. The international shop and spot names also usually refer to the owners' past or present stay *outside*, often seen as a kind of quality guarantee. Amanfo is thus full of *Borgas* and people who desire to become *Borgas* themselves.

## Hope and Uncertainty in High-Risk Migration

Kwaku was one of many young men in Amanfo longing for *Borga* status. When I first met him, he explained: 'I want to be a *Borga*, you know, Canada *Borga*. I want to be a *Borga* because they do things. They build houses. They drive big cars'. Going to Libya would be a first step in realizing this life. Kwaku thus decided to brave the desert, knowing full well that the journey could be dangerous. What he had not realized was the extent of the difficulties and suffering he would encounter—kidnapping, detention, and then overland deportation to Agadez in Niger, where he and several hundred other sub-Saharan Africans were transported in pick-up trucks and then dumped and left to survive on the streets.

The high-risk nature of the overland migration through the Sahara undertaken by Kwaku and many other West African migrants must be seen within the overall context of increasingly restrictive mobility regimes (Glick Schiller and Salazar 2013) in Europe and Africa which have made legal migration hard to achieve for most Ghanaian migrants with destinations outside ECOWAS. It has also made traveling or living in irregular ways more difficult and dangerous, affecting many townspeople in Amanfo. Whereas a few have the opportunity to travel to Western countries and other attractive destinations through family reunification or on educational or tourism visas, the majority do not. Instead, much migration from Amanfo takes place outside the legal circuits of international migration, entailing the risk of abuse, assault, detention, and deportation[9]—even death (cf. Amnesty International 2015; Bredeloup and Pliez 2011; Hamood 2006; Lucht 2011). The mobile livelihoods and high-risk nature of much migration from Amanfo imply that migration projects are often temporary, disrupted, and in flux, rather than permanent emigration, and that involuntary return migration is common. In 2011, for instance, 20,000 Ghanaian labor migrants were evacuated from or fled the conflict in Libya (Bob-Milliar and Bob-Milliar 2013; Kleist forthcoming), of whom about 1,000 alone returned to Amanfo. Deportees like Kwaku add to this number.

The effects of restrictive mobility regimes are aggravated by conflict and political instability in transit zones and destinations, making overland migration from places like Amanfo to Libya more uncertain and more risky but, as we have seen, it does not stop it. Risk has been defined as the 'known probabilities of outcomes' (Williams and Baláz 2012, 168). However, migrants rarely have full knowledge of the conditions of their migration. This makes Horst and Grabska suggest that 'under conditions of mobility in conflict, a focus on uncertainty rather than risk is more appropriate' (2015, 5)—an argument that could be extended to most migration situations. 'Risk-taking', in this sense, relates to how migrants manage and relate to uncertainty (cf. Hernández-Carretero and Carling 2012) which, again, relates to different modes of hope.

In his taxonomy of five modes of hope, Webb (2007) distinguishes between hope with an open-ended orientation towards the future and goal-oriented hope with specific objectives. Overland migration to Libya can be seen as an example of the latter, which Webb again divides into estimative, resolute, and utopian modes of hope. Estimative hope refers to an assessment of the probability of a positive outcome of an action or process, e.g., to informed risk assessment, which is problematic in contexts of outspoken uncertainty. Webb's notion of resolute hope as taking a chance in spite of a 'less than fair gamble' (2007, 81) is more helpful, pointing to how migrants (and others) approach and handle a high degree of uncertainty. The question is not only the kinds of challenge and obstacle that migrants expect (or fear) to encounter but also the notions of the life and future that they hope to realize through migration—their social hope, in other words.

When I discussed this question with my interlocutors in Amanfo, their initial response focused on material outcomes: houses, cars, businesses, and consumer goods. During interviews and participant photography,[10] deportees, returnees from Libya, prospective migrants, and migrant family members consistently expressed the same hopes for the good life: to have one's own house, to have a steady income, to own a car, and to be able to send the children to good schools. Such visions of the good life reflect the material outcomes of being a *Borga* (or other kinds of successful migrant) or having a *Borga* in the family, and are in line with a perhaps increasingly universal, middle-class lifestyle. The focus on cars and houses could, indeed, be seen as an expression of what Thompson has called the 'privatization of hope' in relation to 'economic reductionism in its consumer-capitalist form' (2013, 1). The deportees and their families were hoping for a prosperous and comfortable lifestyle and future—reaching out for the promises of wealth and modernity, seemingly without questioning the overall political and economic structures which constrain their access to realizing these hopes. Certainly, Webb suggests that resolute hope tends to be self-efficacious and private, serving a socially conservative function (2007, 71).

However, I posit that the social hope underpinning migration from Amanfo should not primarily be understood in terms of consumption or the material aspects of becoming a *Borga*. Cars and houses not only constitute material goods and comfort but also represent security and autonomy for the individual and his or her family. There are several aspects to this. First, money and material resources enable people to invest in social relations and hence engage in long-term patterns of reciprocity which may provide support in future times of need (Awedoba and Hahn 2014; Thorsen 2014). Second, my interlocutors explained that the cars were meant both for personal transport and also for serving as commercial vehicles—granting an income—and the houses were for accommodation for the family, who would thus be independent from the moods of a landlord, as well as for renting out. Whereas the few interlocutors who were in relatively more privileged positions, with good jobs or wealthy backgrounds, expressed personal ambitions in terms of their careers, the remainder hoped for stability and social and economic security for themselves and their families. Fancy cars and big houses were both a means to this end and objects of desire in their own right. Finally, it should be noted that autonomy, accumulation, and economic independence are established cultural values among the Akan (Arhin 1983; Clarke 2000; Fortes 1963), the biggest ethnic group in this part of Ghana.

The prominence of high-risk migration as a means to provide these goods and hence to enable security and autonomy, must be seen in the light of the lack of opportunities for people without much education and of poor backgrounds in Amanfo and elsewhere in Ghana (and in Africa). They do not find themselves in a position where they can easily 'do things', as Kwaku said, at least not all the things they would like to do. On the contrary, many of the interlocutors described their situation as 'being stuck', with few or no opportunities, money, educational diplomas, or connections. This feeling of being stuck in life can be perceived as existential immobility when 'a person suffers from both absence of choices or alternatives to the situation [he or she] is in and an inability to grab such alternatives even when they present themselves' (Hage 2009, 4). As shown above, the societal hope distributed by the government and main political parties in Ghana is linking education, oil money, and (future) prosperity, locating a promising future *and* the means to reach it in Ghana. This topography of societal hope, however, is not shared by many people in Amanfo. Although many do perceive the ideal future as located in Ghana, they do not think that they can actually realize a promising future through staying in the country.

## Disrupted Migration Projects: Life after Deportation

Most interlocutors in Amanfo did indeed describe Ghana as a nice place but were quick to add that 'money is a problem'. Whereas migration to attractive destinations like Europe or North America might entail long-term residency, none of the deportees I talked to expressed a desire to actually live their entire life *outside*. Rather, they envisioned their long-term future in Ghana as a successful returnee, as a *Borga*. In Akyeampong's words: '"Success" in the immigrant community comes to depend on one's exertions, and material accumulation is open to all [. . .] The successful migrant returns home as an "upper-class" citizen, respected for her/his wealth' (2000, 187). Migration abroad is a means to realize (at least) two overall goals: to take care of one's family and oneself and to be able to return with a status of respect. Ghana thus constitutes a place of potential pleasure, security, and well-being in the local topography of hope *after* successful migration, when the migrant has transformed his or her social and economic status. Conversely, returning involuntarily and empty-handed is seen as catastrophic and shameful, as the ultimate failure of the migration project. This failure is embodied by deportees who are sometimes called *Borga lose* or *Borga useless* (cf. Kabki et al. 2004, 90; Nieswand 2013, 15–16). The hopeful *Borga* has turned into a loser, suffering a drastic decline in status, turning into 'deportee trash' in the public imaginary, as Sørensen has described with reference to Latin America (Sørensen 2011).

Shame and failure are recurrent themes in studies of post-deportation, whether focusing on Africa (Alpes 2011; Drotbohm 2015; Peutz 2010; Tiilikainen 2011), Central America (Brotherton and Barrios 2009; Sørensen 2011; Walter *et al.* 2004), or Asia (Koshravi 2009; Majidi 2012; Schuster and Majidi 2015). Shame is 'evoked by failure of an individual or group to live according to their values or commitments, especially the ones concerning their relations to others and goods which others also value' (Sayer 2005, 953–954). As Sayer further notes, shame is the most likely to occur when experiencing disrespect from 'those whose values and judgements one most respects' (2005, 954). Returning empty-handed to one's family and local community, with nothing but debt and worries galore, represents the epitome of failure, aggravated by public ridicule and shaming from other people in the hometown. Whereas the suffering experienced on the way to Libya and back again—being kidnapped, imprisoned, fearing death, and begging for survival in the streets of Agadez—was extremely painful for Kwaku, he did not articulate it as shameful. This indicates that shame is not an attribute of deportation itself (cf. Galvin 2015; Schuster and Majidi 2015). Rather, shame relates to how certain activities and experiences are perceived and evaluated in the moral universe of the deportee and his family and surroundings with regard to conceptions and expectations of migration and its outcomes, including the economic gain and loss.

An understanding of shame as related to an individual's significant others also shed light on why many migrants refrain from disclosing degrading life and working conditions abroad to family or community members and, conversely, that family members often do not enquire about them. Such an economy of appearance (Cole 2014b) makes it possible to uphold the *Borga* status through collaborative silences (Nieswand 2013) about disgraceful or shameful conditions and activities abroad (see also Bredeloup, this volume; Hernández-Carretero and Carling 2012). It is effectively destroyed, however, when migrants return empty-handed. The shame may be further aggravated by the often collective aspects of migration in terms of financing the journey of a family member and the expectations of subsequently benefiting from its outcome. It is not only the social repositioning of the migrant which has failed but potentially that of the entire family. Deportation thus demonstrates how social hope can turn into social hopelessness, so to speak; how the potentiality of hope may evaporate and leave only uncertainty.

Despite the challenging nature of life after deportation, deportees described their return in different ways. Whereas Kwaku was caught and deported before starting to work, other deportees had managed to save money. Pastor Emmanuel had worked in several European countries before he was deported from Norway in 2002 and was widely described as a successful returnee. Working for a farmer in a Norwegian village and keeping his expenses to a minimum, he had managed to save 22,000 USD, which he sent back to Amanfo, enabling him to buy a house and start small-scale farming. Furthermore, he came back with some money in his pocket and 'exposure' from his traveling. Now he was doing well, having married and started a family, owning his own house, and being respected as a pastor. When I asked him to describe his deportation, he explained:

> I was feeling happy, yeah. Even the majority of them [townspeople in Amanfo] thought my goods were coming on their way. They thought that because they think I am looking fine. I don't normally eat any common food so they prepare food for me nicely, because they think I am having money. So if you come home like that, people know that you are a traveler, and they will come to you for advice. Yeah, they will be coming for advice here and there.

Contrary to Kwaku's story, Pastor Emmanuel's account highlights success and admiration. He came back with money, and people thought that his belongings from Europe were on their way because of his confident appearance. He described his migration as a transformational experience where he learnt several European languages and gained important experience that he now uses to give advice to people in relation to traveling and to other important life choices. Pastor Emmanuel even claimed to have changed his eating habits, preferring fruit and light meals, rather than the heavy meals and staples that many Ghanaians prefer, setting him apart from the ordinary townspeople in Amanfo. He thus embodied the successful returnee, the *Borga*, who had managed to transform himself during his journey abroad and who had returned with the resources and experience to become a big man. His success shows that savings and investments made during migration, in combination with the comportment of the deportee, are significant in relation to how the deportee is perceived by his or her surroundings (cf. Alpes 2011; Drotbohm 2015). It also demonstrates that migrant success revolves not only around economic achievement but also around the broadening of horizons through 'exposure' to *outside* and the acquisition of competences. However, it should be added that Pastor Emmanuel's deportation took place ten years ago, indicating the importance of a temporal perspective in any analysis of post-deportation.

## The 'Safe Migration' Position: Locating Societal Hope in Ghana

The stories of Kwaku and Pastor Emmanuel illustrate how the public evaluation of success or failure of *Borgas* and deportees relates to what they (are believed to) have achieved during their migration project. Furthermore, this evaluation tends to focus on individual virtue and discipline, or the lack thereof, rather than linking deportation to restrictive regimes of mobility and global and local inequalities—despite the fact that the hardship of traveling to or living in Libya (and other destinations) is well-known in Amanfo and, more generally, in Ghana. As Schuster and Majidi note in relation to deportation from Europe to Afghanistan, such a response can be perceived as 'a way of holding on to the dream of a better life in a distant destination, a dream challenged by deportation' (2015, 14). In the Ghanaian context, this translates into holding on to the social hope that a family member will become a *Borga* and thereby transform the life of the family still in Ghana. It can thus be seen as an expression of the conflict between local and state topographies of hope and the structures of opportunities and constraint that shape how and whether these hopes can be realized.

However, Pastor Emmanuel did not encourage prospective migrants and deportees in Amanfo to follow his example. Quite the contrary, he told them to stay and seek their fortune in Ghana through education, hard work, and prayer, sharing the societal hope distributed by the Ghanaian state. This may be a way of distinguishing himself from other deportees, positioning himself as a respectable man in society. He and a number of other persons in Amanfo—usually in elite, middle-class, or otherwise relatively well-off positions—were part of what can be termed the 'safe migration position' or, when more organized, the 'safe migration industry' (cf. Gammeltoft-Hansen and Sørensen 2013). Consisting of individuals, NGOs, and institutions that promote safe migration through information campaigns and advice, the safe migration industry can be found all over Ghana and, indeed, in most countries from where there is (what may become) irregular international migration.[11] The overall premise of such interventions is first, and usually quite mistakenly, that prospective migrants do not know the risks and hardship which their migration projects entail and, second, that a life in Ghana offers better prospects for the future.

Proponents of the safe migration industry thus share the visions of Ghanaian politicians who locate societal hope in Ghana. However, the Ghanaian state does not discourage migration as such. Changing Ghanaian governments have particularly embraced high-skilled migrants in Western countries with regularized statuses since 2001 and initiated a range of policy initiatives to encourage migrants' contributions to development in Ghana (Kleist 2013; Kleist 2015). Some types of migration are thus seen as acceptable, even desirable, in the state's topography of hope. This does not apply to unskilled migrants, however. Rather, the Ghanaian state is discouraging and aiming to prevent high-risk and (what eventually becomes) irregular migration through an increasing emphasis on migration management, partly funded by European countries as part of the externalization of border controls.

Whether focusing on preventing the loss of lives or on the legal aspects, both high-risk and irregular migration were discouraged by safe migration proponents, while they articulated a sedentary lifestyle as a safer, better, and sometimes morally superior choice. In 2012 and 2013 the safe migration proponents in Amanfo and elsewhere repeatedly explained to me that there is a bright future in Ghana for those who work hard and for those who are educated—especially in the light of the recent economic growth and the oil reserves in Ghana, on the one hand, and the economic crisis in Southern

Europe, which make life less promising there, on the other. Likewise, they emphasized that, if only the migrants would use the money they would otherwise spend on the journey to Libya on investment in Ghana, and if they would exercise the same work ethics back home as they do *outside*, they would easily be able to succeed in Ghana. Migration was not discouraged *per se*, as legal migration 'with a purpose'—such as obtaining a degree at a foreign university followed by return to Ghana—is seen as a positive phenomenon. However, this kind of migration is rarely available for poor and low-skilled persons such as deportees and prospective migrants in Amanfo. Whereas they shared the end goal of living a comfortable, prosperous, and respectable life in Ghana, they did not share the belief that they could actually realize it without traveling outside the country.

The implication is that high-risk migration to places like Libya remains an element in the local topographies of hope in places like Amanfo, at least partly because of the lack of a convincing alternative. Nevertheless, the *Borga* position seems to be changing and becoming more ambivalent. Not only has it become more difficult to enter Europe, find work, and save money, and hence be able to perform '*Borganess*' in Ghana, but the growth and unequal but visible wealth in Ghana in recent years also means that the social distinctiveness of *Borgas* is becoming less conspicuous. Whereas *Borgas* were generally respected and admired in Amanfo, their position was in the process of changing, as explained to me by Kwame, the brother of a deportee. This change is outspoken in major cities. 'Accra doesn't have any regard for *Borgas*', he said, 'there are people there who live big lives without ever having traveled outside Ghana, so they don't respect *Borgas* at all'. Kwame himself had traveled no further than a neighboring country but had obtained a university degree and subsequently landed a good government job in Amanfo, earning well, driving a nice car, and living in a comfortable house, owned in fact by a Ghanaian living in Italy. He had realized much of the *Borga* position, in other words, without going through the hardships of traveling. Stories like his, Kwame further continued, are beginning to change the *Borga* status, even in Amanfo:

> One thing about the *Borgas* is that, when they come home, we who have lived in the system for a while . . . we are able to sustain ourselves economically for a long time. But when they come, they are not able to do that. Because some want to show off and, before they know it, the few thousand euros or dollars they bring are gone, and they get a bit miserable.

According to Kwame, the disenchantment of the *Borga* position is based on the growing wealth and opportunities for living 'big lives' in Ghana, meaning that the *Borgas*' demonstration and, sometimes, squandering of money is no longer seen as exceptional or respectable. Even in Amanfo, persons like Kwame, who had 'lived in the system'—i.e., studied and obtained a good job—were doing better, being able to sustain themselves rather than spending all the money at once and then being impoverished. Achievement in Ghana is possible, according to Kwame, if you live and work with 'the system', rather than going aimlessly outside and risking your life crossing the desert and the sea. He thus adhered to the societal distribution of hope and its focus on prosperity in Ghana through hard work and educational achievement.

## Conclusion

In this chapter I have attempted to establish an analytical framework that combines the concepts of social hope (Hage 2003) and topographies of hope (Mar 2005) and hence links the temporal and spatial dimensions. Focusing on Ghana, I have shown a tension between the Ghanaian state's topography of *societal hope* and local topographies of *social hope* among deportees in the context of high-risk migration and restrictive mobility regimes. The narratives of societal hope are embedded in messages of economic optimism after the finding of oil in 2007, and revolve around a prosperous future in Ghana achieved through hard work and educational excellence, rather than migration. However, economic growth in Ghana is highly unequal, and there is a widespread sense of dissatisfaction with the lack of economic opportunities for large swathes of the population. This is indeed the case for poor and low-skilled deportees and prospective migrants, who find themselves in a situation in which they have no access to legal migration and few prospects for prosperity through educational achievement. The potential of societal hope—that the hoped-for future may happen—is not distributed to this group, who find themselves in a schism between 'the culturally expected and the socially possible' (Vigh 2009, 95) in terms of expectations from families, the local community, and the migrants themselves. Becoming a *Borga* or having one in the family is perceived as a pathway for social mobility but this pathway is considered illegitimate in the visions of societal hope generated and distributed by the state. Nevertheless, migration to Libya and other destinations remains a central element in the local topographies of hope—a risky but potentially possible way of supporting one's family and progressing in life.

The chapter thereby accentuates the importance of examining deportation as a process and of including the local context of reception (Drotbohm and Hasselberg 2015). I have shown how post-deportation status depends on achievement and resource mobilization: deportees can become 'big men' or *Borgas* if they return with money, consumer goods, and 'exposure'—like Pastor Emmanuel. However, most deportees—like Kwaku—return empty-handed and face difficulties, shame, and ridicule, and the same as or worse economic conditions than before their migration. This indicates a high degree of individualization of deportees' situations that downplays structural constraints. From the point of view of safe migration proponents, deportation demonstrates the non-viable nature of high-risk migration as a livelihood strategy and a means to establishing a promising future. However, when aspiring migrants and family members individualize the causes of deportation, they maintain the social hope of high-risk migration as a pathway to a better life, in the absence of convincing alternatives, despite its uncertain nature. They thus demonstrate the continuing importance of migration in the local topography of social hope.

## Acknowledgements

I thank all interlocutors in Amanfo and elsewhere in Ghana for their help and time. I have received helpful questions and comments on previous versions of the chapter at the ECAS conference, Lisbon, 2013; the IUAES Congress, Manchester, 2013; the Interdisciplinary Network's workshop on Hope, Prague, 2014; the ESA network on emotions, Rhodes, 2014; and the Precarious Futures workshop, Tisvildeleje, 2015. I also thank the two reviewers and Dorte Thorsen, Robin May Schott, and Ulla Holm for valuable feedback. The research was funded by a grant from the Danish Council of Independent Research—Humanities.

## Notes

1. All names have been changed to protect the privacy of the interlocutors.
2. http://hdrstats.undp.org/en/countries/profiles/gha.html.
3. http://news.bbc.co.uk/2/hi/africa/6766527.stm.
4. See Darkwah (2013) for a fascinating analysis of how a youth training program for working in the oil industry was keeping hope alive for this group.
5. http://www.worldbank.org/en/publication/global-economic-prospects/data?region=SST.
6. http://www.worldbank.org/en/publication/global-economic-prospects/data?region=SST (accessed 03 September 2015).
7. Libya has become a less attractive destination in recent years because of the civil war in 2011 and the outbreak of conflict again in 2014; however, Libya-bound migration is still ongoing.
8. Interview with the local NADMO (National Disaster Management Organisation) representative, March 2013.
9. Mass deportation from Libya also took place in May 2013, when almost 800 sub-Saharan Africans were deported to Agadez in pick-up trucks: http://www.rfi.fr/afrique/20130529-centaines-clandestins-nigeriens-refoules-libye.
10. I held 15 sessions of participant photography with deportees, involuntary return migrants, and their family members, asking them to take photos of their everyday life and what they would like to achieve in the future.
11. In the cases where the focus is explicitly on preventing irregular migration, a more appropriate term would be 'anti-illegal-migration industry'.

## References

Akyeampong, E. 2000. Africans in the diaspora: The diaspora and Africa. *African Affairs* 99 (395): 183–215.

Alpes, M. J. 2011. *Bushfalling: How young Cameroonians dare to migrate*. PhD thesis, University of Amsterdam, Institute for Social Science Research.

Amnesty International. 2015. 'Libya is full of cruelty': Stories of abduction, sexual violence and abuse from migrants and refugees. London: Amnesty International

Arhin, K. 1983. Rank and class among the Asante and Fante in the nineteenth century. Africa 53 (1): 2–22.

Awedoba, A. K., and H. P. Hahn. 2014. Wealth, consumption and migration in a West African society: New lifestyles and new social obligations among the Kasena, Northern Ghana. Anthropos 109 (1): 45–55.

Bob-Milliar, G. M., and G. K. Bob-Milliar. 2013. The politics of trans-Saharan transit migration in the Maghreb: Ghanaian migrants in Libya, c.1980–2012. African Review of Economics and Finance 5 (1): 60–73.

Bredeloup, S., and O. Pliez. 2011. The Libyan migration corridor. Fiesole: Robert Schuman Centre for Advanced Studies, European University Institute, Research Report.

Brotherton, D. C., and L. Barrios. 2009. Displacement and stigma: The social-psychological crisis of the deportee. Crime Media Culture 5 (1): 29–55.

Clarke, G. 2000. Mothering, work and gender in urban Asante ideology and practice. American Anthropologist 101 (4): 717–729.

Cole, J. 2014a. The téléphone malgache: Transnational gossip and social transformation among Malagasy marriage migrants in France. American Ethnologist 41 (2): 276–289.

Cole, J. 2014b. Producing value among Malagasy marriage migrants in France: Managing horizons of expectation. Current Anthropology 55 (S9): S85–S94.

Darkwah, A. 2013. Keeping hope alive: An analysis of training opportunities for Ghanaian youth in the emerging oil and gas industry. International Development Planning Review 35 (2): 119–134.

Drotbohm, H. 2015. The reversal of migratory family lives: A Cape Verdean perspective on gender and sociality pre- and post-deportation. Journal of Ethnic and Migration Studies 41 (4): 653–670.

Drotbohm, H., and I. Hasselberg. 2015. Deportation, anxiety, justice: New ethnographic perspectives. Journal of Ethnic and Migration Studies 41 (4): 551–562.

Fortes, M. 1963. Time and social structure: An Ashanti case study. In Social structure: Studies presented to A. R. Radcliffe-Brown, ed. M. Fortes, 54–84. New York: Russell and Russell.

Galvin, T. M. 2015. 'We deport them but they keep coming back': The normalcy of deportation in the daily life of 'undocumented' Zimbabwean migrant workers in Botswana. Journal of Ethnic and Migration Studies 41 (4): 617–634.

Gammeltoft-Hansen, T., and N. N. Sørensen, eds. 2013. The migration industry and the commercialization of international migration. London and New York: Routledge.

Glick Schiller, N., and N. B. Salazar. 2013. Regimes of mobility across the globe. Journal of Ethnic and Migration Studies 39 (2): 183–200.

Hage, G. 2003. Against paranoid nationalism: Searching for hope in a shrinking society. Annandale, NSW and London: Pluto Press and Merlin.

Hage, G. 2009. Waiting out the crisis: On stuckedness and governmentality. In Waiting, ed. G. Hage, 97–106. Melbourne: Melbourne University Press.

Hamood, S. 2006. African transit migration through Libya to Europe: The human cost. Cairo: The American University in Cairo, Research Report.

Hernández-Carretero, M., and J. Carling. 2012. Beyond 'kamikaze migrants': Risk taking in West African boat migration to Europe. Human Organization 71 (4): 407–416.

Horst, C., and K. Grabska. 2015. Introduction. Flight and exile—Uncertainty in the context of conflict-induced displacement. *Social Analysis* 59 (1): 1–18.

Kabki, M., V. Mazzucato and E. Appiah. 2004. 'Wo benanE a EyE bebree': The economic impact of remittances of Netherlands-based Ghanaian migrants on rural Ashanti. *Population, Space and Place* 10 (2): 85–97.

Kleist, N. 2013. Flexible politics of belonging: Diaspora mobilization in Ghana. *African Studies* 72 (2): 285–306.

Kleist, N. 2015. Policy spectacles: Promoting migration–development scenarios in Ghana. In *Mobility makes states: Migration and power in Africa*, eds. J. Quirk and D. Vigneswaran, 125–146. Pennsylvania: University of Pennsylvania Press.

Kleist, N. 2017. Disrupted migration projects: The moral economy of involuntary return to Ghana from Libya. Forthcoming in *Africa*.

Koshravi, S. 2009. Sweden: Detention and deportation of asylum seekers. *Race and Class* 50 (4): 38–56.

Lucht, H. 2011. *Darkness before daybreak: African migrants living on the margins in Southern Italy today*. Berkeley, Los Angeles and London: University of California Press.

Majidi, N. 2012. *The myth of return and reintegration in Afghanistan*. Oslo: Peace Research Institute Oslo, paper given to the conference Return Migration and Transnationalism: Alternatives or Complements?, 4–5 September.

Mar, P. 2005. Unsettling potentialities: Topographies of hope in transnational migration. *Journal of Intercultural Studies* 26 (4): 361–378.

McCaskie, T. C. 2008. The United States, Ghana and oil: Global and local perspectives. *African Affairs* 107 (428): 313–332.

Nieswand, B. 2013. The burger's paradox: Migration and the transnationalization of social inequality in southern Ghana. *Ethnography* 15 (4): 403–425.

Osei-Assibey, E. 2014. *Inequalities country report—Ghana*. Accra: Report presented to the Pan-African Conference on Inequalities in the Context of Structural Transformation, 28–30 April.

Peutz, N. 2010. 'Criminal alien' deportees in Somaliland: An ethnography of removal. In *The deportation regime: Sovereignty, space and the freedom of movement*, eds. N. de Genova and N. Peutz, 371–409. Durham and London: Duke University Press.

Quartey, P. 2009. *Migration in Ghana: A country profile 2009*. Geneva: International Organization for Migration.

Sayer, A. 2005. Class, moral worth and recognition. *Sociology* 39 (5): 947–963.

Schuster, L., and N. Majidi. 2015. Deportation stigma and re-migration. *Journal of Ethnic and Migration Studies* 41 (4): 635–652.

Smith, L., and V. Mazzucato. 2009. Constructing homes, building relationships: Migrant investments in houses. *Tijdschrift voor Economische en Sociale Geografie* 100 (5): 662–673.

Sørensen, N. N. 2011. The rise and fall of the 'migrant superhero' and the new 'deportee trash': Contemporary strain on mobile livelihoods in the Central American region. *Border-Lines* 5: 90–120.

Thompson, P. 2013. Introduction: The principle of hope and the crisis of negation. In *The privatization of hope: Ernst Bloch and the future of utopia*, eds. P. Thompson and S. Zizek, 1–20. Durham and London: Duke University Press.

Thorsen, D. 2014. Jeans, bicycles and mobile phones: Adolescent migrants' material consumption in Burkina Faso. In *Child and youth migration: Mobility-in-migration in an era of globalization*, eds. A. Veale and G. Donà, 67–90. Basingstoke: Palgrave Macmillan.

Tiilikainen, M. 2011. Failed diaspora: Experiences of *Dhaqan Celis* and mentally ill returnees in Somaliland. *Nordic Journal of African Studies* 20 (1): 71–89.
Turner, S. 2015. 'We wait for miracles': Ideas of hope and future among clandestine Burundian refugees in Nairobi. In *Ethnographies of uncertainty in Africa*, eds. E. Cooper and D. Pratten, 173–191. Basingstoke: Palgrave Macmillan.
Van Hear, N. 1998. *New diasporas: The mass exodus, dispersal and regroup of migrant communities*. Seattle: University of Washington Press.
Vigh, H. 2009. Wayward migration: On the imagined futures and technological voids. *Ethnos* 74 (1): 91–109.
Walter, N., P. Bourgois and H. M. Loinaz. 2004. Masculinity and undocumented labor migration: Injured Latino day laborers in San Francisco. *Social Science and Medicine* 59 (6): 1159–1168.
Webb, D. 2007. Modes of hoping. *History of the human sciences* 20 (3): 65–85.
Weiss, B. 2002. Thug realism: Inhabiting fantasy in urban Tanzania. *Cultural Anthropology* 17 (1): 93–124.
Williams, A. M., and V. Baláz. 2012. Migration, risk and uncertainty: Theoretical perspectives. *Population, Space and Place* 18 (2): 167–180.

# Index

*Abidjan* (song) 64–5
ACS (American Colonization Society) 80–1, 82, 84
adventure: as context for hope 139–44; diamond trade framed as 140; dignity and shame dynamics in 144–9; emic notion of 134, 150; as epic journey 142–4; faith and 140–2, 150; as social construction 134, 135; stories of 137, 141; stress of 138; Western and African connotations for 136; as youthful endeavor 138–9
affect 36, 41, 46, 52
Africa, mobility in 2–3, 22, 24–5
age, impact on migration plans 29, 33, 138–9; *see also* youth, African
agency: in adventure 138, 143; in 'anthropology of the good' 157; defeatist 156; dependence on external sources of 60, 71, 120, 140; religious framework for 50, 51, 53, 108; in waiting 128, 129; of youth 61, 71
American Colonization Society (ACS) 80–1, 82, 84
'anthropology of the good' 157
Appadurai, Arjun 8, 60
Argentina: 'brokers of hope' in 43; as destination country 40; regularization of undocumented migrants in 9, 44–7, 52; Senegalese migrants' attitudes in 47–54
aspiration/ability model of migration plans 28

back-to-Africa movement 79–85, 89, 90
*badenya* 143
belonging, sense of: of African slaves in America 80; disrupted by forced displacement 59; otherness as asset for 58, 68–9; *see also* shame; social status

Berger, John 162
Biyaoula, Daniel 149
Bjarnesen, Jesper 9–10, 58ff
Bloch, Ernst 7–8, 11, 12, 41–2, 76, 79
bluff, as social performance 68
*Borga lose/Borga useless* 183
*Borgas*: cultural influence 180; deportees as 185; locals' respect for 178–9, 181; material goods owned by 182–3; state views of 187, 188
Bourdieu, Pierre 8, 43, 47, 156, 171
Brazil 49
Bredeloup, Sylvie 9, 10, 14, 134ff
brokers, migration 43–4, 99, 159
'brokers of hope' 9, 43, 48, 49, 50–1, 54
Browne, Craig 7
bureaucracies 9, 22, 27, 30–1, 35; *see also* papers, legal
Burkina Faso: *diaspo* experience in 65–71; interdependence with Côte d'Ivoire 58, 61–2

Cabot, Heath 34
'capacity to choose' 129
Cape Verde 24–5
Cape Verde, visa application process: biographical unevenness in 21, 26–8, 29, 31–2, 33; classificatory performances in 9, 30–5, 36; delayed interviews in 31, 33–4; difficulty of 9, 22, 26; organization of knowledge in 30, 35; social network support needed for 28–30, 35
capitalism 42–3, 61–2, 65, 123
Carling, Jørgen 28
China: legal permit and visas in 99–100; Nigerian migration to 98–101; *see also* Pentecostalism
Christianity *see* faith; Pentecostalism; religious institutions

classificatory performances 9, 30–5, 36
Côte d'Ivoire 58, 60–1, 68; *see also* Zouglou music
Crapanzano, Vincent 127, 140, 156
critical phenomenology 157–8

danger: in adventure stories 140, 141; in migrant brinkmanship 161–2, 170, 171; *see also* migration, high-risk
death of migrants: adventurer and hero relationships to 143; as beginning rather than end 168–70; funeral arrangements 160–1; as iconoclasm 157–8, 171; risk of 5–6, 154, 161–2
defeatist agency 156
de Gaulejac, Vincent 149
Delaney, Martin 84
deportation: as aim of American Colonization Society 85; Argentinian policy for 45; conflicting notions of the good life and 174, 175, 176, 182, 187–8; coping with 174, 184–5, 186; faith seen as protection from 106; family rejection 146–7, 149, 150; language for 147, 148, 183; of Nigerian migrants in Asia 98–9; preparation for 148; public evaluation of deportees 185–6; shame surrounding 146, 148, 183–4; stranded deportees in Niger 154ff; as ultimate failure of migration project 15, 173
Desjarlais, Robert 157
despair: as breakdown of moral economy 154, 167; faith and 53–4, 95, 103, 142; proactive form of 156
destination countries: changes in 1, 24–5; livelihood challenges in 10, 48, 55, 66, 100–1, 128, 130
diamond smugglers 140, 142–3
diasporan identities: as assets 58, 68–9; rejection of 80–1, 84–5, 88; *see also* diasporicity
diasporicity: core propositions 78, 91n2; as embodiment of spatialized variant of hope 76, 77, 89–90; in historical past 84–5; origin mythologies informing 77, 78, 80; in present 85–9; relationship to mobility 79; structural violence as driver of 77–8, 81–4, 85, 89–90
*diaspo* youth culture 66, 67, 68–71
differentiation, social 83–4, 89–90
dignity: aided by migration 125, 144; language for 147–8; of triumphant return 144–5; in works of fiction 149; *see also* shame; social status
Di Nunzio, Marco 115
Diome, Fatou 149
displacement, social 59–60, 66–7
dispositional hopefulness 60, 67–8
Douglass, Frederick 84
Drotbohm, Heike 9, 10, 21ff
Duval, Martin 46
Dwyer, Peter 129

epic journey, migration as 142–4, 150
*Espoir 2000* 64–5
estimative hope 182
Europe: collective African memory of 137; migrants "stuck" in 126–9; restrictive immigration policies in 5, 6, 40, 118, 126, 181
exclusion, social: of contemporary Americo-Liberians 86–7; *diaspos'* response to 66–9; *see also* structural violence
exile, in migration narratives 141, 142, 143
existential (im)mobility: entrapment abroad 126–9; faith during 53; high-risk migration and 183; migration as solution to 117; role of hope in 13–15, 16
existential reciprocity 154, 156, 158, 167–8, 170
expectations: about costs of failure 130; of family 12, 13, 25, 48, 145, 149, 184, 186, 188; gender-based 125; about high-risk migration 173, 181; about improved conditions 127–8, 129; patience and 128, 129; about reciprocity 25, 29, 45–6, 145, 167, 184; of societies and peers 12, 130, 136, 184, 188; about support from church 102; about triumphant return 145

*fadenya* 143–4
failure, language for 147–8
faith: agency through 50, 51, 53; patience as display of 128; relationship to adventure 140–2, 150; relationship to despair 53–4, 95, 103, 142; in situations of hardship and death 169; *see also* Pentecostalism; religious institutions
family: church as replacement for 103, 105–6; deportees rejected by 146–7, 149, 150; disconnection

from 145, 154, 184; in epic stories 143; expectations of 12, 13, 25, 48, 145, 149, 184, 186, 188; gendered inequality in 29; migration as care for 183; as regulatory authority for migration 29; reunification as factor in migration 29; shame borne by 184; support for migration projects 29, 117, 124, 147, 184; *see also* social networks; social status, remittances to family
fiction, migration in 136, 148–9
future, near *vs.* distant 10–13, 76, 83, 97

Gaibazzi, Paolo 14, 28–9
Gambia 28–9
Gandoulou, Jean-Daniel 139
Gasparini, G. 128, 129
gender: endurance and 128; expectations and 125; impact on migration plans 9, 28, 29, 35; in Liberian diasporic identity 88–9, 90; in Senegalese migrant population 115
Ghana: inequality in 178, 187, 188; migration from 154ff, 173ff, 180–3; political context in 176–7, 178, 186; post-deportation life in 183–5; safe migration industry in 185–8; societal hope in 15, 176–9, 183, 185–8; *see also* Borgas
globalization, stratified: inequality and uncertainty in 3–5, 175; migration as factor in 136–7; perseverance of hope in 156–8
good life: conflicting notions of 176, 181–3, 188; mobility paradox and 1; societal views of 8–9, 174; *see also* societal hope
Goudé, Charles Blé 63
Goudiaby, Abba 45
Guéladio, Samba 142–3
Guyer, Jane 11

Hage, Ghassan: dispositional hopefulness 60, 67–8; distribution of hope 42–3, 60, 116, 175; on existential mobility 13, 117; hope and capitalism 42, 61, 65; on hopefulness 118; migration as expression of hope 155; social hope 7–8, 61, 174; societal hope 8, 42–3, 174–5; on waiting and endurance 128, 129
Haugen, Heidi Østbø 12, 94ff
Hernández-Carretero, María 12, 113ff
heroes, relationship to death 143

Heyman, Josiah 32
hope: as active and imaginative 7, 41–2; adventure as context for 139–44; as analytical framework for mobility paradox 1–2, 15–16; in capitalist context 61, 65, 182; in death 168–70; as embodied practice 107–10; in existential immobility 13–15, 16, 53, 117; existential reciprocity and 154, 156, 158, 167–8, 170; faith and 140–2, 169; in high-risk migration 178–9, 181–3, 188; inherited 62, 70; interpersonal dimension of 124–6; method of 68, 97, 108, 110; modes of 59, 60–1, 64, 181–2; as moral value 103–5, 109; as passive counterpart to desire 139–40; Pentecostal churches' production of 95–7, 103–10; perseverance through hardship 155, 158, 166–7; privatization of 182; situated nature of 7–8, 36; social distribution of 60–1, 64; as social imaginary for navigating present realities 77, 83; spatial distribution of 116–17; state distribution of 7–8, 41, 42–3, 174–5, 177–8; topographies of 174–6, 178, 183, 186, 187, 188; uncertainty mediated by 113–14, 117–19, 129; waiting and 126–9; work of 118; youth agency and 71; *see also* repositories of hope; social hope; societal hope; spatial dimensions of hope; temporal dimensions of hope
hope, brokers of 9, 43, 48, 49, 50–1, 54
hopefulness 60, 68, 118

identity narratives 68–71; *see also* diasporicity
immigration policies, restrictive *see* mobility regimes, restrictive
immobility, physical 13–14
inequality: gendered 29; racial 85; in social distribution of uncertainty 60–1; stratified globalization and 3, 4–5, 175
inherited hope 62, 70
integration into host society: of *diaspos* in Burkina Faso 58, 70; religious proselytization at odds with 104; of Senegalese migrants in Argentina 46
Islam 50, 104, 141

Jackson, Michael 51, 155, 168
Jonnson, Gunvor 144

Kane, Ousmane 142
Kierkegaard, Søren 53
kinship 28–9
Kleist, Nauja 1ff, 15, 173ff
Kufuor, John 177, 178

liberation theology 96–7
Liberia 79–85, 86
Libya: as desirable destination 180, 189n7; high-risk migration to 6, 154, 181–2; mass deportation from 189n9; migrants stranded in 145
liminal legality 36
livelihood: challenges in destination countries 10, 48, 55, 66, 100–1, 128, 130; of *diaspos* 69; migration as strategy for 1, 5, 6, 25, 178, 188; of stranded migrants 160; uncertainty after return 115, 121, 122–3, 124; uncertainty in country of origin 113, 115, 128
Lubkemann, Stephen 1, 11, 76ff
Lucht, Hans 14, 154ff
luck 115, 119, 120, 125, 127, 130

Malraux, André 139
Mar, Phillip: hope in religious traditions 140; on religious foundation for hope 51; social hope 22–3; spatialization of aspirations 90n1; topologies of hope 175
*marabout* 9, 50–2
Mauss, Marcel 45, 49
Mbodji, Mamadou 125
media 136, 139
Melly, Caroline 119
method of hope 68, 97, 108, 110
migrant brinkmanship 161–2, 170, 171
migrants, stranded 1, 13, 14, 145
*migrason* 25–6
migration: dignity and shame dynamics in 144–9; as element of social hope 7–8; as epic journey 142–4, 150; as expression of hope 155; individual *vs.* collective frameworks for 30, 135, 137, 143; as livelihood strategy 1, 5, 6, 25, 178, 188; as moral or mystic experience 135, 140–2; as rite of passage 25, 150; in works of fiction 148–9; *see also* adventure; mobility regimes, restrictive
migration, high-risk: conflicting notions of good life and 173, 181–3, 188; as context for social hope 178–9, 181–3, 188; discouraged by safe migration proponents 186–7; effect of restrictive mobility regimes on 1, 5–6, 118, 181; West African routes 154, 180, 181
migration, irregular or unauthorized: discouraged by safe migration proponents 186–7; effect of restrictive mobility regimes on 5–6, 99–101; EU migration management and 6; fatality rates for 5–6
migration projects, failed: language for 147–8; postponed returns and 126–9; shame surrounding 15, 125–6, 145–50, 184; *see also* deportation
migration rights 22, 25
Miyazaki, Hirokazu 12, 23, 62, 68, 97, 110, 118
mobility: as element of social hope 7–8; hindered by fear of unsuccessful return 126; importance in contemporary Africa 2–3, 22, 24–5; promised by Pentecostal pastors 94, 102, 106; relationship to diasporicity 79
mobility, existential *see* existential (im)mobility
mobility, physical 13–14
mobility paradox 1, 3, 5–6, 13
mobility regimes, restrictive: in China 99–101; in Europe 5, 6, 40, 118, 126, 181; high-risk migration resulting from 1, 5–6, 118, 181; ignored in public evaluation of deportees 185–6; mobility limited by 1, 5–6, 58; state sovereignty and 22; unauthorized migration and 100–1; *see also* Cape Verde, visa application process
modes of hope 59, 60–1, 64, 181–2
Moltmann, Jürgen 96
moral breakdown 77–8, 81–4, 85, 89–90

Nairobi (Kenya) 23
Newell, Sasha 68
Nigeria: migration from 94ff, 98–100; political context in 97; visa application and brokerage in 31, 99; *see also* Pentecostalism
*nouchi* slang 68

Okane, Ike 98

papers, legal: bureaucracies and social hope 9, 22, 27, 30, 35; in China 99–100; classificatory performances and social hope 9, 30–5, 36; in

Nigeria 31; previous studies relating hope to 22–3; social networks and hope 28–30, 35; *see also* Cape Verde, visa application process; mobility regimes, restrictive
patience 127–9
Pedersen, Morten 118, 157
Pentecostalism: deliverance from past in 103–4, 105–6; Exodus narrative for migration in 141–2; hope as embodied practice in 107–10; hope as moral value in 103–5, 109; hope without restraint in 105–7; migration process aided by 95–6, 102; not-yet-geographical referents in 107; ontology of time in 96–7; physical *vs.* cerebral emphasis of 108, 110; proselytization-integration tension in 104; Prosperity Gospel in 94, 96, 103, 105, 106–7; spiritual warfare perspective in 101–2, 103; theology of hope in 95–7
physical (im)mobility 13–14
Piot, Charles 22
potentiality 2, 7–8, 11
prayer, Pentecostal view of 108–9
'privatization of hope' 182
prospective moments 95, 97, 104, 107
prospective momentum 12, 108, 110
Prosperity Gospel 94, 96, 103, 105, 106–7

reciprocity: with destination country 46–7; existential 149, 154, 156, 158, 167–8, 170; with family and community 25, 29, 145, 182; obligations within 45–6
religious institutions: as brokers of hope 9, 50–2; endurance supported by 52–5; Islam 50, 104, 141; moral support for visa process through 35; *see also* faith; Pentecostalism
remittances: African Pentecostal perspective on 103–4, 105–6; expectations for 25, 103, 113, 147; government restrictions on 48–9; hope nurtured by 36; mobility paradox and 13; social status and 87, 179
repositories of hope 8–10, 124; *see also* papers, legal; religious institutions; social networks; Zouglou music
resolute hope 182
return to country of origin: in back-to-Africa movement 79–85, 89, 90; bureaucratic challenges in 100; cautious attitudes about 113, 121–2, 129–30; as conclusion of adventure narratives 143, 145; after deportation 15, 146, 148, 183–5, 188; discouraged by African Pentecostal churches 101, 103, 104–5, 109; interpersonal pressures affecting 124–6, 130; livelihood uncertainty and 115, 121, 122–3, 124, 130; migration eligibility and likelihood of 31–2; migration status risked in 121–2; postponement of 126–9; as rest from adventure and risk 138; shameful 15, 125–6, 145–50; social reintegration 144; successful 121, 145, 147, 175, 178–9, 181, 182–3
risk: adventurous disposition toward 139; defined 181; in migrant brinkmanship 161–2; shame as motivation for 145; *vs.* uncertainty 181; *see also* adventure; 'taking chances' on migration; uncertainty
rite of passage, migration as 25, 150
Robbins, Joel 157

sacrifices, reciprocity and 154, 156, 158, 167–8, 170
'safe migration' position 185–8
savings 113, 122, 175, 185
Schopenhauer, A. 155
Senegal: livelihood uncertainty in 116–17, 128; migration to Argentina from 9, 40ff; migration to Spain from 12, 113ff, 119–20; social hope in 124; uncertainty of return to 12, 113ff, 121–2, 130
shame: *vs.* culpability 149; after deportation 146, 148, 183–4; after failed migration projects 15, 125–6, 145–9, 150; language for 147–8; mitigated by appearance 148, 185; as motivating factor 145; in works of fiction 148–9; *see also* dignity; social status
Simmel, Georg 137, 138
slavery 79–85
social differentiation 83–4, 89–90
social hope: erased by deportation 184; Hage's characterization of 7–8, 61, 174; high-risk migration and 178–9, 181–3, 188; Mar's characterization of 23; migration and mobility as elements of 7–8; origin of term 14n2; repositories of 8–10; as resolute hope

182; role of material goods in 182–3; topographies of 174–6, 188; *see also* papers, legal; Zouglou music
social imaginaries: hope as posture for navigating present realities 77, 83; situatedness of hope and 7–8, 36
social networks: deportees evaluated by 183–5, 188; as repositories of hope 27, 28–30, 35; as social attachments in diasporicity 36, 78, 80, 81–2, 83, 89, 91n4; *see also* social status
social performance 68–9, 71
social status: appearance and 148, 185; of *Borgas* 178–9, 181, 185, 187; of deportees 146, 148, 183–5, 188; after failed migration projects 15, 125–6, 145–50; humiliating jobs abroad and 144, 184; remittances to family and 87; reversed through migrant brinkmanship 171
societal hope: defined 8; as distribution of hope by state 8, 42–3, 174–5, 188; in Ghana 176–9, 183, 188; reciprocity expected for 46–7, 49–50; topographies of 175–6, 183, 188
Soum Bill 64
Spain 114, 121–2, 126–7
spatial dimensions of hope: in diasporicity 76, 77, 79, 89–90, 90n1; effect of global stratification on 136–7; hope's migration "ahead of the migrants" 155; mobility necessary for survival 24; for Senegalese migrants in Spain 114, 116–17, 127; structural violence as context for 77–8, 81–4, 85, 89–90; *vs.* temporal reorientations of hope 13; in topographies of hope 175, 188
spiritual warfare 101–2, 103
stranded migrants 1, 13, 14, 145, 154ff, 158–60
structural violence 77–8, 81–4, 85, 89–90; *see also* exclusion, social
subjectivity 135, 150, 157, 168, 170
subjunctivity 60

'taking chances' on migration: affordability of 122–3, 130; *vs.* hesitation about returning 113, 121–2, 129–30; as proactive engagement with uncertainty 115–16, 118, 119–20, 129
temporal dimensions of hope: hope's migration 'ahead of the migrants' 155; in Liberian-American

transnational field 76, 83, 85, 89; limitations of 77, 84, 89; near *vs.* distant futures 10–13, 76, 83, 97; in Pentecostal *vs.* liberation theology 96–7; *vs.* spatial transposition of hope 13; in tension with spatialization 89; in topographies of hope 174, 188; in waiting 114, 116, 127, 129
Tidjaniya 142, 151n8
'topographies of hope' 174–6, 178, 183, 186, 187, 188
Tounkara, Mamoutou 147
Tukulors 140, 151n4
Turner, Simon 23

Umar Tall, El Hadj 142, 151n9
uncertainty: definitions of 115; in high-risk migration 181–3; hope invoked by 2, 59; mediated by hope 113–14, 117–19, 129; about return 12, 113ff, 121–2, 130; *vs.* risk 181; social displacement as cause of 59–61; sources of 4; stratified globalization and 3–5, 175; taking chances on migration despite 115–16, 118, 119–20, 129; temporal and spatial responses to 114, 116–17, 127, 129; temporary *vs.* persistent 114, 128
United States: Americo-Liberian migration to 86–9; back-to-Africa movement 79–85, 89, 90; linked with Liberia 78
upward symbolic mobility *see* existential (im)mobility

Vammen, Ida Maria 9, 40ff
Vigh, Henrik 114, 155
visa application 31, 99–100; *see also* Cape Verde, visa application process; papers, legal

Waberi, Abdourahman 137, 151n3
waiting: active *vs.* passive 41, 64, 127, 128–9; hope and faith during 139–44; immobility during 6, 117; patience and 126–9; as temporal hope 114, 127, 129; uncertainty during 129
Webb, D. 181–2
West Africa: epic story in 142; high-risk migration routes in 154, 180, 181; shaped by mobility practices 2–3
Whitehouse, Bruce 144, 145
Whyte, Susan Reynolds 60

Willen, Sarah 157
'work of hope' 118

youth, African: as adventurers 138–9, 143–4; agency of 61, 71; *diaspo* youth culture 66, 67, 68–71; hierarchical social context for 61, 64–5, 144; migration as rite of passage for 25, 150; *see also* Zouglou music

Zigon, Jarrett 77, 155
Zouglou music: as bridge between *diaspos* and neighbors 68–9; *diaspo* youth experience reflected in 65, 67; hope as theme of 67, 71; origins and social context of 62–3; political themes in 62, 63, 64–5, 69, 70; as repository of knowledge 67; in social performance of *diaspos* 68–71; social values conveyed in 67

For Product Safety Concerns and Information please contact our EU representative  GPSR@taylorandfrancis.com
Taylor & Francis Verlag GmbH, Kaufingerstraße 24, 80331 München, Germany

www.ingramcontent.com/pod-product-compliance
Ingram Content Group UK Ltd.
Pitfield, Milton Keynes, MK11 3LW, UK
UKHW022001220326
11408UKWH00003B/409